Democracy Fatigue

Democracy Fatigue

An East European Epidemy

Edited by
Carlos García-Rivero

Central European University Press
Budapest–Vienna–New York

© Carlos García-Rivero, 2023

Published in 2023 by
CENTRAL EUROPEAN UNIVERSITY PRESS

Nádor utca 9, H-1051 Budapest, Hungary
Tel: +36-1-327-3138 or 327-3000
E-mail: ceupress@press.ceu.edu
Website: www.ceupress.com

All rights reserved. No part of this publication may be reproduced, stored in a retrieval system, or transmitted, in any form or by any means, without the permission of the Publisher.

ISBN 978-963-386-639-9 (hardback)
ISBN 978-963-386-640-5 (ebook)

Library of Congress Cataloging-in-Publication Data

Names: García-Rivero, Carlos, editor.
Title: Democracy fatigue : an East European epidemy / edited by Carlos García-Rivero.
Description: Budapest ; New York : Central European University Press, 2023. | Includes bibliographical references and index.
Identifiers: LCCN 2023026917 (print) | LCCN 2023026918 (ebook) | ISBN 9789633866399 (hardback) | ISBN 9789633866405 (ebook)
Subjects: LCSH: Democracy--Europe--Case studies. | Populism--Europe--Case studies. | Europe--Politics and government--1989- | BISAC: POLITICAL SCIENCE / Political Ideologies / General | HISTORY / Modern / 21st Century
Classification: LCC JN40 .D456 2023 (print) | LCC JN40 (ebook) | DDC 320.56/62094--dc23/eng/20230706
LC record available at https://lccn.loc.gov/2023026917
LC ebook record available at https://lccn.loc.gov/2023026918

Contents

List of Figures VII
List of Tables IX

Introduction: European Democracy at the Crossroads
Carlos García-Rivero 1

Part I
Populism in Europe: Concept and Context

Chapter 1
Quality of Democracy in Europe
Enrique Clari and Carlos García-Rivero 15

Chapter 2
Populism: Theoretical Foundations
Ángel Rivero 36

Chapter 3
Mapping European Populism and Its Association with Anti-Pluralism: Descriptive Evidence in Time and Space
Enrique Clari 51

Chapter 4
On the Persistence of Radical Right Populism in Europe: The Role of Grievances and Emotions
Hans-Georg Betz 75

Part II
Political Participation under Populism: Trends and Limits

Chapter 5
The Limits of Democratic Competition: Time-Series, Cross-Sectional Evidence of the Asymmetrical Impact of Polarization on Europeans' Political Attitudes and Behavior
Enrique Clari and Carlos García-Rivero 99

Chapter 6
POPULIST VOTER PROFILES IN DIFFERENT ELECTORAL CALLS: LESSONS FROM SPAIN
   Javier Antón-Merino, Sergio Pérez-Castaños, and Marta Méndez-Juez 125

Chapter 7
IDEOLOGICAL CONGRUENCE BETWEEN POPULIST RIGHT PARLIAMENTARY ELITES AND THEIR VOTERS: AN ANALYSIS OF POLAND, SWEDEN, AND GERMANY
   Carlos García-Rivero and Hennie Kotzè 146

Chapter 8
INTERNAL SANCTIONS FOR RULE OF LAW BREACHES UNDER ARTICLE 7 TEU: WHY IS THE EU DRAGGING ITS FEET?
   Clara Portela and Ruth Ferrero-Turrión 172

Part III
POPULIST PARTIES IN DIFFERENT EUROPEAN REGIONS

Chapter 9
POPULISM IN WESTERN VERSUS EASTERN EUROPE
   José Rama and Andrés Santana 193

Chapter 10
POPULISM IN SOUTHERN EUROPE
   Belén Fernández-García and Ángel Valencia-Sáiz 215

Chapter 11
NORDIC POPULISM: CONJOINING ETHNO-NATIONALISM AND WELFARE CHAUVINISM
   Eirikur Bergmann 240

CONCLUSION: WHAT LIES AHEAD
   Carlos García-Rivero 262

ABOUT THE CONTRIBUTORS 267
INDEX 273

Figures

Figure 1.1	Trends in satisfaction with democracy and the level of liberal democracy in Europe, 2002–2018	19
Figure 1.2	Uncritical attitudes toward democracy in Europe, 2004–2018	25
Figure 1.3	Observed political cultures by country, 2004–2018	25
Figure 1.4	Political trends across Europe, 2002–2018	26
Figure 1.5	Social and structural predictors of an uncritical political culture	28
Figure 3.1	Vote share of populist parties by country and year	58
Figure 3.2	Populism and anti-pluralism correlation in Western (grey) and ex-communist (black) Europe	60
Figure 3.3	Party types by region and year	61
Figure 3.4	Economic positions	62
Figure 3.5	"Cultural" positions (I)	64
Figure 3.6	"Cultural" positions (II)	66
Figure 3A.1	Vote share of populist parties in most recent general elections, 2019	70
Figure 5.1	Within-country trends in authoritarianism and polarization	111
Figure 5.2	Effect of polarization on engagement conditional on authoritarianism	115
Figure 5.3	Effect of polarization on mobilization conditional on authoritarianism	116
Figure 6.1	Model summary in different electoral arenas	137

Figures

Figure 9.1 Effect of democratic preferences on the probability of voting for a populist radical right in Western and Eastern Europe 204

Figure 9.2 Effect of democratic satisfaction on the probability of voting for a populist radical right party in Western and Eastern Europe 205

Figure 9.3 Democratic profile of the voters of each populist radical right party. 206

Figure 9.4 Effect of democratic support and satisfaction on the probability of voting for each populist radical right party in Western Europe 209

Figure 9.5 Effect of democratic support and satisfaction on the probability of voting for each populist radical right party in Eastern Europe 210

Figure 10.1 Favorable mentions of democracy and direct democracy in the election manifestos of 2018–2019 222

Figure C.1 Political polarization in Europe 265

Tables

Table I.1	Vote share of radical right parties in the latest elections	2
Table I.2	Support for military rule	3
Table I.3	Estimated postcrisis deflection of potential output of Europe in 2014	5
Table 1.1	Political cultures in relation to the quality of democracy	22
Table 1A.1	Full results from logistic regression models	30
Table 2.1	Liberal democracy versus Populist democracy	46
Table 3.1	Party types across two dimensions	55
Table 3A.1	List of PAP parties by country	69
Table 5.1	Descriptive summary	107
Table 5.2	Variance at each level in the three-level hierarchical structure	109
Table 5.3	Summary of results	112
Table 5.4	Summary of hypotheses, results, and their possible effect on democracy	117
Table 5A.1	Participation in the European Social Survey by country and year	119
Table 5A.2	Wording of items in index variables	120
Table 5A.3	Populist radical right parties by country	121
Table 6.1	Independent variables in the model	135
Table 6.2	Summarization of voter profile by electoral scenario	140
Table 7.1	Positions of party representatives and voters before and after the economic crisis	158
Table 7.2	Congruence differences of party leaders and party voters before and after the economic crisis	159
Table 7.3	Ideological congruence	160

Table 7.4	Ideological congruence (only extremists)	161
Table 7.5	Ideological congruence (only moderates)	162
Table 7.6	Vote for populist parties	163
Table 7A.1	Information on survey sample, variables, and countries	166
Table 9.1	Populist radical right parties in Western and Eastern Europe that contested in the 2019 elections to the European Parliament	198
Table 9.2	Descriptive statistics and variance inflation factors of the variables	200
Table 9.3	Effects of democratic support and satisfaction on the propensity to vote for populist radical right parties in Western and Eastern Europe, 2019 European elections	203

Introduction: European Democracy at the Crossroads

Carlos García-Rivero

INTRODUCTION

Democracy in the world is under assault. Institutional safeguards are collapsing, and democratically elected leaders are ignoring and dismantling the rights of minorities. Most democracy research institutes have, for a long time, been warning of a steady democratic deterioration. Freedom House (2021) has found a steady decline in global freedom for 15 years in a row. The Swedish Varieties of Democracy Institute[1] also identified a slow and profound legal deterioration of democracy.

Although the negative impact of this process is most visible near at the bottom of the scale of democracies, the negative pattern has affected all regime types and regions worldwide, and Europe is not an exception. Populist parties[2] are expanding their influence in institutions from Portugal to Poland and from Sweden to Italy. Although populism[3] is not a new phenomenon,[4] their electoral success in recent years has provided them with a significant degree of democratically gained institutional power, which is unprece-

---

1 Lührmann and Lindberg (2019). This autocratization is accelerating and deepening (Hellmeier et al. 2021 or Maerz et al. 2020).
2 For a definition of populist parties, work of Mudde (2004) has been followed.
3 See Ángel Rivero's Chapter 2 in this volume for a theoretical foundation of populism.
4 On the result of the European Parliament (EP) 2019 elections and the evolution of populist parties at the European elections since 1979, see Zulianello and Larsen (2021), among others. On the impact of the EP success of populist parties on their success in national elections, see Schulte-Cloos (2018).

Table I.1 Vote share of radical right parties in the latest elections

Country	% votes	Political party
Austria	17.2	Freedom Party of Austria
Belgium	3.7	Vlaam Belang
Bulgaria	9.4	National Union of Attack
Cyprus	3.7	National Popular Front
Czech Republic	10.6	Freedom and Direct Democracy
Denmark	8.6	Danish People's Party
Finland	17.48	True Finns
France	17	Rassemblement national
Germany	12.6	Alternative für Deutschland
Greece	2.9 (3.7)	Golden Dawn (Greek Solution)
Hungary	53.3	Fidesz
Italy	17.4 (4.3)	Liga (Fratelli d'Italia)
Netherlands	10.8	Party for Freedom
Norway	11.7	Progress Party
Poland	37.6 (8.8)	Prawo i Sprawiedliwość (Kukiz)
Portugal	7.18	Chega
Romania	1.5	Greater Romania Party
Slovakia	8	People's Party Our Slovakia
Spain	11	Vox
Sweden	17.5	Sweden Democrats
Switzerland	26.6	Swiss People's Party
United Kingdom	2.4	UKIP

Source: Own research.

dented in recent history. Table I.1 below shows the percentage of vote in the latest elections.

How they manage to attain such electoral strength is open to debate, and both contextual and cultural factors are certainly behind the transformation of the concept of democracy over the past two decades. This introduction presents the scenario and major changes during the past two decades in Europe, leading to the current situation where democracy is questioned by both parties and values.

Table I.2 Support for military rule

Country	Support for military rule 2000	Support for military rule 2020
Austria	1	5
Belgium	n.a.	n.a.
Bulgaria	12	15
Cyprus	n.a.	5
Czech Republic	5	9
Denmark	1	5
Finland	6	8
France	4	13
Germany	1	1
Greece	10	6
Hungary	3	12
Italy	5	10
Netherlands	1	3
Poland	17	22
Portugal	7	13
Romania	28	36
Slovakia	8	16
Spain	7	10
Sweden	6	6
Switzerland	5	4
United Kingdom	7	16
Average	*7*	*11*

Note: Entries in the table represent the percentage of people who were "much" or "very much" in support of military rule as a form of government. The survey offered four options to the interviewees: nothing, something, much, or very much in support of the military rule.

Source: World Values Survey (www.worldvaluessurvey.org).

Illiberal and anti-pluralist ideas are now spread throughout society, and this has an impact on the level of support for and satisfaction with democracy as well as support for alternative, nondemocratic forms of government that have significantly modified the *playing field*. Table I.2 shows support for military rule[5] in European countries from 2000 to the present. Figures indicate that when researchers declare that democratic quality has decreased, this is only half of the story. The remaining half is that citizens' demand for an alternative, nondemocratic form of government is, in several countries at least, on the rise. At present, democracy is no longer the *only game in town*.

In this new scenario of increasing illiberal and anti-pluralist values and escalating electoral success of populist parties, a major turning point was the 2008–2012 subprime mortgage economic crisis that boosted a *cultural backlash* and ultimately strengthened populism and consolidated populist parties in the electoral arena. Table I.3 below shows the major impact of the crisis on European countries.

The crisis forced many countries to implement a series of tough austerity measures and structural reforms of the welfare estate and labor market. These policies were very often explicitly enforced by external actors like the EU, leaving national governments and legislative bodies little or no room to maneuver in national politics and the national economy. It also left citizens without the capacity for autonomous decision-making (Beckert and Streeck 2012) and had an impact on citizens' confidence in the European Union. The acceptance or refusal of the new fiscal, labor, and social policies by both citizens and civil society organizations was mainly irrelevant, eroding the legitimacy of liberal democracy (Armingeon and Baccaro 2012).

The common response of the citizenry to the imposed measures of austerity was social unrest, upheaval, and political instability, all of which had a significant effect on the legitimacy of democratic regimes (Armingeon and Guthmann 2014). In some countries, such as Spain, Greece, and Italy, social unrest gave rise to new political parties that claimed to represent civil society and ordinary citizens, thus revealing a confrontation between the state and civil society. It was in this disconnection between civil society and state, between voters and traditional parties, that populism and populist parties found fertile ground to flourish and carry the voice of the disenchanted citizen and the voter who was excluded from the decision-making process back to the institutions. It widened the division

---

[5] See Chapter 7 for the impact of support for military rule on voting for populist radical right parties.

Table I.3 Estimated postcrisis deflection of potential output of Europe in 2014

Country	Productivity	Capital/worker	Total factor productivity	Employment	Labor force participation	Structural unemployment	Total
GRC	**-15.2**	-1.2	-14.3	**-8.6**	-2.4	-6.2	**-23.8**
EST	**-9.1**	-8.6	-0.4	**-4.9**	-4.5	-0.3	**-13.9**
HUN	**-16.3**	-3.3	-13	**2.7**	4.5	-1.9	**-13.6**
SVN	**-8.6**	-2.2	-6.3	**-4.6**	-2.5	-2.2	**-13.2**
PRT	**-12.5**	-1.6	-10.9	**1.6**	1	0.7	**-10.9**
CZE	**-5.3**	-1	-4	**-4.9**	-2.3	-2.6	**-10.2**
IRL	**-5.3**	-1	-4	**-4.9**	-2.3	-2.6	**-10.2**
SVK	**-8.3**	0.8	-8.7	**-1.1**	1.5	-2.6	**-9.4**
FIN	**-10.1**	0.8	-10.8	**1.5**	1.3	0.1	**-8.6**
UK	**-7.6**	-1.9	-5.5	**0.6**	1.2	-0.5	**-6.9**
SWE	**-6.8**	-1.1	-5.6	**0.2**	0.8	-0.5	**-6.6**
SPA	**2.1**	1.3	1	**-8.4**	-2.9	-5.6	**-6.4**
DNK	**-3.3**	-1.4	-1.8	**-2.3**	-1.4	-0.9	**-5.6**
LUX	**-4.4**	-2.1	-2.2	**-0.3**	1.6	-1.9	**-4.7**
NLD	**-3.3**	-0.3	-2.9	**-1.4**	-0.3	-1.1	**-4.7**
NLD	**-3.3**	-0.3	-2.9	**-1.4**	-0.3	-1.1	**-4.7**
NOR	**-5.2**	-0.9	-4	**0.5**	0.6	-0.1	**-4.7**
BEL	**-4.2**	-0.6	-3.4	**-0.2**	-0.1	-0.1	**-4.3**
ITA	**-3**	-2.4	-0.7	**-0.8**	0.6	-1.4	**-3.8**
CHE	**-4.1**	-1.6	-2.4	**0.9**	1.2	-0.2	**-3.2**
AUT	**-3.5**	-1.6	-1.8	**2**	2.2	-0.1	**-1.5**
FRA	**-1.1**	-0.1	-0.9	**0.5**	1.6	-1.1	**-0.6**
POL	**-6.7**	-0.8	-5.5	**7**	4.8	2.3	**0.3**
GER	**-0.8**	-0.7	0.1	**5.5**	2.9	2.7	**4.7**

Source: Ollivaud and Turner (2014).

between *we-the-people* and the *corrupt elite*, and democracy as we knew it lost legitimacy.

Populists view themselves as sole representatives of ordinary citizens and blame the established political elites for betraying the people and disrespecting their genuine interests. At a glance, populism undermines and hollows out liberal democracy by discrediting formal institutions and functions. The malfunctioning and erosion of liberal democracies is part of a broader downward shift in the whole spectrum of regimes, which show increasing signs of illiberalism, deconsolidation, and deinstitutionalization.

Although populist parties have previously had the opportunity to enter government as junior coalition partners—Lega in Italy from 2001 to 2006 and from 2008 to 2011, the FPÖ in Austria from 2000 to 2006, PiS in Poland between 2005 and 2007—their definitive takeoff came after 2010, as the victories of Fidesz in Hungary, PiS in Poland, SYRIZA in Greece, and M5S in Italy evidence. As this book goes to press, Europe is witnessing its final consolidation with its recent electoral success in Italy and Sweden in 2022.

Against this background, this book aims to analyze this whole process of political change from different perspectives to reach some conclusions regarding both the pernicious impact on democracy and the chances for consolidation of these parties in Europe.

The book is divided into three parts. The first part, "Populism in Europe: Concept and Context," focuses on the scenario and the idea of populism. In the first chapter of this section, titled "Quality of Democracy in Europe," Enrique Clari and Carlos García-Rivero analyze the political scenario generated in the past 15 years. Interestingly, the democratic decline in Europe during this period has run parallel to a strange phenomenon: an increase in satisfaction with democracy where democracy is deteriorating. In other words, not only is democracy deteriorating in Europe but, in some countries, citizens are increasingly satisfied with the way this democracy is evolving. Drawing on aggregate survey and institutional data, the authors show descriptive evidence of the ambiguous stance of Europeans toward liberal-democratic principles. Their key finding is that "uncritical" political cultures—that is, citizens' dissatisfaction with increasing levels of democratic quality and/or their satisfaction with democratic erosion—are most prevalent in those settings where a majority of the population holds authoritarian values,[6] and this helps explain why cases of democratic backsliding in the continent have not faced much popular contestation.

In Chapter 2, "Populism: Theoretical Foundations," Ángel Rivero discusses the idea of populism, its meaning, and the differences between liberal democracy and populist democracy. He demonstrates that populism is a set of ideas that inform political action that pretends to redemocratize an existing democracy when it is the opposite of liberal democracy. Populism states that societies are divided into oligarchy and the people, and the gap between the two is insurmountable. Hence, politics is a zero-sum game: it is basically a battle between the two models of government: oligarchy versus democracy. When oligarchy rules, there is no democracy. When democracy wins, oligarchy is defeated.

Following clarification of this notion, Chapter 3, "Mapping European Populism and Its Association with Anti-Pluralism: Descriptive Evidence in Time and Space" by Enrique Clari, argues that the recent success of populist parties poses a direct threat to European democracies. Contrary to previous works suggesting that populism has an ambivalent effect on democracy—it can act both as a "threat" to liberal checks and balances and as a "corrective" on representative institutions—the author uses V-Party data to show that European populist parties are mostly *also* anti-pluralist, and their illiberal drift has only grown stronger in the last few years.

In Chapter 4, "On the Persistence of Radical Right Populism in Europe: The Role of Grievances and Emotions," the last chapter in this part, Hans-Georg Betz explains why these parties have managed to remain successful in Europe for so long based on the role of grievances and emotions. At a glance, concepts like anxiety, concern, recognition, dignity, and respect have played a fundamental role in the capacity of populism to attract the disadvantaged and previously excluded into their area of influence.

Part II, "Political Participation under Populism: Trends and Limits," of this volume focuses on the political participation of voters for populist parties and the possible sanctions at hand when these parties, in office, chal-

---

6   The reference is to what Adorno et al. (1950) called an "authoritarian personality," which is an explanatory factor for the rise of fascism during the interwar period (see also Altemeyer 1988).

lenge political rights and civil liberties. On one hand, it analyzes the effect of polarization, and on the other, the congruence among voters themselves and the congruence between the party elite and the party voter. In the first chapter of this section, Chapter 5, titled "The Limits of Democratic Competition: Time-Series, Cross-Sectional Evidence of the Asymmetrical Impact of Polarization on Europeans' Political Attitudes and Behavior," Enrique Clari and Carlos García-Rivero draw on comparative and longitudinal evidence from the European Social Survey for the 2002–2018 period and show that polarization has an asymmetrical effect on the political attitudes of liberal and authoritarian citizens, respectively. Whereas it makes the former grow disaffected and disengaged, the latter feel emboldened by the hostile environment that polarization brings about, and this process disproportionately benefits the populist radical right parties compared to moderate, mainstream forces. Thus, polarization's illiberal reverberations through the democratic system are both wider and deeper than previously thought.

Chapter 6, "Populist Voter Profiles in Different Electoral Calls: Lessons from Spain" by Javier Antón-Merino, Sergio Pérez-Castaños, and Marta Méndez-Juez, seeks to test whether a different electoral arena manifests a different profile of the populist radical right electorate by using Spain as a case study. The higher the level of congruence in voter patterns of different electoral calls (local, regional, national, or European elections), the stronger the link between the party and the voter and, hence, the higher the expectation of the party's electoral success. The authors present evidence that this seems to be the case, at least in Spain. The fact that Vox is a strongly centralized party and that it has not had time to develop a party structure in all the territories has penalized this electoral brand in local elections, as well as in the regional elections of some Spanish autonomous communities. The entry of Vox into the government of Castilla y León represents a new milestone for the Spanish populist radical right, which for the first time in its short history has managed to form part of a regional government.

In a similar vein, in Chapter 7, "Ideological Congruence between Populist Right Parliamentary Elites and Their Voters: An Analysis of Poland, Sweden, and Germany," Carlos García-Rivero and Hennie Kotzè analyze the level of political congruence, but at the elite-voter level. The higher the level of congruence between party representatives (parliamentarians in this case) and their voters, the lower the probability of electoral volatility. The research makes extensive use of quantitative data gathered from citizens and parliamentarians of Poland, Sweden, and Germany before and after the 2008–2013 economic crisis. The chapter shows that there is evidence of strong ideological congruence between populist right party voters and their party representatives. In the core value system (liberties and intolerance), the level of congruence of parliamentarians and voters of populist right parties is even more evident and much more pronounced compared to that of the other parties.

The analysis of Spain as well as of Poland, Sweden, and Germany show a very high level of consistency through different elections and of political elite-voter congruence, respectively. This justifies the rising electoral success[7] of the populist parties, from 2001 to the present, becoming a threat to liberal democracy. In this regard, it is worth considering whether there is any legal instrument at hand to inhibit this challenge to liberal democracy once such a party is in office. This is explained in Chapter 8, "Internal Sanctions for Rule of Law Breaches under Article7 TEU: Why Is the EU Dragging Its Feet?," by Clara Portela and Ruth Ferrero-Turrión, who conclude that, unfortunately, there is not much room for hope in this regard: in terms of EU internal sanctions, once a populist party comes to power in one of the member states, the EU is ultimately unwilling to do anything about it. They contrast the EU's active sanctions practice in external relations with its reticence to activate internal sanctions. At a glance, the EU's commitment to discipline those members seems to be considerably weaker than in extra-European organizations.

The last part of this volume, Part III, titled "Populist Parties in Different European Regions" is composed of three chapters, each of which analyzes populist parties in different regions of Europe. José Rama and Andrés Santana, in Chapter 9, "Populism in Western versus Eastern Europe," explore the reasons behind electoral support for populist parties in Western Europe versus those in Eastern Europe, devoting special attention to the effect of support for democracy and satisfaction with democracy. Their results uncover both similarities and differences in the relationship between democratic attitudes and the electoral support of the populist radical right in the two regions. On the one hand, support for democracy hinders the vote for populist radical

---

7 According to the Timbro Institute (2019) from Sweden, populist electoral share has doubled from 11.8% to 22.3% in the past two decades, becoming the third ideological force in European politics.

right parties both in Western and Eastern Europe. On the other hand, satisfaction with democracy works in different, opposite, directions in the West and the East: while it further impairs the vote for these parties in Western Europe, it increases rather than curtails their electoral prospects in Eastern Europe. These results side with those encountered in Chapter 1 in terms of satisfaction with democracy when analyzing the quality of democracy in Eastern versus Western Europe.

Belén Fernández-García and Ángel Valencia-Sáiz in Chapter 10, "Populism in Southern Europe," analyze the situation in Southern Europe, focusing in particular on the impact of the 2008–2012 economic crisis and the subsequent situation, especially in the 2018–2022 elections in Spain, Portugal, Italy, and Greece and the democratic agenda of populist parties. They conclude that populist parties in Southern Europe are similar in terms of their promises to improve the representativeness of the system while they show differences in their notions of democracy. Basically, left-wing parties defend participatory democracy and promise to strengthen its plebiscitary character, whereas radical right parties in Portugal and Spain uphold a more representative vision of democracy, based on national sovereignty and their hostility toward pluralism and civil society.

Finally, in Chapter 11, "Nordic Populism: Conjoining Ethno-Nationalism and Welfare Chauvinism," Eirikur Bergmann analyzes the situation in the Nordic countries in the past half a century, with special emphasis on immigration, welfare policies, and nativism. He presents some relevant differences between Nordic populist parties and their counterparts in Western Europe. Nordic populist parties, rather than referring to the economic situation of the ordinary citizenry, combine socioeconomic left-oriented policies with hard-core conservative sociocultural ideas.

A chapter on *what lies ahead* summarizes the conclusions reached and presents the possible scenario in years to come. In a nutshell, the reader can anticipate that populism and populist parties have come to Europe to stay and to rule; they are not merely a temporary fad or simple protest groups.

Bibliography

Adorno, T. W., E. Frenkel-Brunswik, D. Levinson, and N. Sanford. 1950. *The Authoritarian Personality*. Studies in Prejudice Series. New York: Harper & Row.

Altemeyer, B. 1988. *Enemies of Freedom: Understanding Right-Wing Authoritarianism*. San Francisco, CA: Jossey-Bass.

Armingeon, K., and L. Baccaro. 2012. "The Sorrows of Young Euro: Policy Responses to the Sovereign Debt Crisis." In *Coping with Crisis: Government Reactions to the Great Recession*, edited by N. Bermeo, and J. Pontusson, 162–200. New York: Russell Sag.

Armingeon, K., and K. Guthmann. 2014. "Democracy in Crisis? The Declining Support for National Democracy in European Countries, 2007–2011." *European Journal of Political Research* 53 (3): 423–442.

Beckert, J., and W. Streeck. 2012. "Die Fiskalkrise und die Einheit Europas." *Aus Politik und Zeitgeschichte* 62 (4): 7–17.

Freedom House. 2021. *Freedom in the World 2021. Democracy under Siege*. New York: Freedom House.

Hellmeier, S., R. Cole, S. Grahn, P. Kolvani, J. Lachapelle, A. Lührmann, S. F. Maerz, S. Pillai, and S. I. Lindberg. 2021. "State of the World 2020: Autocratization Turns Viral." *Democratization* 28 (6): 1053–1074. https://doi.org/10.1080/13510347.2021.1922390.

Lührmann, A., and S. I. Lindberg. 2019. "A Third Wave of Autocratization Is Here: What Is New about It?." *Democratization* 26 (7): 1095–1113. https://doi.org/10.1080/13510347.2019.1582029.

Maerz, S. F., A. Lührmann, S. Hellmeier, A. Grahn, and S. I. Lindberg. 2020. "State of the World 2019: Autocratization Surges—Resistance Grows." *Democratization* 27 (6): 908–927. https://doi.org/10.1080/13510347.2020.1758670.

Mudde, C. 2004. "The Populist Zeitgeist." *Government and Opposition* 39 (4): 541–563. https://doi.org/10.1111/j.1477-7053.2004.00135.x.

Ollivaud, P., and D. Turner. 2014. "The Effect of the Global Financial Crisis on OECD Potential Output." *OECD Economics Department Working Papers* 1166. https://doi.org/10.1787/18151973.

Schulte-Cloos, J. 2018. "Do European Parliament Elections Foster Challenger Parties' Success on the National Level?." *European Union Politics* 19 (3): 408–426. https://doi.org/10.1177/1465116518773486.

Timbro Institute. 2019. *Timbro Authoritarian Populism Index: Annual Report*. Stockholm: Timbro Institute.

Zulianello, M., and E. G. Larsen. 2021. "Populist Parties in European Parliament Elections: A New Dataset on Left, Right and Valence Populism from 1979 to 2019." *Electoral Studies* 71 (June): 1–8. https://doi.org/10.1016/j.electstud.2021.102312.

PART I

Populism in Europe: Concept and Context

CHAPTER 1

Quality of Democracy in Europe

Enrique Clari and Carlos García-Rivero

INTRODUCTION

A wave of "democratic backsliding" (Norris and Inglehart 2019) or "autocratization" (Lührmann and Lindberg 2019) haunts political regimes around the globe. The era of optimism ushered by the fall of Western communism and the end of the Cold War has come to an abrupt end in recent times, as signaled by the concatenation of such concerning events as the Eurosceptic exit of the United Kingdom from the EU, the rise of populist radical right parties (PRRPs) in Europe and their access to government, the widespread violation of constitutional norms by authoritarian leaders during the global COVID-19 pandemic, and, perhaps most disturbing of all, Putin's imperialist and ultranationalist military campaign in Ukraine. As recently summarized by Boese et al. (2022, 991), "6 out of 27 EU member states are now autocratizing [and three] EU neighbors to the east are also autocratizing."

But what is even more concerning is that recent studies have found experimental evidence (García Rivero 2022, appendix) that challenges the long-standing belief that there is a diffused support for democracy (Easton 1965) and that "emancipative values" (Welzel and Inglehart 2006) are widespread in European societies. To analyze this trend, an important question that emerges is how one should go about measuring people's attitudes toward democracy. As pointed out by Linde and Ekman (2003, 395; emphasis in original), consolidated democracies need "support for the *regime principles* (i.e., support for democracy, as a principle or an ideal, as the most appropriate form of government), as well as support for the performance of the regime (i.e., support for how it functions in practice)." Stated differently, democracies need *support for* and *satisfaction with* democracy.

In this regard, although researchers have found an overall decreasing satisfaction with democracy parallel to the above-mentioned deteriorating level of democracy (Wike and Schumacher 2020), others have found diverging trends depending on the level of democracy, but parallel to this level of democracy. Foa and colleagues (2020) have found a small sample of countries (Anglo-Saxon democracies) that bucked the (dissatisfaction) trend by recording high levels of satisfaction with democracy. To summarize, where democracies are run better, citizens tend to show a higher level of satisfaction with democracy and vice versa. However, in this chapter, we present evidence of a different *species*: countries with a growing satisfaction with democracy's performance despite its fading institutional quality.

As Claassen and Magalhães (2022) point out, most previous studies delving into satisfaction with democracy have employed static, cross-sectional research designs, without controlling its evolution over the years, and they tend to focus on a single variable, namely satisfaction with democracy (SWD).[1] However, to our knowledge, no study combines the level of SWD *and* the level of democracy as a dependent variable, let alone the evolution of these two variables over the years. In this chapter, we fill this gap by combining SWD *and* the quality of democracy in a single dependent variable, and we analyze it longitudinally. This approach allows us to investigate why some citizens are satisfied with a *decaying* democracy. We merge survey data from the European Social Survey (ESS) with institutional and political party indicators to provide comparative and longitudinal evidence of the growth of both purely uncritical attitudes and authoritarian values, thus lending credence to recurring warnings about the decline of support for democracy in supposedly "consolidated" regimes (e.g., Foa and Mounk 2016; Foa et al. 2021, 2022).

First, we review the literature on the concept as well as sources on satisfaction with democracy in order to present an overall picture of the current situation in Europe in terms of the quality of democracy and satisfaction with it. We then lay out the theory and formulate hypotheses. We then

---

[1] Or at most, combine it with support for democracy (Claassen and Magalhães, for example)

present descriptive evidence of increasing satisfaction with decaying democracy and then use logistic regression models to uncover the underlying factors that explain this anomaly. The last section summarizes our findings and presents conclusions drawn from this study.

Satisfaction with Democracy

Despite its initial use as a proxy for "diffuse support" (Easton 1965) for democracy as a political system, answers to the question on satisfaction "with the way democracy works" (SWD) have been shown to gauge instrumental rather than principled evaluations (Linde and Ekman 2003). When asked about their SWD, individuals tend to base their responses on their perception of the system's effectiveness and representativeness, that is, their opinion on how the state's machinery is working rather than on how legitimate or desirable democracy is as a form of government.

Linz and Stepan (1996, 42, 223) distinguish between a regime's legitimacy (support for democracy) and efficacy (satisfaction with democracy). Although it is obvious that the legitimacy and efficacy of a democracy are closely related, it should be borne in mind that they measure different things. Support for a regime refers to the legitimacy of the regime, whereas satisfaction with the way a regime works refers to the efficacy of such a regime. As pointed out by Linde and Ekman (2003, 395), consolidated democracies need "support for the regime principles (i.e., support for democracy, as a principle or an ideal, as the most appropriate form of government), as well as support for the performance of the regime (i.e., support for how it functions in practice)."

According to Norris (2006), satisfaction with a regime means public evaluations of how well autocratic or democratic governments work in practice. It refers to the capacity of a democratic regime to deliver what citizens expect from it. In other words, it refers not to *legitimacy*, but to performance, to the *efficacy* of the regime. In other words, if a regime performs well, then its citizens will be satisfied.

However, there is no unanimity about the factors that propel SWD as researchers have reached contradictory evidence. In democratic regimes, it is expected that the higher the democratic quality, the higher the SWD. However, things are not always that straightforward. In fact, economic recessions, crime waves, and disease epidemics shine an unforgiving light on the effectiveness of governments [and there is a] demand [for] a coherent and sustained response. Indeed, it now seems clear that ineffective governance substantially reduces government support and executive approval. Less clear is whether these effects spill over to the regime itself. In autocratic contexts, the effectiveness of governments does appear to enhance support for the regime, [however], evidence is more ambiguous when it comes to attitudes in democracies: although some scholars have linked evaluations of democracy with effective government, many others find little to no relationship. Is it the case that citizens in democracies have built up loyalty to their political system because it kept the peace and swelled their pocketbooks? Or does the presence of fair elections, which allow citizens to replace governments, prevent ineffective governance from corroding public attachment to the democratic system? (Claassen and Magalhães 2022, 870)

Against this background, what is the situation in Europe and how has it evolved? Figure 1.1 shows the evolution over the years of satisfaction with democracy (data from ESS) and the level of liberal democracy (data from Varieties of Democracy [V-Dem]) in 29 countries. Interestingly, the trends in Eastern Europe and Western Europe seem different. Whereas in most of Western Europe satisfaction with democracy runs parallel to the level of democratic quality, in Eastern Europe, the opposite trend can be observed: a growing satisfaction with democracy is seen in a decaying liberal democracy. This is especially evident in countries such as Hungary and Poland—the two countries with the highest electoral support for PRRPs in recent elections (Figure 1.1).

In general, there is no consensus about which factors propel satisfaction with democracy, let alone, satisfaction with a degenerating democracy. Stated differently, what this picture portrays is a growing satisfaction with what Lührmann and Lindberg (2019) called the "third wave of autocratization" (see also Freedom House 2021). The question that emerges, then, is: why are people satisfied with a rising authoritarianism that undermines their own rights and liberties?

Under a conventional form authoritarianism, violence and terror substitute democratic accountability and responsiveness (Morgenbesser 2016).

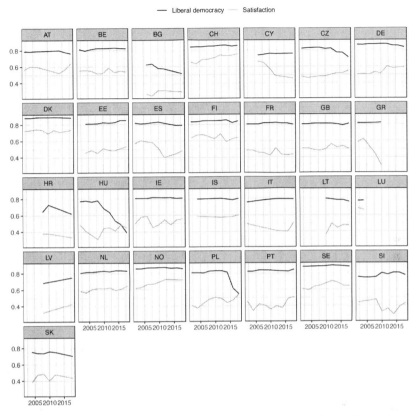

Figure 1.1 Trends in satisfaction with democracy and the level of liberal democracy in Europe, 2002–2018

However, none of the countries analyzed is a classical authoritarian regime, but is a democracy with a deteriorating level of rights and liberties. If, in general, explaining satisfaction with democracy "is more complicated than many scholars perhaps would like to admit" (Linde and Ekman 2003, 404), explaining satisfaction with a deteriorating democracy becomes an even more complex task.[2]

---

2   For now, this image discredits the idea that right-wing authoritarianism is widely supported by disaffected citizens (Arzheimer and Carter 2006; Kriesi 2020), with democratic dissatisfaction often predicting support for populist parties (Werts et al. 2013), as in some of these countries (i.e., Hungary and Poland), the highest level of support has been found for populist right parties.

Satisfaction with democracy: Literature review

Although the literature on SWD is vast, it has been found to depend on several issues related to the regime's *effectiveness*. Effectiveness refers both to economic and institutional performance since citizens are perfectly aware of the intimate connection between the two. Economic performance is a straightforward category encompassing both egotropic and sociotropic perceptions on growth, unemployment, and inequality (Armingeon and Guthmann 2014), whereas institutional performance has, to a great extent, been equated with a particular definition of "quality of government" (van der Meer 2017). Thus, the relative weight of each category will ultimately depend on their interaction with other factors ranging from economic management (Magalhães 2017) to the effect of the media (Van Aelst 2017) to social capital (Hooghe and Kern 2017). However, some authors suggest that institutional performance ultimately takes the upper hand, since "where [it] is high the impact of economic indicators is marginal, but where the quality of government is low, political support is quite sensitive to economic outcomes" (Andeweg and Aarts 2017, 198; see also Magalhães 2017; Rothstein and Teorell 2008; Magalhães 2017; Börang et al. 2017).

Other factors that come to the front when explaining SWD are institutional design and the feeling of representativeness that relates to issues such as proportional or presidential systems (Christmann and Torcal 2018), polarization (Dahlberg and Holmberg 2014; Ridge 2022; Simonovits et al. 2022; Graham and Svolik 2020), and incumbency or party affinity. In this regard, the partisan effect is stronger among electoral winners (Ezrow and Xezonakis 2011; Mayne and Hakhverdian 2017; Harteveld et al. 2021; Mazepus and Toshkov 2021).

All of the above-mentioned factors are instrumental, not principled (Linde and Ekman 2003), and so, depending on the outcome, SWD will grow or not. However, in consolidated democracies, we should expect a sizeable share of the population whose SWD is determined, at least partially, by the regime's respect for and action in accordance with democratic principles. Individuals may defend democracy irrespective of contextual factors for two reasons. First, they may be convinced that liberal regimes, despite their chronic crises, are still a better conduit for long-term prosperity than autocracies are, what Knutsen calls the "business case for democracy" (Knutsen

2021). And second, liberal ideals of individual freedom and protection from state intervention may be so ingrained in the mindsets of some citizens that they would perceive an attack against democratic institutions as an assault on themselves and their highly priced lifestyles. Stated simply, the reference here is to cultural issues—relating to a general mentality of the population—that influence the behavior and structure of the political and social institutions in the society (Brooks 1935; Brooker 1995). By "cultural issue" in a context of degrading democracy and increasing satisfaction with democracy, we refer here to the so-called authoritarian values or authoritarian personality. Empirical research suggests that some people's personality gives them strong authoritarian tendencies. Researchers have long investigated why certain individuals appear more prone to follow orders from authority figures, even if it means that they must sacrifice their own rights.

After World War II, Adorno[3] and colleagues (1950) analyzed how German people were able to turn into obedient mass murderers under Nazi rule. They developed the so-called F-scale (F stood for fascism), focusing on issues such as traditional values, anti-intellectualism, superstition, a willingness to submit to authorities, and authoritarian aggression. An individual scoring high on the scale was labeled an "authoritarian personality." Concretely, they identified several traits that were believed to cluster together. These traits include conventionalism, authoritarian submission, authoritarian aggression, anti-intellectualism, power and "toughness," anti-intraception, superstition and stereotypy, destructiveness and cynicism, projectivity, and exaggerated concerns over sex (Adorno et al. 1950, 228). However, this index was criticized as the indicators did not correlate with each other, and they did not result in a single entity or single personality.

Following this, Altemeyer (1981) later refined their work, reducing the original nine dimensions to three, namely *submission toward authorities* (a high degree of submissiveness to the authorities who are perceived to be legitimate in the society—*hierarchy*); the *endorsement of aggressive behavior if sanctioned by authorities* (a general aggressiveness directed against deviants and people who are targets according to established authorities—*intolerance*); and a high level of *conventionalism* (namely, conforming to old traditions and values—*tradition*) (Altemeyer 1981, 1988).

---

3   This line of research had already been developed by Frenkel-Brunswik et al. (1947).

Compared to individuals ranking low on the scale, authoritarians are, for example, more racist (Duriez and Van Hiel 2002), more discriminatory (Parkins et al. 2006), more aggressive, (Carnahan and McFarland 2007), more prejudiced (Ekehammar et al. 2004), more sexist (Begany and Milburn 2002), as well as more likely to follow unethical orders (Milgram 1963), to support restrictions on civil liberties (Cohrs et al. 2005), to approve of capital punishment (McKee and Feather 2008), and to follow unethical decisions when they are promoted by a socially dominant leader who perceives society as a hierarchy in which the domination of inferior groups by superior groups is legitimized (Son Hing et al. 2007).

These attitudes and values of the authoritarian personality "were usually transmitted, on one hand, by a monolithic system of propaganda, so that everyone would believe the same absolute 'truths', and, on the other, basic attitudes and values transmitted through family" traditions and practices where the parents serve as a model for the authority relations in society (Meloen 2000,108; see also Horkheimer et al. 1936). In this way, "these regimes could claim to represent the people without being held accountable by a democratic electoral system" (Meloen 2000, 109).

Methods, data, and hypotheses

To build our *dependent variable*, we classify the political cultures of different countries based on the average social reaction (in terms of SWD) to changes in the quality of democracy. Table 1.1 summarizes the possible combinations.

We use the generic label "critical citizens" to refer to those who supposedly "grasp some of the basic procedures of liberal democracy, who hold democratic values as important to their lives, and who are simultaneously dissatisfied by the performance of democracy in their own country" (Norris 2011, 34). And so, we see a political culture as "critical" when either (1) a decline in democratic quality leads to greater dissatisfaction (critical citizens

Table 1.1 Political cultures in relation to the quality of democracy

	Satisfaction grows	*Satisfaction falls*
Democracy grows	Satisfied citizens	Cynical citizens
Democracy falls	Illiberal citizens	Critical citizens

stricto sensu) or (2) SWD grows when democratic quality improves (satisfied citizens).

In contrast, *uncritical* political cultures are those in which a majority of citizens either respond positively to the erosion of democracy (illiberal citizens) or become more dissatisfied despite the growing quality of their democratic institutions (cynical citizens). Thus, uncritical political cultures can be the product of the prevalence of authoritarian or nativist values (Harteveld et al. 2021; Kokkonen and Linde 2021) or, simply, of an overall lack of diffuse support for democracy among "credulous" (Norris 2022) or "majoritarian" (Grossman et al. 2022) citizens. Consequently, our dependent variable is coded as a dummy taking the value "1" for any country-year observation in which either (1) democracy grows and average satisfaction falls (cynical citizens) or (2) democracy falls and average satisfaction grows (illiberal citizens), and the value of "0" otherwise and, we hypothesize as follows:

Hypothesis 1a: Uncritical political cultures are driven by illiberal conceptions of the system's representativeness (*input-hypothesis*).

Also, it is possible that factors such as dissatisfaction with the economy or with one's income may reduce SWD even when democracy grows. In this case:

Hypothesis 1b: Uncritical political cultures are driven by cynical evaluations of the system's effectiveness (*output-hypothesis*).

Alternatively, a number of contextual factors different from average individual attitudes, such as the quality of government, political polarization, liberal democracy, the electoral strength of anti-pluralist political parties, being an ex-communist country, GDP per capita, or unemployment may also have an effect on a country's political culture. In this case:

Hypothesis 2: Uncritical political cultures are structured by institutional and economic factors (*context-hypothesis*).

The independent variables are an array of social attitudes, effectiveness evaluations, and contextual factors such as institutional and economic issues. More specifically,

Social attitudes which include

1. *Representativeness evaluations*: *Authoritarianism* measured by the country-year mean in Schwartz's (1992) conservation factor that measures adherence to tradition, conformity, and security (ESS data); *Nativism* measured by country-year mean in index measuring negative views toward immigrants (ESS data); *Political trust* using the country-year mean in index measuring trust in political parties and the legislative (ESS data); and, finally, *Political interest* using the country-year mean (ESS data)
2. *Effectiveness evaluations*: *Satisfaction with the way the economy is doing* measured by the country-year mean (ESS); *Satisfaction with one's income* measured by the country-year mean (ESS)

Contextual factors including

1. *Institutional factors* such as *Quality of government* measured by experts' evaluations (QoG dataset) and *Liberal democracy index* measured by experts' evaluations (V-Dem); *Political polarization* measured by experts' evaluations (V-Dem); and the presence of *Anti-pluralist parties* measured by the product of a party's score in the anti-pluralism index (rated by experts) times its vote share (V-Party), and finally, if the country is or not an *Ex-communist country* with two possible values 1="yes," 0="no"
2. *Economic factors* including *GDP per capita* measured in 2010 dollars (World Bank data) and the level of *Unemployment* measured in percentage (World Bank data)

Finally, we use *Control variables* like *Time* measured in ESS waves.

We first use descriptive statistics and then use a conventional logistic regression analysis to regress our dependent variable on the battery of the above-explained independent variables. Although we use nested data and multilevel analysis is more appropriate when using this type of data, preliminary analysis reveals an intraclass correlation coefficient (ICC) below 5%, which suggests that observations across countries are independent enough to use a conventional logistic regression model. The following section presents the analysis.

Analysis

We first present a descriptive analysis of the dependent variable. Figures 1.2, 1.3, and 1.4 illustrate the results.

Quality of Democracy in Europe

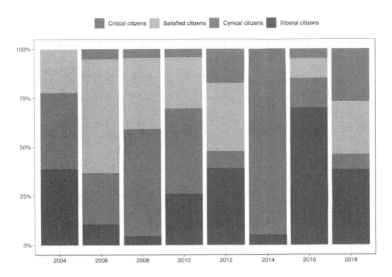

Figure 1.2 Uncritical attitudes toward democracy in Europe, 2004–2018
Note: The plot shows the yearly percentage of countries classified as having either a critical (democracy falls and so does mean satisfaction), a satisfied (democracy grows and so does mean satisfaction), a cynical (democracy grows yet mean satisfaction falls), or an illiberal (democracy falls yet mean satisfaction grows) political culture. Results should be taken with caution since countries participating in the ESS vary across rounds.

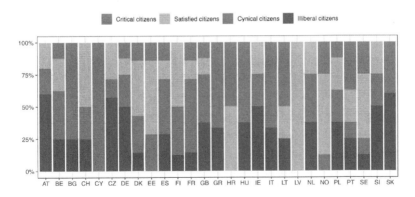

Figure 1.3 Observed political cultures by country, 2004–2018
Note: The plot shows the relative frequency with which each value of the dependent variable has been observed across countries.

25

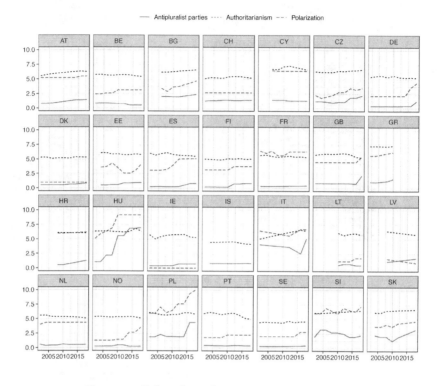

Figure 1.4 Political trends across Europe, 2002–2018

Figure 1.2 shows a steady decrease in the number of satisfied citizens following the 2008 financial crisis coupled with an increase in the number of cynical citizens, which is consistent with previous findings about the record levels of disaffection sparked by the Great Recession, especially in Southern Europe (e.g., Cordero and Simón 2016; Teixeira et al. 2014). However, starting in 2015–2016, we see a dramatic surge of illiberal political cultures, probably due to citizens' initial positive reaction to PRRP leaders breaking through many European Parliaments. Finally, 2018 seems to usher in a phase of deep polarization between European political cultures, pitting critical and illiberal citizenships against each other.

Figure 1.3 allows us to see the relative strength of each kind of political culture across countries—but it must be emphasized that not all countries have participated in all ESS waves and, therefore, the analysis that follows should be taken with a grain of salt. As we just suggested, there is a strong presence of *cynical* citizens in Southern Europe—in Cyprus, Spain, Greece, and Italy—where democratic quality has remained high despite the many years of economic turmoil. *Illiberal* citizens, on the other hand, have an important presence not only in ex-communist countries such as Czechia, Hungary, Poland, Slovenia, and Slovakia but also in Western countries like Austria, Germany, and the Netherlands. In some of them (e.g., Hungary, Lithuania, and Slovakia), *critical* citizens appear to raise their voice from time to time, but overall, it is by no means clear that there is a mass of liberal citizens ready to defend their democratic institutions in European countries.

Figure 1.4 helps us understand what has been going on behind the scenes in the two previous figures. It shows standardized levels of three different variables: the strength of anti-pluralist parties, authoritarian values among citizens, and political polarization. What is concerning is that in many European countries, all of them have risen together in the past ten years. This is the case, for instance, in Austria, Bulgaria, Czechia, Hungary, Poland, Slovenia, and Slovakia. Likewise, anti-pluralist parties and polarization—but not authoritarian values—have grown in Germany, Spain, and Italy. The picture that emerges, therefore, is one of spiraling threats to liberal democracy across the whole continent, even if such dangers are especially pervasive in the ex-communist bloc. Overall, this casts doubt on the hypothesis that European citizens are clear defenders of democracy or that they should "carry the creed" of democracy (García-Rivero and Kotze 2020, 452).

To investigate which of these factors actually propel the rise of an uncritical political culture, Figure 1.5 plots the results of our logistic regression analysis (see also Table A1.1 in the Appendix) with a set of both social attitudes and structural variables as predictors. The main finding is that only authoritarianism is positively and significantly associated with an uncritical political culture, while the remaining variables measuring society's evaluations of the system's representativeness fail to reach significance—this is the case for nativist values, political trust (our proxy for diffuse support), and interest in politics (our proxy for democratic engagement). Furthermore, none of the coefficients of variables related to instrumental evaluations of the regime's performance, such as satisfaction with one's income and with the way the economy is doing, is statistically significant—although satisfaction with the economy is significant in Model 1 (Est.=-0.796, p-value=0.027, see Table 1A.1). And, interestingly, contextual factors appear to have no effect.

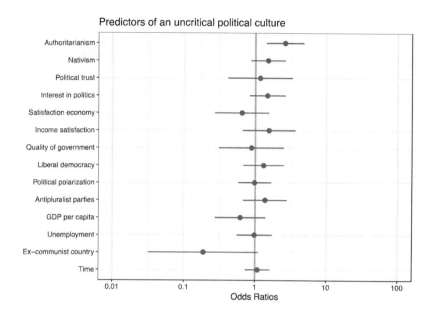

Figure 1.5 Social and structural predictors of an uncritical political culture

Note: Coefficients derived from Model 3 in Table 1A.1 in the Appendix, which includes institutional and longitudinal controls. The plot shows odds-ratios with their 95% confidence interval. Odds-ratios greater than one (blue) represent a positive association between the predictor and the dependent variable, whereas odds-ratios smaller than one (red) correspond with a negative association. Confidence intervals that cut across the grey vertical line are not statistically significant.

What this means is that the democratic commitment of European societies and their response to changes in the quality of democracy are mostly driven by their position in a spectrum that ranges from completely liberal to completely authoritarian political values. In those countries where a majority of citizens embrace a reactionary, traditionalist, and intolerant worldview, uncritical conceptions of democracy are more likely to emerge, whereas exactly the opposite is the case in liberal, tolerant, and inclusivist countries. Thus, authoritarian societies are less likely to mobilize against the democratic transgressions of their political leaders and to counterbalance any antidemocratic threat from power.

The explanatory power of social attitudes is clearly stronger than that of contextual factors, as evidenced by the much higher R^2 of Model 1 compared to Model 2. Still, the total variance accounted for by Model 3—which includes both kinds of variables—is also rather low (R^2=0.166), and this poses an important limitation to some of our claims. In particular, we are cautious not to interpret our results as evidence of a link at the individual level between authoritarian values and a lack of support for democracy. This is because all of our variables relating to social attitudes have been built as aggregated scores by country-year, which does not allow us to test any individual causal mechanisms. All we can say while avoiding the ecological fallacy is that countries with higher average scores of authoritarianism are significantly more likely to produce an uncritical political culture, even after controlling for a number of possible confounders.

In Chapter 9, Rama and Santana offer a compelling explanation of the motivations that may drive illiberal citizens in uncritical political cultures. Addressing the Central European case, they suggest that "Poles and Hungarians would [not] necessarily feel better in any environment that is less democratic. They may feel better, however, in those scenarios where the democratic backlash is the result of measures undertaken by the party they voted for."

Also, since our dependent variable is dichotomous, we cannot be sure about which kind of the two "uncritical" political cultures—cynical or illiberal—our models explain. All in all, our results lend support to Hypothesis 1a (*"Uncritical political cultures are driven by illiberal conceptions of the system's representativeness"*), whereas Hypotheses 1b (*"Uncritical political cultures are driven by cynical evaluations of the system's effectiveness"*) and 2 (*"Uncritical political cultures are structured by institutional and economic factors"*) are not compatible with our findings.

Conclusion

In most of the world, democracy is declining and also in most countries, satisfaction with democracy follows a similar path. Some countries where democracy is not achieving satisfaction with democracy also seem to stick to this path. However, in some areas, especially in Eastern Europe, a new *species* has been found, namely countries with a declining quality of democracy have citizens showing satisfaction with this trend. In this chapter, we have presented evidence of this trend and attempted to analyze the underlying reasons for this anomaly. The only overall explanation points to the spread of authoritarian values across society. Should this situation continue, democracies will most probably consolidate as low-quality democracies with limited rights and liberties.

Our results nonetheless face a number of limitations. We have already discussed the most obvious one: the causal mechanism at the individual level driving authoritarian citizens toward antidemocratic, uncritical positions. Furthermore, our argument assumed that citizens are capable of identifying changes in democratic quality and that they do in fact react to such changes. And even though there are powerful reasons to believe that uninformed citizens cannot hold critical evaluations, the correspondence between objective and subjective evaluations of democracy's quality deserves further investigation. Further research in this direction is needed, hopefully with a new and more specific dataset.

Yet again, history is repeating itself, and authoritarian values are spreading throughout society undermining the principles of democracy, paving the way to—legitimately—dismantling democracy.

Appendix

Table 1A.1 Full results from logistic regression models

	Model 1		Model 2		Model 3	
	Odds-Ratios	95% CI	Odds-Ratios	95% CI	Odds-Ratios	95% CI
(Intercept)	1.49*	1.05 – 2.13	2.23*	1.23 – 4.27	2.64**	1.32 – 5.75
Social attitudes						
Authoritarianism	2.35***	1.45 – 3.99			2.63**	1.47 – 5.05
Nativism	1.41	0.89 – 2.27			1.51	0.87 – 2.67
Political trust	1.39	0.61 – 3.20			1.17	0.41 – 3.39
Interest in politics	1.44	0.84 – 2.52			1.48	0.83 – 2.69
Satisfaction economy	0.45*	0.22 – 0.89			0.65	0.26 – 1.55

(*Continued*)

	Model 1		Model 2		Model 3	
Income satisfaction	1.75	0.89 – 3.57			1.56	0.67 – 3.76
Contextual factors						
Quality of government			0.80	0.35 – 1.72	0.88	0.30 – 2.48
Liberal democracy			1.28	0.71 – 2.36	1.31	0.68 – 2.58
Political polarization			1.26	0.79 – 2.05	0.98	0.57 – 1.68
Anti-pluralist parties			1.57	0.81 – 3.30	1.38	0.69 – 2.88
Ex-communist country			0.26	0.05 – 1.05	0.19	0.03 – 1.03
GDP per capita			0.74	0.37 – 1.43	0.62	0.26 – 1.38
Unemployment			1.12	0.73 – 1.76	0.98	0.56 – 1.75
Time control						
Time	1.03	0.71 – 1.50	0.92	0.63 – 1.35	1.08	0.72 – 1.63
N country-year	162		162		162	
R^2 Tjur	0.136		0.067		0.166	
AIC	214.130		227.756		222.837	

Source: European Social Survey (ESS), Quality of Government (QoG), and V-Dem.

Note: * $p<0.05$ ** $p<0.01$ *** $p<0.001$.

Bibliography

Adorno, T. W., E. Frenkel-Brunswik, D. J. Levinson, and R. N. Sanford. 1950. *The Authoritarian Personality*. New York: Harper & Row.

Altemeyer, B. 1981. *Right-wing Authoritarianism*. Winnipeg: University of Manitoba Press.

Altemeyer, B. 1988. *Enemies of Freedom: Understanding Right-Wing Authoritarianism*. New York: Jossey-Bass.

Andeweg R. B., and K. Aarts. 2017. "Studying Political Legitimacy: Findings, Implications, and an Uneasy Question. In *Myth and Reality of the Legitimacy Crisis*, edited by C. Van Ham, J. Thomassen, K. Aarts, and R. B. Andeweg, 193–206. Oxford: Oxford University Press.

Armingeon, K., and K. Guthmann. 2014. "Democracy in Crisis? The Declining Support for National Democracy in European Countries, 2007–2011." *European Journal of Political Research* 53 (3): 423–442. https://doi.org/10.1111/1475-6765.12046.

Arzheimer, K., and E. Carter. 2006. "Political Opportunity Structures and Right-Wing Extremist Party Success." *European Journal of Political Research* 45 (3): 419–443. https://doi.org/10.1111/j.1475-6765.2006.00304.x.

Begany, J. J., and M. A. Milburn. 2002. "Psychological Predictors of Sexual Harassment: Authoritarianism, Hostile Sexism, and Rape Myths." *Psychology of Men and Masculinity* 3 (2): 119–126. https://doi.org/10.1037/1524-9220.3.2.119.

Boese, V. A., N. Alizada, M. Lundstedt, K. Morrison, N. Natsika, Y. Sato, H. Tai, and S. I. Lindberg. 2022. *Autocratization Changing Nature? Democracy Report 2022*. Sweden: Varieties of Democracy Institute (V-Dem).

Boräng, F., M. Nistotskaya, and G. Xezonakis. 2017. "The Quality of Government determinants of Support for Democracy." *Journal of Public Affairs* 17 (1–2): e1643. https://doi.org/10.1002/pa.1643.

Brooker, P. 1995. *Twentieth-Century Dictatorships: The Ideological One-Party States*. London: Macmillan.

Brooks, R. C. 1935. *Deliver Us from Dictators!* Philadelphia: University of Pennsylvania Press.

Carnahan T., and McFarland S. 2007. "Revisiting the Stanford Prison Experiment: Could Participant Self-Selection Have Led to the Cruelty?" *Personality and Social Psychology Bulletin* 33 (5): 603–614. https://doi.org/10.1177/0146167206292689.

Christmann, P., and Torcal, M. 2018. "The Effects of Government System Fractionalization on Satisfaction with Democracy." *Political Science Research and Methods* 6 (3): 593–611. https://doi.org/10.1017/psrm.2017.23.

Claassen C., and P. C. Magalhães. 2022. "Effective Government and Evaluations of Democracy." *Comparative Political Studies* 55 (5): 869–894. https://doi.org/10.1177/00104140211036042.

Cohrs, J. C., S. Kielmann, J. Maes, and B. Moschner. 2005. "Effects of Right-Wing Authoritarianism and Threat from Terrorism on Restriction of Civil Liberties." *Analyses of Social Issues and Public Policy* 5 (1): 263–276. https://doi.org/10.1111/j.1530-2415.2005.00071.x.

Cordero, G., and P. Simón. 2016. "Economic Crisis and Support for Democracy in Europe." *West European Politics* 39 (2): 305–325.

Dahlberg, S., and S. Holmberg. 2014. "Democracy and Bureaucracy: How Their Quality Matters for Popular Satisfaction." *West European Politics* 37 (3): 515–537. https://doi.org/10.1080/01402382.2013.830468.

Dahlberg, S., J. Linde, and S. Holmberg. 2015. "Democratic Discontent in Old and New Democracies: Assessing the Importance of Democratic Input and Governmental Output." *Political Studies* 63:18–37. https://doi.org/10.1111/1467-9248.12170.

Dassonneville, R., and I. McAllister. 2020. "The Party Choice Set and Satisfaction with Democracy." *West European Politics* 43 (1): 49–73. https://doi.org/10.1080/01402382.2019.1609286.

Duriez, B., and A. Van Hiel. 2002. "The March of Modern Fascism. A Comparison of Social Dominance Orientation and Authoritarianism." *Personality and Individual Differences* 32:1199–1213. https://doi.org/10.1016/S0191-8869(01)00086-1

Easton, D. 1965. *A Framework for Political Analysis*. Englewood Cliffs, NJ: Prentice-Hall.

Ekehammar, B., N. Akrami, M. Gylje, and I. Zakrisson. 2004. "What Matters Most to Prejudice: Big Five Personality, Social Dominance Orientation, or Right-Wing Authoritarianism?." *European Journal of Personality* 18 (6): 463–482. https://doi.org/10.1002/per.526.

Ezrow, L., and G. Xezonakis. 2011. "Citizen Satisfaction with Democracy and Parties' Policy Offerings." *Comparative Political Studies* 44 (9): 1152–1178. https://doi.org/10.1177/0010414011405461.

Foa, R., and Y. Mounk. 2016. "The Danger of Deconsolidation: The Democratic Disconnect." *Journal of Democracy* 27 (3): 5–17.

Foa, R. S., A. Klassen, M. Slade, A. Rand, and R. Collins. 2020. *The Global Satisfaction with Democracy Report 2020*. Cambridge: Centre for the Future of Democracy.

Foa, R. S., X. Romero-Vidal, A. J. Klassen, J. Fuenzalida Concha, M. Quednau, and L. S. Fenner. 2022. *The Great Reset: Public Opinion, Populism, and the Pandemic*. Cambridge: Centre for the Future of Democracy

Freedom House. 2021. *Freedom in the World*. Washington: Freedom House.

Frenkel-Brunswik, E., D. J. Levinson, and R. N. Sanford. 1947. "The Anti-Democratic Personality." In *Readings in Social Psychology*, edited by T. M. Newcomb and E. L. Hartley, 96–124. New York: Holt.

García-Rivero, C. 2022. "Authoritarian Personality vs Institutional Performance—Understanding Military Rule in Africa." *Politikon* 49 (2): 175–194. https://doi.org/10.1080/02589346.2022.2072582.

García-Rivero, C., and H. Kotzé. 2020. "The 2007–2009 Financial Crisis." *Comparative Sociology* 19 (4–5): 437–464. https://doi.org/10.1163/15691330-BJA10005.

Graham, M., and M. Svolik. 2020. "Democracy in America? Partisanship, Polarization, and the Robustness of Support for Democracy in the United States." *American Political Science Review* 114 (2): 392–409. https://doi.org/10.1017/S0003055420000052.

Grossman, G., D. Kronick, M. Levendusky, and M. Meredith. 2022. "The Majoritarian Threat to Liberal Democracy." *Journal of Experimental Political Science* 9 (1): 36–45. https://doi.org/10.1017/XPS.2020.44.

Harteveld, E., A. Kokkonen, J. Linde, and S. Dahlberg. 2021. "A Tough Trade-Off? The Asymmetrical Impact of Populist Radical Right Inclusion on Satisfaction with Democracy and Government." *European Political Science Review* 13 (1): 113–133. https://doi.org/10.1017/S1755773920000387.

Hooghe, M., and Kern, A. 2017. "Social Capital and the Development of Political Support in Europe." In *Myth and Reality of the Legitimacy Crisis: Explaining Trends and Cross-National Differences in Established Democracies*, edited by C. van Ham, J. J. Thomassen, K. Aarts, and R. B. Andeweg, chapter 4. Oxford: Oxford University Press.

Horkheimer, M., E. Fromm, and H. Marcuse. 1936. *Studien über Autorität und Familie*. París: Librairie Felix Alcan.

Knutsen, C. H. 2021. "A Business Case for Democracy: Regime Type, Growth, and Growth Volatility." *Democratization* 28 (8): 1505–1524. https://doi.org/10.1080/13510347.2021.1940965.

Kokkonen, A., and J. Linde. 2021. "Nativist Attitudes and Opportunistic Support for Democracy." *West European Politics*: 1–24. https://doi.org/10.1080/01402382.2021.2007459.

Kriesi, H. 2020. "Is There a Crisis of Democracy in Europe?." *Politische Vierteljahress-chrift* 61 (2): 237–260. https://doi.org/10.1007/s11615-020-00231-9.

Linde, J., and J. Ekman. 2003. "Satisfaction with Democracy: A Note on a Frequently Used Indicator in Comparative Politics." *European Journal of Political Research* 42 (3): 391–408. https://doi.org/10.1111/1475-6765.00089.

Linz, J., and A. C. Stepan. 1996. "Toward Consolidated Democracies." *Journal of Democracy* 7 (2): 14–33. https://doi.org/10.1353/jod.1996.0031.

Lührmann, A., and S. I. Lindberg. 2019. "A Third Wave of Autocratization Is Here: What Is New about It?." *Democratization* 26 (7): 1095–1113. https://doi.org/10.1080/13510347.2019.1582029.

Magalhães, P. 2017. "Economic Outcomes, Quality of Governance, and Satisfaction with Democracy." In *Myth and Reality of the Legitimacy Crisis: Explaining Trends and Cross-National Differences in Established Democracies*, edited by C. van Ham, J. J. Thomassen, K. Aarts, and R. B. Andeweg, chapter 9. Oxford: Oxford University Press.

Mayne, Q., and A. Hakhverdian. 2017. "Ideological Congruence and Citizen Satisfaction: Evidence from 25 Advanced Democracies." *Comparative Political Studies* 50 (6): 822–849. https://doi.org/10.1177/0010414016639708.

Mazepus, H., and D. Toshkov. 2022. "Standing up for Democracy? Explaining Citizens' Support for Democratic Checks and Balances." *Comparative Political Studies* 55 (8): 1271–1297. https://doi.org/10.1177/00104140211060285.

McCoy, J., G. Simonovits, and L. Littvay. 2020. "Democratic Hypocrisy: Polarized Citizens Support Democracy-Eroding Behavior When Their Own Party Is in Power." Paper prepared for the American Political Science Convention. Panel on Seeking Solutions to Polarization: The U.S. in Comparative Perspective. September 10–14.

McKee, I. R., and N. T. Feather. 2008. "Revenge, Retribution, and Values: Social Attitudes and Punitive Sentencing." *Social Justice Research* 21:138–163 https://doi.org/10.1007/s11211-008-0066-z.

Meloen, J. D. 2000. "The Political Culture of State Authoritarianism." In *Political Psychology Cultural and Cross-Cultural Foundations*, edited by S. Renshon and J. Duckitt, 108–127. New York: New York University Press.

Milgram, S. 1963. "Behavioral Study of Obedience." *Journal of Abnormal and Social Psychology* 67 (4): 371.

Morgenbesser, L. 2016. *Behind the Façade: Elections under Authoritarianism in Southeast Asia*. New York: State University of New York Press.

Norris, P. 2011. *Democratic Deficit: Critical Citizens Revisited*. Cambridge: Cambridge University Press.

Norris, P. 2022. "Trust in Government Redux: The Role of Information Environments and Cognitive Skills." HKS Faculty Research Working Paper Series.

Norris, P., and R. Inglehart. 2019. *Cultural Backlash: Trump, Brexit, and Authoritarian Populism*. Cambridge: Cambridge University Press.

Parkins, I. S., H. D. Fishbein, and P. N. Ritchey. 2006. "The Influence of Personality on Workplace Bullying and Discrimination" *Journal of Applied Social Psychology* 36 (10): 2554–2577.

Ridge, H. M. 2022. "Just Like the Others: Party Differences, Perception, and Satisfaction with Democracy." *Party Politics* 28 (3): 419–430. https://doi.org/10.1177/1354068820985193.

Rose, R. 1997. *Survey Measures of Democracy*. Glasgow: University of Strathclyde Studies in Public Policy.

Rothstein, B. O., and J. A. Teorell. 2008. "What Is Quality of Government? A Theory of Impartial Government Institutions." *Governance* 21 (2): 165–190. https://doi.org/10.1111/j.1468-0491.2008.00391.x.

Schwartz, S. H. 1992. "Universals in the Content and Structure of Values: Theoretical Advances and Empirical Tests in 20 Countries." *Advances in Experimental Social Psychology* 25:1–65.

Simonovits, G., J. McCoy, and L. Littvay. 2022. "Democratic Hypocrisy and Out-Group Threat: Explaining Citizen Support for Democratic Erosion." *Journal of Politics* 84 (3): 1806–1811. https://doi.org/10.1086/719009.

Son Hing, L. S., D. R. Bobocel, M. P. Zanna, and M. V. McBride. 2007. "Authoritarian Dynamics and Unethical Decision Making: High Social Dominance Orientation Leaders and High Right-Wing Authoritarianism Followers." *Journal of Personality and Social Psychology* 92 (1): 67–81. https://doi.org/10.1037/0022-3514.92.1.67.

Teixeira, C. P., E. Tsatsanis, and A. M. Belchior. 2014. "Support for Democracy in Times of Crisis: Diffuse and Specific Regime Support in Portugal and Greece." *South European Society and Politics* 19 (4): 501–518.

Van Aelst, P. 2017. "Media Malaise and the Decline of Legitimacy." In *Myth and Reality of the Legitimacy Crisis: Explaining Trends and Cross-National Differences in Established Democracies*, edited by C. van Ham, J. J. Thomassen, K. Aarts, and R. B. Andeweg, chapter 6. Oxford: Oxford University Press.

Van der Meer, T. 2017. "Dissecting the Causal chain from Quality of Governance, and Satisfaction with Democracy." In *Myth and Reality of the Legitimacy Crisis: Explaining Trends and Cross-National Differences in Established Democracies*, edited by C. van Ham, J. J. Thomassen, K. Aarts, and R. B. Andeweg, chapter 8. Oxford: Oxford University Press.

van Ham, C., and Thomassen, J. 2017. "The Myth of Legitimacy Decline: An Empirical Evaluation of Trends in Political Support in Established Democracies." In *Myth and Reality of the Legitimacy Crisis: Explaining Trends and Cross-National Differences in Established Democracies*, edited by C. van Ham, J. J. Thomassen, K. Aarts, and R. B. Andeweg, chapter 2. Oxford: Oxford University Press.

van Ham, C., J. J. Thomassen, K. Aarts, and R. B. Andeweg, eds. 2017. *Myth and Reality of the Legitimacy Crisis: Explaining Trends and Cross-National Differences in Established Democracies*. Oxford: Oxford University Press.

Welzel, C., and R. Inglehart. 2006. "Emancipative Values and Democracy." *Studies in Comparative International Development* 41 (3): 74–94. https://doi.org/10.1007/BF02686237.

Werts, H., S. Peer, and M. Lubbers. 2013. "Euro-Scepticism and Radical Right-Wing Voting in Europe, 2002–2008: Social Cleavages, Socio-Political Attitudes and Contextual Characteristics Determining Voting for the Radical Right." *European Union Politics* 14 (2): 183–205. https://doi.org/10.1177/1465116512469287.

Wike, R., and S. Schumacher. 2020. "Democratic Rights Popular Globally but Commitment to Them Not Always Strong." *Pew Research Center*.

Chapter 2

Populism: Theoretical Foundations

Ángel Rivero

The ideology of populism

In this chapter, I would like to show that, contrary to what many commentators such as Aslanidis say, populism is a distinctive set of ideas and, as such, constitutes a full-fledged ideology. These ideas have a long history that can be traced back to the inception of modern democracy more than two hundred years ago. The core idea of populism is the conception of democracy as a means to politically express the collective will of the people. In this sense, populism embodies an alternative definition of democracy that goes against the grain of what liberal democracy stands for. As aptly pointed out by Rosanvallon (2021, 14), "its ideology [of populism] has been characterized as soft or weak [but] these qualifications are deceptive, as Populism's capacity to mobilize supporters make clear ... We have to recognize Populism as the rising ideology of the twenty-first century."

In a liberal democracy, political participation is instrumental in the protection of individual rights. Thus, democracy is about protecting freedom. On the contrary, in the populist understanding of democracy, the plebiscite is seen as the manifestation of the single will of the people: democracy is about implementing the will of a sovereign collective being.

In this chapter, I will describe the origins of this alternative notion of democracy, provide a detailed analysis of its core notions, present a comparison of populist democracy with liberal democracy, and finally, explain why there is a strong connection between populist democracy and authoritarianism.

A POPULIST UNDERSTANDING OF DEMOCRACY

Before explaining the populist understanding of democracy, it is necessary to point out that populism and demagoguery are not the same, and that populism and autocracy are not interchangeable concepts either. Demagoguery is as old as democracy, but it can also appear in other political regimes. The demagogue is a politician who flatters or scares the people to gain political support and legitimacy. As shown by Berend (2020, 1; emphasis in original), the demagogue can be a democrat, a fascist, or a communist, but, contrary to what he or she states, the demagogue is not always a populist: The "term *demagogue* comes from the Greek *demos agein* (leader of people), but in modern times it has a much darker meaning, *leader of the mob* ... a demagogue is a political agitator who appeals to the passions and prejudices of the mob in order to obtain power."

In my view, it is more useful for the purposes of conceptual clarification to restrict the use of the term "populist" to a more limited group of demagogues. A demagogue can be labeled "populist" when, in a democratic setting, he or she appropriates the voice of the people to denounce what he or she describes as a false democracy. The suggested alternative definition has two main implications. First, populism can happen only in democracies; second, the ideal climate for populist demagoguery is created by a defective or weakened democracy. In this sense, one can see populism as a parasitic ideology of democracy and, further, that populism is endemic to only democracy.

If we take for granted the preceding ideas, there are two basic assumptions in the populist understanding of democracy. The first one is that democracy is "the government in the name of the people" or "Au nome du people," which was Marine Le Pen's slogan in the French presidential elections of 2017. However, the definition was coined by the French Jacobin Constitution of 1793: "The laws, decrees, sentences, and all public transactions are superscribed: In the name of the French people, in the—year of the French Republic" (article 61).

Contrary to what we consider to be essential while defining an advanced democracy (checks and balances, fair elections, separation of powers, free speech, civil and political rights, and, thus, a complex definition of democracy), populism allows for an instant, straightforward definition: the government in the name of the people. This is extraordinarily effective under certain circumstances in eroding political trust when, in a democracy, social distress is triggered by an economic, political, social, or cultural crisis. Characteristically, discontent is voiced by populism denouncing that democracy is no longer in place, and the government is accused of being illegitimate; in other words, when it comes to "the common good," people's will is not the effect of its actions. As stated by Juan Domingo Perón in his famous speech of October 17, 1950, at the Plaza de Mayo: "True democracy is the system where the Government carries out the will of the people defending a single objective: the interests of the people."

The second basic assumption of populism as an ideology is that societies are split into two opposing closed groups: the people and the oligarchy. Populism is, therefore, an ideology of conflict according to which there is a social division between the two antagonistic camps in every society. Here, antagonistic means that one group is defined in opposition to that of the other. According to populism, this divide between the groups is permanent and unbridgeable. In this sense, politics is not understood as a device to solve social conflicts but as the battleground where these two sides fight for hegemony. In Greek, the term hegemon means a "supreme leader." Hegemony means the dominance of a social group over others; in the case of populism, it is the people versus the oligarchy. Eva Perón's last public speech, delivered on May 1, 1952, was a war cry against the "enemies of the people" who were "insensitive and repugnant" and "as cold as toads and snakes." She exalted the "holy fire of fanaticism" and ordered the people of Argentina to "fight the oligarchy." A year before, in her "Speech to the Descamisados" on October 17, 1951, she noted thus: "I know that God is with us because he is with the humble and despises the arrogance of the oligarchy. Therefore, victory will be ours. We will achieve it sooner or later, whatever the cost, whoever may fall."

Ernesto Laclau (2005, 125), a contemporary defender of populism and political advisor to presidents Néstor Kirchner and Cristina Fernández de Kirchner of Argentina, stresses this idea in fashionable academic language by pointing out that "the only features I retain from the usual notion of democracy are: (1) that [the] demands are formulated to the system by an underdog of sorts—that there is an equalitarian dimension implicit in them; (2) that their very emergence presupposes some kind of exclusion or deprivation (what I have called 'deficient being')."

Underlying Laclau's "idiosyncratic" understanding of democracy is the idea of a struggle between the oppressed and the oppressors, between those included and those excluded in society. But the goal of this struggle is not a comprehensive integration of all but for the dispossessed to achieve hegemony.

This second feature of populism is also associated with a moral or Manichean understanding of politics. "Oligarchy" encompasses the evil and corrupt part of society that pretends to impose domination over the people, while, on the contrary, "the people" constitute the healthy, virtuous, and good part of society that is always just. In this sense, when the oligarchy is in power, there is no democracy or, in some cases, there is a "false democracy." However, "real democracy" is a government in the name of the people, and it is assumed that provided the people's will is followed, all social problems will be solved. As aptly expressed by Russell Kirk (1988, 1), the basic conviction of a populist is that "the cure for democracy is more democracy" and, as I will show later, this explains why populists are always suspicious of liberal or representative democracy and why they feel more comfortable with direct or plebiscitary democracy.

In a sense, this second basic assumption of populism qualifies the first one: democracy understood as a government of the people means government in the name of the healthy, virtuous part of society: in other words, democracy is good government for the good people.

Given that in a representative democracy there is always a functional division between those that govern and those who are governed, the banner denouncing "fake democracy" can be raised easily in times of crisis, whereas, in a plebiscitary regime, the leader's self-presentation as the people's voice can be disguised as democracy. I will deal with this in greater detail later in the chapter while explaining the authoritarian drive of populism. For now, it is sufficient to highlight the fact that in a liberal democracy, when the relationship between the representatives and the represented is no longer founded in trust, the faith in existing democracy deteriorates, and the democratic pendulum swings toward populism in search of a restoration of democracy.

As mentioned earlier, the roots of populism can be traced back to the very inception of democracy in ancient Greece but, above all, they can be clearly discerned in the foundation of contemporary democracy in the American and French Revolutions.

According to Aristotle's classification of political regimes, democracy is a deviant form of government of pluralities working in their own interest and disregarding the common good. He also defined oligarchy as a corrupt government of a minority that, for its own sake, once again, neglects the common good. In the populist view, these are the only two possible forms of government, and politics is seen by them as the permanent struggle between "democracy" and "oligarchy."

In modern times, this struggle focused on sovereignty, the supreme power or authority. Sovereignty, in the past, was the main attribute of a monarch, but the French Revolution of 1789 transferred it to the people; the sovereign people were named "nation." Since then, there has been a long intellectual and political history of democracy understood as a government in the name of a sovereign people. The most important among its intellectual defenders was Jean-Jacques Rousseau, the archenemy of representative democracy.

The political instances of the realization of this idea can be seen in the Jacobin stage of the French Revolution and, above all, in Bonapartism in French political history. As explained by Pombeni (1997, 50), populism can be seen in European history as the attribution of "souveraineté (c'est-à-dire de la capacité d'engendrer commandement et obligation politique) à ceux qui peuvent se considerer en harmonie avec le peuple" (sovereignty [i.e., the ability to generate command and political obligation] to those who can consider themselves in harmony with the people).

Nadia Urbinati (2019) has noted that "populism is not new. It emerged along with the process of democratization in the nineteenth century ... What *is* novel today is the intensity and pervasiveness of its manifestations" (1; emphasis in original)

It is striking that despite the European roots of populism, it was considered, until recently, a political phenomenon restricted to America, as if it were a tropical plant incapable of growing and developing in the old continent. See, for instance, the absence of Western Europe in the classic book by Ionescu and Gellner (1969) on populism. In a sense, there is a forgotten history of populism in Europe that can be explained by the postwar consensus that defined politics in the western part of the continent between 1945 and the 1970s. During this period of European history, populism was almost absent in political life, but populism was a part of earlier European history that is now back and here to stay, perhaps, for a long time. According to Ivan Krastev (2011),

> It would be a major mistake to analyse the current rise of populism in Europe as a kind of pathology or as a temporary phenomenon. Populism is here to stay and, in the age of populism, tensions between the directions of the democratisation of society and their impact on the effectiveness of democratic governance will be the principal tensions in shaping the future of democracy. (15; for more on European history of populism and its future in Europe, see Rivero 2018)

The Populist Constellation of Ideas and Attitudes

Beyond these two core ideas of populism mentioned earlier—democracy and the division of society into oligarchy and people—there are other aspects of this ideology that need consideration. A constellation is defined as a group of stars forming a recognizable pattern that is traditionally named after its apparent form or a group of associated or similar people or things. Ideologies can be seen as constellations of ideas in the sense that they are not united by a system but by their political performance in everyday politics forming a recognizable pattern.

But prior to presenting these other ideas of the ideology of populism, it is important to discuss the populist understanding of "the people." According to Cas Mudde, "populism is a thin-centered ideology that considers society to be ultimately separated into two homogenous and antagonistic groups: *the pure people* and *the corrupt elite* and argues that politics should be an expression of the *volonté générale* (general will) of the people" (Mudde 2004, 543; emphasis in original). Putting aside this definition of populism as a "thin ideology" (a topic much discussed by Schroeder [2020] and even by Freeden [2017]), in Mudde's view, the people and the elite are divided along moral lines: the healthy part of the society is the people, *the pure people*, whereas the rotten one is the elite, *the corrupt elite*, namely, the oligarchy. Thus, in populism, the people are no longer seen mainly as a social class but as moral agents.

This moralization of politics is essential in the populist ideology. As noted earlier, Laclau was perhaps the most important contemporary ideologue of populism. While he understands the people as an "empty signifier," he still retains this moral dimension of the concept of "the people," without specifying their features as such, representing all those who resent the social divisions of society. To him, all those who perceive themselves as victims of the system can identify with "the people." In this sense the people are no longer, as mentioned, a social strata or class, but rather an all-encompassing concept to aggregate all the groups that resent the "domination of the oligarchy."

Laclau argues that populism aims to mobilize these groups simplifying social pluralism and complexity in foes and friends—oligarchy and the people. For him, a successful populism is one that is able to divide society in an antagonist sense entirely: the people and the anti-people, that is, the oligarchy:

> Populism, it is argued, "simplifies" the political space, replacing a complex set of differences and determinations by a stark dichotomy whose two poles are necessarily imprecise. In 1945, for instance, General Perón took a nationalistic stand and asserted that the Argentinian option was to choose between Braden (the American ambassador) and Perón. And, as is well known, this personalized alternative features in other discourses through dichotomies such as the people versus the oligarchy, toiling masses versus exploiters, and so on. (Laclau 2005, 18)

Another important facet of populism is anti-politics. According to Bernard Crick (1962), anti-politics is the public expression of negative feelings toward the politicians, political parties, and institutions of representative democracy as well as the vocal defense of the value of "real democracy." Or, as defined by Matthew Wood (2022, 28), "anti-politics [can be seen] as coherent sets of political attitudes and ideas (political belief systems) containing preferences for unmediated mechanisms of democratic representation, informed by distrust in mediated democratic representation." Populism is anti-political in the sense that

> populists are explicitly distrustful of elites they accuse of being corrupted by the material rewards of office, which allegedly put them in opposition to the interests of "the people." This sets up populism to be explicitly distrustful of mediated representation, because, for populists, the people cannot ever entrust its morally pure singular will to the corrupted whims of elected elites. (Wood 2022, 31–32)

To sum up this point, instances of populist anti-politics can be seen when the political system is assessed as corrupt and when politicians are described as members of a corrupt class that kidnapped democracy for their own benefit. This anti-political stance explains why populists tend to avoid identifying themselves with politicians and perform the role of the common man or the ordinary people. This can be done, for example, by dressing casually or by speaking like an ordinary man. As shown by Susan Hunston (2017), for instance, Donald Trump's language was striking for a president of a major power, "Trump's language appears to be designed to align him with non-politicians, to assert his identity as a 'common man' … Although his language, both in content and in style, is odd for a political leader, it is familiar to his audience. It is the true language of populism."

Another important feature of populism, as mentioned above, is the vocal defense of direct democracy vis-à-vis representative or liberal democracy—an aspect that needs to be discussed in detail. Direct democracy is presented by populists as real democracy whereas, in contrast, liberal democracy is allegedly a false democracy. In the populist view, societal problems arise from a lack of democracy, and liberal democracy is essentially nonradical, that is, it does not aim to eliminate the causes of social unrest but to deal with the effects of social conflict. The objective of liberal democracy is to resolve conflicts in society while protecting individual liberty and rights and, in this sense, it falls short of the normative expectations of the populist understanding of democracy. Accordingly, populist ideology states that liberal democracy needs to be democratized, and this can be done by the implementation of direct democracy tools.

For populism, to "democratize" a liberal democracy entails introducing "direct democracy" procedures, such as referenda or, even better, plebiscites. For instance, it is this affinity that Robert Zaretsky (2022) uses while defending Marine Le Pen from being branded a fascist. On the contrary, he notes that Le Pen is carrying on the French *bonapartist* tradition in which authoritarian power is made democratic by using the plebiscite. During the French presidential election campaign of 2022, "sitting behind a wall of microphones, she declared that France faced an *unprecedented democratic crisis* and that referendums were its cure. After becoming president, Le Pen vowed that she would 'organize a referendum on the essential questions of the control of immigration, the protection of the French identity, and the primacy of national rights'" (Zaretsky 2022).

As mentioned by Katherine Collin (2019, 1), "referendums are often seen as a tool that empowers populist authoritarians. Globally, democratic backsliding has coincided with increased use of popular votes." While stating that referenda can be a useful tool in the checks and balances system of liberal democracy, she admits that, with the exception of a few countries in Europe, not all referenda are instrumental in the consolidation of authoritarianism.

This point is clearly argued by Penadés and Velasco (2022) who note that "the comparative study of authoritarianism has neglected plebiscites, and the comparative study of referendums tends to see in them a form of direct democracy regardless of the regime." In a nutshell, referenda are best suited to disguise authoritarianism as democracy. And, in fact, what populism calls referenda are, to define them accurately, plebiscites: "plebiscites are government-initiated popular voting processes on government-formulated questions ... Most plebiscites were won by overwhelming majorities; they were likely to be manufactured and unlikely to be taken at face value" (Penadés and Velasco 2022, 74). Plebiscites are much-appreciated instruments used to legitimize power not only in autocracies but also by populists in search of democratic acquiescence. The effect, as can be seen in many instances, is an authoritarian drive of democracy. As Zaretsky (2022) says, "Just as the elder Napoleon employed a plebiscite to ratify his self-promotion from first consul to emperor, the younger Napoleon harnessed it to transform himself from former president to future emperor. What had been, under the Roman Republic, a device of democracy had become, under the Bonapartes, an accomplice of autocracy." The very word "plebiscite" triggers populist resonances: it comes from the Latin *plēbiscītum*, a decree of the people; the populace, *plēbs*; and from *scītum*, decree or approbation.

Finally, another word very much cherished by populism is sovereignty. "Sovereignty" refers to the supreme power—a power that is above all other powers in a society and that is not limited or constrained by them. A state is defined as sovereign when its decisions are not limited by other states or powers. In the populist view, sovereignty and democracy are closely linked: there is no democracy without sovereign people. This way, the defense of sovereignty forms a part of the basic demands of populism. For instance, the three pillars of the Peronist political creed were *social justice, economic independence, and political sovereignty*, and Le Pen promised "restaurer la souveraineté de la France" (To restore the sovereignty of France) as a way of restoring democracy.

According to the liberal understanding of sovereignty, if "the power of a small number is sanctioned by the assent of all, then that power becomes the general will" (Constant 1988, 175). But here there is an important proviso: this power cannot be unlimited and cannot be used against the rights of individuals because "when sovereignty is unlimited, there is no means of sheltering individuals from governments" (179). But this is not the way populism understands the concept.

Following Schmitt, contemporary populism maintains that the only principle of legitimacy today is democracy. So, to justify a supreme power prior to the rule of law, sovereignty should be democratized. Schmitt, in his *Dictatorship: From the Origin of the Modern Concept of Sovereignty to the Proletarian Class Struggle* (1931/2013), maintains that the sovereign dictator draws his authority not from himself but from invoking the name of the people.

Thus, a sovereign dictatorship is seen as fully democratic when the will of the people is ascertained and exercised. Before Schmitt, Robert Michels (1911), in his book titled *Zur Soziologie des Parteiwesens in der modernen Demokratie* (Political Parties: A Sociological Study of the Oligarchical Tendencies of Modern Democracy), explores democracy without representation by formulating the *iron law of oligarchy*, in which he states that democracy and representation are incompatible in the sense that representation creates a new governing class whose interests are above those of the people. The iron law, a permanent law for all countries and times, reiterates that representation always means oligarchy.

In his quest for democracy as the political expression of the will of the people, Michels arrived at the conclusion that real democracy can be identified as the communion of a leader and mass and seen as the perfect realization of the people's will, without the corrupt mediation of the elites; he concluded by declaring his "democratic enthusiasm" for fascism.

The contemporary rehabilitation of Schmitt was carried out, among others, by prominent populist ideologues such as Ernesto Laclau and Chantal Mouffe (1999). In a purely populist vein, Mouffe (1999, 6) encourages one to read Schmitt on how to improve liberal democracy: "The strategy is definitively not to read Schmitt to attack liberal democracy, but to ask how it could be improved." In Mouffe's (1999) view, it is necessary to read Schmitt because existing liberal democracy is imperfect, and the sovereignty of the people needs to be restored. But her vision clouded her understanding of what liberal democracy really is. Liberal democracy is not defective in giving strength to the people's voice because it is not an abstract concept. Liberal democracy is the only existing democracy, but it is very different from what populism defends as "real democracy." Both democracies are not different faces of the same coin, the imperfect and the perfect, but refer to totally different understandings of what democracy is and should be. As stated by Takis S. Pappas (2019, 1), populism "seeks to institute a ... form of democratic politics that is antagonistic towards established liberal democracy."

Populist democracy versus liberal democracy

In his book on populism and liberal democracy, Pappas (2019) focuses on this comparison between liberal democracy and populist democracy. However, we will first look at the differences between liberal democracy and populist democracy (Table 2.1).

Table 2.1 Liberal democracy versus Populist democracy

Liberal democracy	Populist democracy
Assumptions: political and social pluralism are recognized and valued. People encompassing all citizens.	**Assumptions**: people are understood as a collective being with a single will. Antagonistic division of society people/elite (*oligarchy*).
Institutions: separation of powers, checks and balances, political accountability. Moderate or limited state power.	**Institutions**: strong executive with supervising control over the legislative and judiciary powers. Unlimited state sovereignty.
	(*Continued*)

Media: Independent press and media groups.	**Media:** State control of media and public communications. Preponderance of public-owned media that is supervised by the executive power.
Elections: regular and competitive.	**Elections:** permanent electoral processes, rigged elections.
Direct democracy: referenda and plebiscites are rare exceptions.	**Direct democracy:** plebiscites are frequent and elections are converted into plebiscites.
Political parties: political pluralism recognized and valued.	**Political parties:** Manichean moralization of political competition: "us" versus. "them." Political polarization and anti-political mood.
Political action: political bargaining in search of agreement.	**Political action:** adversarial politics in search of hegemonic imposition.
Leadership: accountable and limited intime.	**Leadership:** leader/people identification, unlimited sovereignty deployed in the name of the people.

Source: Author's own research.

Populist democracy is not an improved version of liberal democracy. Certainly, it is the case that populism appears in a democratic setting in which political disaffection is present. But populism is not aimed at the restoration of trust in the democratic institutions of a weakened democracy. On the contrary, populism mobilizes anti-political feelings to make room for an alternative model of democracy. For instance, Silvio Berlusconi was named by Gianfranco Pasquino as "the Knight of Anti-politics" because he blamed the Italian political class for the corruption of democracy and presented himself as a "nonpolitical" savior of democracy. But beyond his personalization of power, there is no democratic legacy after Berlusconi: his acrimony against the Italian false democracy was instrumental in his thirst for power to protect himself from judiciary control. There was no better democracy beyond populism.

Similarly, according to populism, all nonelective institutions of liberal democracy are nondemocratic powers devised to limit people's sovereignty and are derisively called "counter-majoritarian." Following this creed, the defense of a "majoritarian democracy" is seen as a legitimate challenge to the rule of law justified by the fact that more importance is given to "democracy" than to the Constitution. In fact, the Constitution is frequently presented by the populist as a "padlock" that prevents people's will from being realized. In this sense, there is another significant difference between liberal democracy and populist democracy. The former understands politics as a bargaining process between different political interests and actors to reach an agreement. The people speak with a single voice only through the law. According to populism, however, politics is about the implementation of the people's will, and the very idea of bargaining to arrive at public decisions with other political actors is seen as an example of corruption. Given that there is only one legitimate position—one that speaks in the name of the people—political bargaining is associated with corruption, namely, the act of treason that betrays the people's will.

Thus, from a populist perspective, the democratization program devised to improve liberal democracy tends to focus on the elimination of all counter-majoritarian institutions and the establishment of a strong executive defined as the people's voice. As expected, the main outcome of the populist promise of democracy is authoritarianism.

Urbinati (2019, 14) has shown that populism is a new form of *democratic* government based on a direct relationship between the leader and the people: "Populist leaders claim to speak to and for the people without the need for intermediaries—in particular, political parties and independent media—whom they blame for betraying the interests of the ordinary many." She explains that populist governments are distinct from dictatorial or fascist regimes, but "their dependence on the will of the leader, along with their willingness to exclude the interests of those deemed outside the bounds of the 'good' or 'right' people, stretches constitutional democracy to its limits and opens a pathway to authoritarianism" (17).

Populist Democracy and Authoritarianism

As discussed thus far, populism can be considered as an ideology owing to the fact that its core ideas form a recognizable pattern, a constellation of ideas, with a discernible character: democracy in the name of the people, people versus oligarchy, direct democracy and plebiscite, the sovereignty of the nation. Indeed, populism as an ideology is instrumental in informing political action because it provides a description of a political system of its own; delivers an assessment of a political system; and lays out a prospective blueprint for political action. In performing all these ideological functions, populism views liberal democracies as divided into people and oligarchy; criticizes liberal democracies as fake democracies; and makes a promise of regeneration by democratizing liberal democracy. When liberal democracy faces an economic crisis, a social crisis associated with growing inequality and poverty, a political crisis or a crisis of presentation, or a cultural crisis (e.g., associated with the cultural change induced by immigration), the social and political preconditions for a populist movement are given.

In consolidated democracies, this populist time can be managed through institutions and can have the positive impact of triggering a repoliticization of democracy. Here populism is a symptom of democracy's decline, but in less-strong democracies, populism is not a symptom of a decaying democracy but rather a threat to the existing weak democracy. Then the ideology of populism can be deployed at the end as democracy paves the way for authoritarianism: the enforcement of strict obedience to authority, and top-down control, at the expense of personal freedom and in the name of the people.

Bibliography

Aslanidis, P. 2016. "Is Populism an Ideology? A Refutation and a New Perspective." *Political Studies* 64 (S1): 88–104. https://doi.org/10.1111/1467-9248.12224.

Berend, I. T. 2020. *A Century of Populist Demagogues. Eighteen European Portraits 1918-2018.* Budapest: Central European University Press.

Collin, C. 2019. "Populist and Authoritarian Referendums: The Role of Direct Democracy in Democratic Deconsolidation." Brookings, February. https://www.brookings.edu/research/populist-and-authoritarian-referendums-the-role-of-direct-democracy-in-democratic-deconsolidation/.

Constant, B. 1988. *Political Writings*. Cambridge: Cambridge University Press.

Crick, B. 1962. *In Defence of Politics*. Chicago: University of Chicago Press.

Freeden, M. 2017. "After the Brexit Referendum: Revisiting Populism as an Ideology." *Journal of Political Ideologies* 22 (1): 1–11. https://doi.org/10.1080/13569317.2016.1260813.

Hunston, S. 2017. "Donald Trump and the Language of Populism." https://www.birmingham.ac.uk/research/perspective/donald-trump-language-of-populism.aspx (Accessed April 17, 2023).

Ionescu, G., and E. Gellner, eds. 1969. *Populism: Its Meaning and National Characteristics.* New York: Macmillan.

Kirk, R. 1988. "The Popular Conservatives." The Heritage Lectures, 168. The Heritage Foundation, Washington. http://thf_media.s3.amazonaws.com/1988/pdf/hl168.pdf.

Krastev, I. 2011. "The Age of Populism: Reflections on the Self-Enmity of Democracy." *European View* 10:11–16. https://doi.org/10.1007/s12290-011-0152-8.

Perón, J. D. 1952. *Peronist Doctrine*. Buenos Aires: Peronist Party.Laclau, E. 2005. *On Populist Reason*. London: Verso.

Michels, R. 1962. *Political Parties: A Sociological Study of the Oligarchical Tendencies of Modern Democracy*. Translated by E. Paul and C. Paul, with an introduction by S. M. Lipset. New York: Free Press.

Mouffe, C., ed. 1999. *The Challenge of Carls Schmitt*. London: Verso.

Mudde, C. 2004. "The Populist Zeitgeist." *Government and Opposition* 39:541–563. https://doi.org/10.1111/j.1477-7053.2004.00135.x.

Pappas, T. S. 2019. *Populism and Liberal Democracy: A Comparative and Theoretical Analysis*. Oxford: Oxford University Press.

Pasquino, G. 2007. "The Five Faces of Silvio Berlusconi: The Knight of Anti-Politics." *Modern Italy* 12 (1): 39–54. https://doi.org/10.1080/13532940601134817.

Penadés, A., and Velasco, S. 2022. "Plebiscites: A Tool for Dictatorship." *European Political Science Review* 14 (1): 74–93. https://doi.org/10.1017/S175577392100031X.

Pombeni, P. 1997. "Typologie des populismes en Europe (19e-20e siècles)." *Vingtième Siècle, Revue d'Histoire* 56 (October–December): 48–76. https://doi.org/10.3406/xxs.1997.4491.

Rivero, Á. 2018. "Populism and democracy in Europe." In *Routledge Handbook of Global Populism*, edited by A. De la Torre, 281–294. London: Routledge.

Rosanvallon, P. 2021. *The Populist Century: History, Theory, Critique*. Oxford: Polity.

Schmitt, C. 2013. *Dictatorship. From the Origin of the Modern Concept of Sovereignty to the Proletarian Class Struggle*. Oxford: Polity Press.

Schroeder, R. 2020. "The Dangerous Myth of Populism as a Thin Ideology." *Populism*, 3 (1): 13–28. https://doi.org/10.1163/25888072-02021042.

Urbinati, N. 2019. *Me the People: How Populism Transforms Democracy*. Cambridge: Harvard University Press.

Wood, M. 2022. "The Political Ideas Underpinning Political Distrust: Analysing Four Types of Anti-Politics." *Representation* 58 (1): 27–48. https://doi.org/10.1080/00344893.2021.195407.

Zaretsky, M. 2022. "Is Marine Le Pen a Fascist?" *Foreign Policy*, April 21, 2022. https://foreignpolicy.com/2022/04/21/france-election-le-pen-ideology/.

CHAPTER 3

Mapping European Populism and Its Association with Anti-Pluralism: Descriptive Evidence in Time and Space

Enrique Clari

INTRODUCTION

The "third wave of autocratization" (Lührmann and Lindberg 2019) that haunts European democracy cannot be understood without a reference to the other political phenomenon it is most often associated with: the rise of populist parties signaling a new *"Zeitgeist"* (Mudde 2004; Akkerman et al. 2016). The connection between populism and democratic backsliding is nowhere clearer than in those countries, such as Hungary and Poland, where populist authoritarian leaders have gained access to government and then used their power to dismantle liberal checks and balances from within the system.

But, in fact, populism's continued growth across the whole continent, which manifests itself in various guises—some authors talk about "radical" parties (Kriesi and Schulte-Cloos 2020), whereas others employ the labels "protest" (Borbáth and Hutter 2021), "anti-political-establishment" (Abedi 2004; Casal-Bértoa and Rama 2021), or "challenger" (Hobolt and Tilley 2016)—has become a matter of concern for all supporters of liberal democracy and forced them to look beyond just Central and Eastern Europe.

Yet, the actual effects of populism on the quality of democratic institutions have been debated for many years, and they remain contentious to this day. In particular, the question separates those who see populism as an inherent threat to democracy from those others who welcome its revitalizing impact on public discussion and herald the "return of the political" (Mouffe 2005).

In this chapter, I use the latest version of the Varieties of Party Identities and Organization (V-Party) dataset (Lindberg et al. 2022) to describe the trajectories of populist parties in Europe, both in the West and in the excommunist region. My main goal is to further test the external validity of the conclusions derived from the "populism-as-a-threat versus populism-as-a-corrective" debate. The rest of the chapter is organized in the following manner: in the first section, I review the literature on the topic. In the second section of the chapter, I analyze the growth of populism's electoral support across regions and time, focusing on the particular trajectory of the populist, anti-pluralist (PAP) party family. Then, I plot PAP parties according to their ideological positions in an attempt to disentangle their real differences across the economic and cultural dimensions. The last section, which concludes the chapter, summarizes the key points and results of the study.

Populist parties and anti-pluralism

The fundamental tension between populism and liberal democracy has been recognized for a long time. Already 40 years ago, Riker (1988, 238–241) wrote about the unattainability of the "populist goal" in liberal democracies, that is, about the impossibility to identify and articulate anything like a "common will" expressed by "the people" in our modern representative regimes owing to their growing complexity and the fallibility of democratic processes of preferences aggregation.

Riker's argument built on social choice theory rather than political philosophy, and even though his concept of populism was not as fine-grained as those developed by current theories (see Rivero's contribution in this volume for a review), his insistence on an irresolvable conflict between the liberal principle of constrained political power and the ideal of popular sovereignty still speaks to us today.

In fact, current understandings of populism have not remained oblivious to this inescapable paradox, as evidenced by Taggart's (2000) early theoretical work. Urbinati (2014), for example, describes populism as a "disfiguration" of democracy and a quite harmful at that, whereas Galston (2018) reminds us of the "populist challenge to democracy." In a different vein, Taggart (2000) sees populism as a symptom of the "pathologies" that afflict liberal democracy, and another author defines it as "an emerging historical phenomenon of late democratic modernity that opposes political liberalism" (Pappas 2019, 1).

Likewise, the "ideational approach to populism" (Mudde 2004; Hawkins et al. 2018) conceptualizes it as a "thin" ideology based on three principles—anti-elitism, people-centrism, and Manicheism—which are, at best, hard to reconcile with the normative core of liberal democracy. In particular, Manicheism or moral monism is clearly at odds with the pluralist principle that reigns supreme in contemporary democratic regimes.

Still, the revival of the study of populism with its new focus on populist *parties* has led to a more ambivalent account of their relationship with liberal democracy, recognizing that populist parties can act, at least in some cases, as a "corrective" rather than as a "threat" (Rovira Kaltwasser 2012).

Not everyone shares this view, of course, as there are many scholars who see populism as inherently detrimental or opposed to liberal democracy (e.g., Müller 2016; Pappas 2019) but most of these accounts refer to an ideological, rather than a practical, incompatibility between liberalism and populism (e.g., Rummens 2017).

Still, there appears to be a growing consensus about the essential difference between the two kinds of populist parties in accordance to their degree of respect for democratic norms, that is, between "inclusionary" and "exclusionary" populist parties (Mudde and Rovira Kaltwasser 2013). The former kind is seen as a predominantly Latin American phenomenon capable of "repoliticizing" the system and giving voice to oppressed minorities, whereas the latter is especially prominent in Europe, where it has manifested itself as a nativistic, deeply illiberal force.

In particular, the current wisdom classifies populist radical left parties located at the GAL (green-alternative-liberal) pole of the new "transnational cleavage" (Hooghe and Marks 2018) as "inclusionary" actors, whereas it stamps the "exclusionary" label on "populist radical right parties" (PRRPs), which share a triad of nativist, authoritarian, and populist attitudes (Rydgren 2004; Mudde 2007). And so, even if "PRRPs have never challenged the bare essence of their democratic systems, this cannot be said of the fundamentals of liberal democracy" (Mudde 2013, 11).

In fact, PRRPs are unanimously seen as the key drivers of democratic backsliding in advanced democracies (Vachudova 2020; Meléndez and Rovira Kaltwasser 2021), and "most observers agree on the undesirability of the radical right, due to its alleged antidemocratic character" (Mudde 2014, 218). PRRPs threaten democracy because they tend to use the "illiberal playbook" (Pirro and Stanley 2022), especially when they gain access to government positions (Albertazzi and Mueller 2013; Huber and Schimpf 2016).

PRRPs also contribute to the deterioration of democratic norms in other ways, too, since "established parties react to the success of radical right challengers by emphasizing more anti-immigrant and culturally protectionist positions" (Abou-Chadi and Krause 2020, 15)—although other authors note that such parties "have an indirect, but modest influence on policy outcomes" (Muis and Immerzeel 2017, 918).

The essentially antidemocratic component of PRRPs as opposed to populist left parties has also permeated several recent projects aimed at producing a database of populist parties. For example, despite their common Eurosceptic attitude, radical left and radical right parties end up in very different party families when classified along the GAL-TAN (Green-Alternative-Libertarian—Traditionalist-Authoritarian-Nationalist) dimension (Bakker et al. 2015; Jolly et al. 2022). Likewise, describing the key findings derived from their own dataset, Meijers and Zaslove (2021, 394) write that "the populist left holds a more pluralistic notion of the people [than the populist right]," which should be understood as evidence of left-wing populism's greater compatibility with liberal democracy.

However, other empirical studies find little support for the idea that populist left and populist right parties are *essentially* different, or that the left-wing kind of populism is *inherently* less threatening to democracy than PRRPs. For instance, Norris (2020, 706) concludes that, in terms of the intensity of their populist rhetoric, "there are important exceptions" in Western Europe to "the conventional association between populism and 'radical-right' parties," which corroborates the contention by Rooduijn and Akkerman (2017, 201; emphasis in original) that "at least in Western Europe, populism and radicalism often go hand in hand—both on the right *and* the left."

Likewise, Zulianello (2020, 343) finds that populism can act as a corrective only under hybrid or fully authoritarian regimes, whereas in liberal democracies its "ideational profile is at odds with both the values of pluralism and the constitutional checks and balances." And even more explicitly, in their analysis merging different databases, Juon and Bochsler (2020, 13) "find no evidence that left-wing populists should be favourably associated with individual liberties and the public sphere ... On the contrary, our results indicate a strong negative effect of left-wing populists on the latter, driven by infringements on constitutional freedoms of association, assembly, speech, and effective freedom of the press." Finally, using V-Party data, Ruth-Lovell et al. (2019, 23) demonstrate that "the negative relationship between populism and electoral, liberal, as well as deliberative democracies holds even if we control for far-right and far-left populist variants."

METHODOLOGY

Conceptual classification and research questions

To further delve into this issue, I propose a classification of parties that is based, on the one hand, on the extent to which they resort to a populist rhetoric and, on the other, on their relative commitment to democratic norms and principles (Table 3.1).

Following this depiction, in most countries *populist, anti-pluralist* (PAP) *parties* will simply correspond with *populist radical right parties* (PRRPs),

Table 3.1 Party types across two dimensions

		Commitment to democracy	
		Pluralist	Anti-pluralist
Populist rhetoric	Non-populist	Mainstream	Radical
	Populist	Populist	Populist, anti-pluralist

Source: Own elaboration.

but there is no reason to believe that this will always the case. With this conceptual scheme in mind, I will try to answer two different research questions:

RQ1: Are populism and anti-pluralism correlated? In other words, does the rise of populist parties necessarily signal the emergence of a *populist, anti-pluralist* (PAP) party family?
RQ2: If the answer is affirmative, then where do PAP parties stand ideologically regarding the most salient economic and cultural dimensions in the current European political system? In particular, relative to the GAL-TAN cleavage, are there any significant differences dividing left-wing and right-wing PAP parties?

Data

The "Varieties of Party Identity and Organization" (V-Party) dataset (Lindberg et al. 2022) is a comparative and longitudinal project that contains evaluations of individual political parties by country experts on the basis of an extensive range of institutional, ideological, and organizational variables.

Rather than just averaging the ratings provided by the different country expert coders, the methodology used in the V-Party dataset to arrive at particular scores for each party relies on item response theory to calculate both point estimates and confidence intervals, and scores are treated as latent constructs rather than as directly observable variables (Pemstein et al. 2020).

The sample used here contains a total of 9,984 observations from 416 political parties in 29 European countries from 2000 to 2019.[1] I have included all democratic regimes from the whole European continent, both EU and non-EU members, and have only excluded a number of smaller states, such as Luxembourg and Malta. The final sample is thus representative of all European regions and political cultures.

---

1   Note, however, that the real number of *unique* observations in the original V-Party dataset is about 75% smaller than my sample's, because, in order to obtain comparable observations across countries, I have filled the gaps between electoral cycles with the data from the latest, prior elections.

KEY VARIABLES

The "populism index" (*v2xpa_popul*) is an interval variable ranging from 0 (not populist at all) to 1 (completely populist party) that tries to measure the extent to which "representatives of the party use populist rhetoric." The index is in turn calculated as the harmonic mean of populism's two fundamental dimensions: anti-elitism and people-centrism.

The "anti-pluralism index" (*v2xpa_antiplural*) measures the "lack of commitment" to democratic principles in a 0–1 scale. Just like the populism index, anti-pluralism scores are derived from a number of different subcomponents: the demonization of political opponents, lack of commitment to free and fair elections, lack of respect for the rights of minorities, and encouragement of political violence.

To compare the positions of PAP parties on *economic issues*, I use both the classical left-right scale (*v2pariglef*), where parties on the left are those favorable to the state's intervention in the market, and right-wing positions refer to *laissez-faire* and deregulatory preferences as well as attitudes toward the welfare state (*v2pawelf*), from comprehensive and universal coverage to minimal provision of welfare policies.

Regarding the GAL-TAN cleavage, the V-Party dataset contains a number of *cultural* variables. First, and as a surrogate of the actual GAL-TAN classification included in the Chapel Hill Expert Survey (Bakker et al. 2015), I use the item on "cultural superiority," which refers to "key non-economic cleavages in society" (Lindberg et al. 2022, 29) and ranges from a strong promotion of the nation's cultural superiority to strong opposition to nativist messages (though I reverse the variable values when necessary to make interpretations easier). Then I compare parties' scores on this item with their positions on a set of other salient cultural issues, such as the promotion or opposition to LGBT rights (*v2palgbt*), immigration (*v2paimmig*), female integration in the workforce (*v2pawomlab*), and reliance on religious principles to justify the party's positions (*v2parelig*).

ANALYSIS

Let us first evaluate the relative strength of populist parties in general, irrespective of their anti-pluralism score.

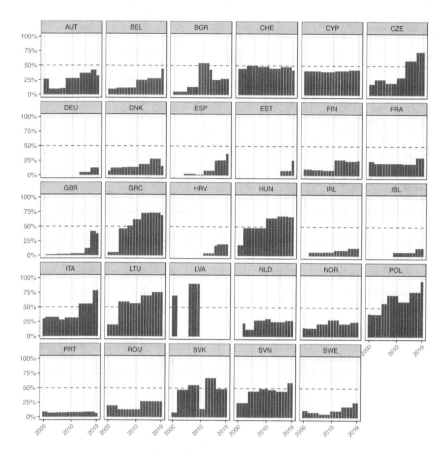

Figure 3.1 Vote share of populist parties by country and year

Note: Populist parties are those scoring in the top 33% in V-Party's *v2xpa_popul* index in the year 2019.

Source: V-Party dataset (Lindberg et al. 2022).

Figure 3.1 shows that throughout the whole European continent there is an upward trend in the electoral success of populist parties. Admittedly, even in 2019, there still was a very high cross-country variation—compare the low percentage in Portugal (6.5%) to the almost complete dive into populism of the Polish party system—but in most countries populists are on the rise.

It also allows us to identify those countries where populism has a longer tradition: in Switzerland, for instance, the Swiss People's Party (SVP)

has enjoyed parliamentary representation since the 1970s, although it turned decidedly Eurosceptic and nativist only some 20 years ago. Likewise, the history of the French Front National (FN) is long enough to even have experienced a generational replacement at its forefront.

In other countries, however, populist parties had no support at all or simply did not exist prior to the Great Recession, and started gaining momentum only with the collapse of traditional party systems. In the Spanish 2011 general elections, for example, the two mainstream parties achieved almost 75% of the vote, whereas in the most recent elections in November 2019 the vote shares of populist radical right Vox and populist radical left Unidas Podemos added up to a total of 25%, only 3 points behind the winning party (PSOE; Partido Socialista Obrero Español or the Spanish Socialist Party) and with Vox only five points behind the mainstream conservative PP (Partido Popular or Popular Party). (for an overview of each party's vote share, see Figure 3A.1 in the Appendix).

Note that our measure of populism encompasses a larger set of parties than those included in the usual scholarly classifications (e.g., Rooduijn et al. 2019), but this in turn allows us to detect those cases in which mainstream parties have also grown populist—be it as a result, for instance, of a more populist public debate in the media (Rooduijn 2014), or of the diffusion of Eurosceptic (Meijers 2017) or anti-immigration (Abou-Chadi and Krause 2020) ideas.

Figure 3.2 plots the average yearly correlation between parties' populism and anti-pluralism in Western and Eastern Europe. In both regions, the association is quite strong (all Pearson correlation estimates are greater than 0.5), but populism and anti-pluralism have become even closer in recent years. In Western Europe, populist parties grew much more anti-pluralist during the hardest years of the Great Recession, as the big jump around 2011 shows. In contrast, in ex-communist countries, the increasing correlation between populism and anti-pluralism goes further back in time and has remained stable but very high since 2007. Interestingly, even if we drop the notoriously illiberal Hungarian and Polish cases, the picture in ex-communist Europe remains quite similar, which suggests that the anti-pluralist trend in the region is not the product of a few outliers.

Furthermore, at the moment there is a big gap between Western and Central-Eastern Europe in terms of the strength of the correlation, as popu-

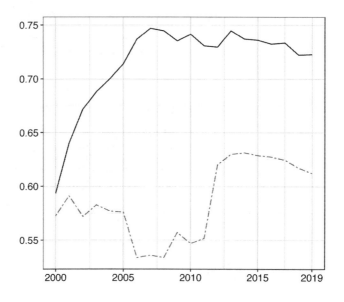

Figure 3.2 Populism and anti-pluralism correlation in Western (grey) and ex-communist (black) Europe

Note: Y-axis values are yearly correlation estimates between parties' populism and anti-pluralism scores and separately calculated for Western and ex-communist European countries (n=8,320).

Source: V-Party dataset (Lindberg et al. 2022).

list parties in the ex-communist bloc are significantly less committed to liberal democratic principles than populist parties in the West are, which may be one of the reasons why the level of democratic backsliding also differs across regions. Overall, we can still conclude that European populist parties have become almost universally anti-pluralist, too, and that they have ultimately coalesced into a single party family, whose exact trajectory is further depicted in Figure 3.3 (for a complete list of all parties falling under the PAP category, see Table 3A.1 in the Appendix).

Turning now to our second research question, how do PAP parties compare to other party families in terms of their ideological positions? And what about differences within the PAP family itself?

Mapping European Populism and Its Association with Anti-Pluralism

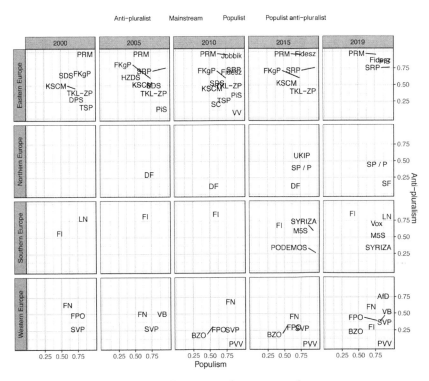

Figure 3.3 Party types by region and year

Note: Individual parties are labeled as "populist" and/or "anti-pluralist" if their respective score is equal to or higher than the 2019 top third for each variable (i.e., >=0.45/1 for populism and >=0.13/1 for anti-pluralism). Due to the figure's size, only PAP parties with a vote share greater than 10% are labeled. *Eastern Europe* includes BGR, CZE, EST, HRV, HUN, LTU, LVA, POL, ROU, SVK, and SVN. *Northern Europe* includes DNK, FIN, GBR, IRL, ISL, NOR, and SWE. *Southern Europe* includes CYP, ESP, GRC, ITA, and PRT. *Western Europe* includes AUT, BEL, CHE, DEU, FRA, and NLD.

Source: V-Party dataset (Lindberg et al. 2022).

Figure 3.4 plots economic positions of parties in Western and Eastern Europe. The X-axis refers to the traditional "left-right" division, measured as the relative preference for public intervention in the economy, whereas the Y-axis reflects support for universal welfare policies. In line with previ-

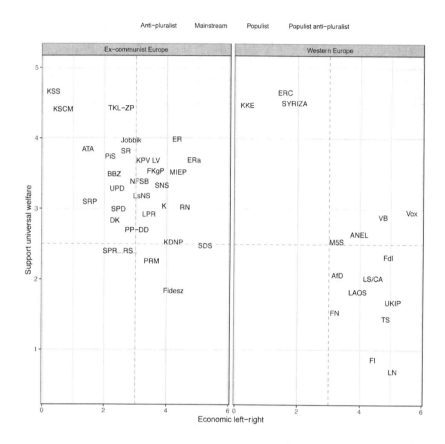

Figure 3.4 Economic positions

Note: *Economic left-right* ranges from "far left" (0=strong defense of state intervention in the economy) to "far right" (6=unconditional support for market liberalization and a reduced government). *Universal welfare* ranges from complete opposition to any public welfare policy (0) to promotion of universalistic welfare policies for all groups in society (5). PAP parties are labeled and highlighted.

Source: V-Party dataset (Lindberg et al. 2022).

ous studies pointing out that left-right divisions no longer capture the fundamental cleavages in European political competition, Figure 3.4 shows that PAP parties are just as likely to embrace left-wing economic policies as right-wing stances, especially in Eastern Europe. This also resonates with Ivaldi et al.'s (2017, 370) conclusion about Western European PAP parties: "whilst embedded in diverse ideological traditions and operating within different contexts, populist parties such as the FN, the Lega, Podemos and the M5S share a common and robust core of ideas that define the structural qualities of the populist ideology."

Likewise, PAP parties from both sides of the ideological spectrum can support universal welfare, although PRRPs tend to adopt so-called welfare chauvinist positions, which Schumacher and van Kersbergen (2016, 301) define as "the view that access to welfare should be restricted to the 'deserving' natives." Furthermore, Krause and Giebler (2020) show that welfare chauvinism can spill from PRRPs over to mainstream right-wing parties, which further blurs the left-right cleavage.

Figure 3.5, in turn, plots position across the cultural dimension. Looking first at the X-axis, we see that right-wing PAP parties are indeed more nationalist than the left-wing PAP parties.[2] The higher score of right-wing PAP parties in the item on cultural superiority is line with a long-standing literature arguing that, despite their equally anti-elitist and people-centric rhetoric, right-wing and left-wing PAP parties actually differ in their particular conceptions of *who* the treacherous elites are (the standard bearers of a globalist, rootless agenda versus the commanding heights of financial capitalism) and exactly which individuals can be considered members of *the* people (the culturally homogeneous national community versus the helpless, ordinary working class).

Scores on the Y-axis of the left-hand side of Figure 3.5 also paint a familiar picture. Besides their different positions in regard to nationalism, right-wing and left-wing PAP parties also hold diverging views in terms of support for LGBT rights. In particular, despite growing acceptance and normalization of same-sex marriage and of homosexuality and nonbinary identities in general, PRRPs still choose to swim against the tide.

Explicitly homophobic programmatic positions are especially prevalent in ex-communist countries, whereas in some Western European countries there are cases, most notably the Dutch PVV (Akkerman 2015; de Lange and Mügge 2015), in which PRRPs try to project a much more progressive posi-

---

2   However, there are some remarkable exceptions like the Catalan independentist party ERC, which combines a strongly leftist economic agenda with a completely nativistic conception of the Catalan ethnicity.

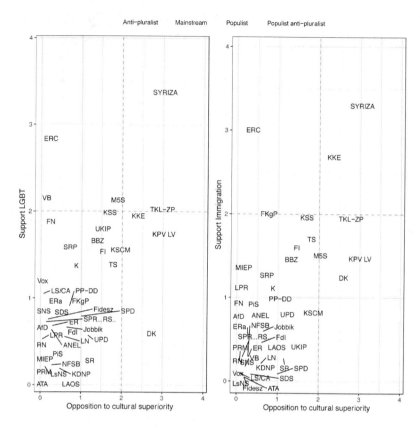

Figure 3.5 "Cultural" positions (I)

Note: We use opposition to cultural superiority (0=promotion of the cultural superiority of the nation, 4=strong opposition to cultural superiority) as a proxy for the GAL-TAN scale, which is also included in the V-Party dataset but misses many of the parties from our sample. Support LGBT goes from strong opposition to LGBT social equality (0) to strong support (4). Support immigration ranges from opposition to all or most forms of immigration into the country (0) to strong support (4). PAP parties are labeled and highlighted.

Source: V-Party dataset (Lindberg et al. 2022).

tion on the issue and even succeed in gaining support from the (admittedly minor) electoral sector composed of "sexually modern nativists" (Spierings et al. 2017).

However, the typical position of Western European PRRPs in this regard is better exemplified by the Spanish Vox, whose leaders try to sell their noticeably discriminatory agenda through a more palatable and even "politically correct" discourse directed against the "lobbies" that have allegedly hijacked the equality movement and perverted it, which is the same kind of strategy they use against the "radical feminists" (Turnbull-Dugarte et al. 2020).

On the contrary, and turning now to the right-hand panel in Figure 3.5, right-wing PAP parties are clearly more opposed to immigration than are left-wing PAP parties. This makes perfect sense, since a xenophobic and nativistic backlash has always been the key element fueling the success of PRRPs, either directly (Lubbers et al. 2002; Rydgren 2004; Iversflaten 2008; Muis and Immerzeel 2017) or indirectly through its diffusion to the positions adopted by mainstream right-wing parties (Abou-Chadi and Krause 2020).

Furthermore, the xenophobic "contagion" of left-wing parties cannot be entirely ruled out, since, in order to please nativist voters, they can have the incentive to infuse their generous social spending policies with a welfare chauvinistic ingredient, especially in a context in which a sector of their electoral base feels "cross-pressured" by the emergence of right-wing PAP parties (Bale et al. 2010; Gidron 2022).

The empirical evidence on the strategies adopted by left-wing parties as a response to the political salience of immigration is, however, inconclusive: some studies find little or no evidence of such contagion (Abou-Chadi and Wagner 2019; 2020; Carvalho and Ruedin 2020) while others argue exactly the opposite (Klüver and Spoon 2020; Hjorth and Larsen 2022).

But how robust are the differences between right-wing and left-wing PAP parties when it comes to other "cultural" issues? A look at support PAP parties for the inclusion of women in the labor market and the adoption of legal norms ensuring gender equality at work show that actually only a share of them oppose this kind of progressive policies. In fact, not only do left-wing PAP parties such as the Czech KSCM or the Italian M5S align in this regard with mainstream parties, but also radical right PAP parties such as the Bulgarian NFSB or the French Front National score relatively high in this item.

This surprising result is even more accentuated when we look at the degree to which parties recur to religious justifications of their political positions. The right-hand panel in Figure 3.6 shows that PAP parties are no more religious than mainstream parties. Again, this applies both to populist left-wing and populist right-wing parties—with the only (and relevant) exceptions of the governing Polish PiS, the Hungarian Fidesz, and Fratelli d'Italia.

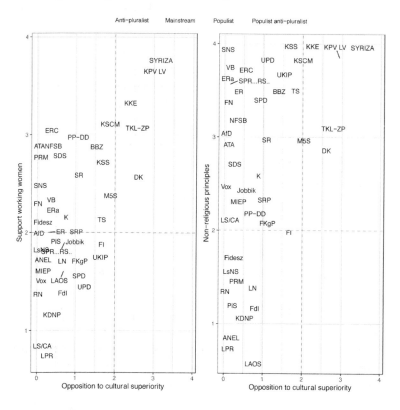

Figure 3.6 "Cultural" positions (II)

Note: We use opposition to cultural superiority (0=promotion of the cultural superiority of the nation, 4=strong opposition to cultural superiority) as a proxy for the GAL-TAN scale, which is also included in the V-Party dataset but misses many of the parties from our sample. Support working women goes from strong opposition to all policies intended to improve gender equality in the access to the labor market (0) to strong support (4). "Nonreligious principles" measures the extent to which party leaders justify their decisions based on religious arguments (0="Always," 4="Never"). PAP parties are labeled and highlighted.

Source: V-Party dataset (Lindberg et al. 2022).

Once again, the case of Vox provides us with a good illustration of this trend: despite its leaders' usual outbursts against the "progressive dictatorship" of the feminist movement, their outlandish evocations of the glorious Reconquista that expelled the infidel "Moors" from the Iberian Peninsula, and their constant appeals to traditional, Christian family values, these religious references look more like a rhetorical device aimed at inflaming the hearts of the masses rather than as an actual call for the revival of Catholicism in Spain.

The most reasonable explanation for this trend is the need PRRPs have felt to adapt their conservative message to the reality of postmaterialist societies. As Ignazi (1992, 19) pointed out early on, "contemporary conservatism does not just recall the traditional moral values of the past" but clearly builds on its opposition to a new left progressivism, and even though the counter-revolution is no longer "silent," PRRPs have still had to adapt to the irrevocable secularization and demand for gender equality in contemporary democracies, which probably explains their success compared to the electoral decline of traditionally conservative Christian democratic parties (Bale and Krouwel 2013; Bale and Rovira Kaltwasser 2021).

Overall, the analysis of these "cultural" issues suggests that the ideology of current PRRPs amounts to something more than just a reactionary ultra-conservatism. Rather, PRRPs today appear to be the distinctive product of postindustrial societies.

Thus, despite their frequent appeal to traditional moral values, shared cultural heritage, and their evocation of a glorious national past, the worldview that (especially Western European) PRRPs adhere to is very different from that of mainstream conservative and Christian democratic parties. For instance, when PRRPs invoke the Judeo-Christian tradition, they do so in opposition to the alleged threat posed by a future cosmopolitan culture or its substitution for an Islamic civilization. Likewise, when they attack LGBT rights and gender equality, their appeal to traditional moral values sometimes masks their deeper reaction against what they see as the rule of a globalist and progressive *elite*. In sum, the "cultural backlash" (Norris and Inglehart 2019) propelled by PRRPs, though ultra-conservative, reactionary, and anti-progressive, points nonetheless to something both bigger and different, namely, to a radically postmodern and original form of authoritarian neo-traditionalism.

Conclusion

Engaging with the "populism-as-a-threat versus populism-as-a-corrective" literature, in this chapter I have used the comprehensive V-Party dataset to describe some of the key trends in the European party system during the past 20 years.

The first finding is that most populist parties are also anti-pluralist, which goes against the common assumption that populist left parties are somehow more committed to democratic norms and principles than populist right parties. What is more, the connection between populism and anti-pluralism has only grown stronger in the last years, so much so that nowadays almost all populist parties belong to a single, illiberal family, which I have called "populist, anti-pluralist" (PAP).

This is not to say that there are no ideological differences across populist parties anymore or that they are all equally contemptuous of democratic norms, but simply that, in terms of their respect for liberal principles, European populist left and populist right parties are increasingly hard to distinguish, since most of them tend to demonize their political opponents, to express a feeble commitment to free and fair elections, and to openly reject political violence.

Second, I have claimed that the ideology espoused by contemporary right-wing PAP parties constitutes a novel worldview and that it is different from classical conservatism since it tries to square a traditionalist, nativist authoritarianism with the need to adapt to the irrevocable secularization of society and demand for gender equality in contemporary democracies.

The main takeaway from this chapter is that the incompatibility between liberal democracy and populist parties from all sides of the spectrum goes beyond the purely theoretical tension between their different political philosophies. Therefore, instead of talking about a "populist" *Zeitgeist* in Europe, it would be advisable to refer to it as an "anti-liberal" (Holmes 1993, 2021) challenge to democracy, which was born in and has ultimately adapted to the particular setting of postindustrial societies.

Appendix

Table 3A.1 List of PAP parties by country

Country	Party
AUT	BZÖ, FPÖ, TS
BEL	PA-PTB, VB
BGR	ATA, BBB, BBZ, NFSB
CHE	SVP
CYP	EDEK, KINHMA
CZE	ANO, KSCM, SPD, SPR-RSC, UPD, VV
DEU	AfD
DNK	DF, Enh
ESP	ECP, ERC, Podemos, Vox
EST	ER, ERa
FIN	SP/P
FRA	FI, FN, PCF
GBR	UKIP
GRC	ANEL, KKE, LAOS, LS / CA, PASOK, SYRIZA
HRV	Most, The Only Option
HUN	Fidesz, FKgP, Jobbik, KDNP, MIEP
IRL	SF
ITA	FdI, FI, LN, M5S
LTU	DK, TT-LDP
LVA	DPS, JKP, KPV LV, LSP, NsL, PCTVL, SC, TKL-ZP, TSP, ZRP
NLD	LPF, PVV
POL	AWS, K, LPR, PiS, RN, ROP, SRP
ROU	PP-DD, PRM, PSDR
SVK	HZDS, KSS, LsNS, OL'aNO, Smer, SNS, SR
SVN	NSi, SDS, SLS, SNS

Source: Popu-List (Rooduijn et al. 2019).

Enrique Clari

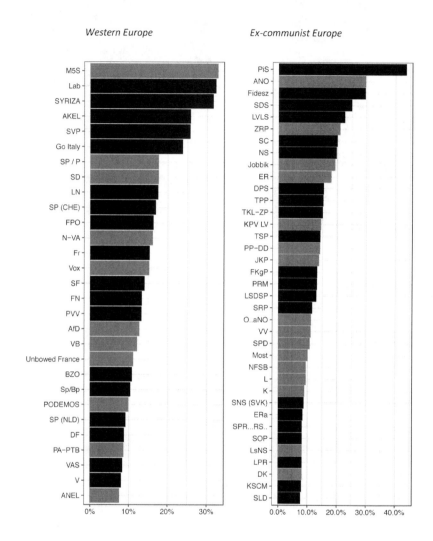

Figure 3A.1 Vote share of populist parties in most recent general elections, 2019

Note: Only parties with a vote share equal to or greater than 7.5% are shown. Parties in black entered Parliament earlier than 2010, whereas parties in grey first gained representation in 2010 or later. *Western Europe* includes AUT, BEL, CHE, CYP, DEU, DNK, ESP, FIN, FRA, GBR, GRC, IRL, ISL, ITA, NLD, NOR, PRT, and SWE. *Ex-communist* countries are BGR, CZE, EST, HRV, HUN, LTU, LVA, POL, ROU, SVK, and SVN.

Source: V-Party dataset (Lindberg et al. 2022).

Bibliography

Abedi, A. 2004. *Anti-Political Establishment Parties: A Comparative Analysis.* London: Routledge.

Abou-Chadi, T., and W. Krause. 2020. "The Causal Effect of Radical Right Success on Mainstream Parties' Policy Positions: A Regression Discontinuity Approach." *British Journal of Political Science* 50 (3): 829–847. https://doi.org/10.1017/S0007123418000029.

Abou-Chadi, T., and M. Wagner. 2019. "The Electoral Appeal of Party Strategies in Postindustrial Societies: When Can the Mainstream Left Succeed?." *Journal of Politics* 81 (4): 1405–1419. https://doi.org/10.1086/704436.

Abou-Chadi, T., and M. Wagner. 2020. "Electoral Fortunes of Social Democratic Parties: Do Second Dimension Positions Matter?." *Journal of European Public Policy* 27 (2): 246–272. https://doi.org/10.1080/13501763.2019.1701532.

Akkerman, T. 2015. "Gender and the Radical Right in Western Europe: A Comparative Analysis of Policy Agendas." *Patterns of Prejudice* 49 (1–2): 37–60. https://doi.org/10.1080/0031322X.2015.1023655.

Akkerman, T., S. L. de Lange, and M. Rooduijn, eds. 2016. *Radical Right-Wing Populist Parties in Western Europe: Into the Mainstream?.* London: Routledge.

Albertazzi, D., and S. Mueller. 2013. "Populism and Liberal Democracy: Populists in Government in Austria, Italy, Poland and Switzerland." *Government and Opposition* 48 (3): 343–371.

Bakker, R., C. De Vries, E. Edwards, L. Hooghe, S. Jolly, G. Marks, and M. A. Vachudova. 2015. "Measuring Party Positions in Europe: The Chapel Hill Expert Survey Trend File, 1999–2010." *Party Politics* 21 (1): 143–152. https://doi.org/10.1177/1354068812462931.

Bale, T., and C. R. Kaltwasser. 2021. "The Mainstream Right in Western Europe: Caught between the Silent Revolution and Silent Counter-Revolution." Cambridge: Cambridge University Press.

Bale, T., and A. Krouwel. 2013. "Down but not Out: A Comparison of Germany's CDU/CSU with Christian Democratic Parties in Austria, Belgium, Italy and the Netherlands." *German Politics* 22 (1–2): 16–45. https://doi.org/10.1080/09644008.2013.794452.

Bale, T., C. Green-Pedersen, A. Krouwel, K. R. Luther, and N. Sitter. 2010. "If You Can't Beat Them, Join Them? Explaining Social Democratic Responses to the Challenge from the Populist Radical Right in Western Europe." *Political Studies* 58 (3): 410–426. https://doi.org/10.1111/j.1467-9248.2009.00783.x.

Bértoa, F. C., and Rama, J. 2021. "The Antiestablishment Challenge." *Journal of Democracy* 32(1): 37–51.

Borbáth, E., and S. Hutter. 2021. "Protesting Parties in Europe: A Comparative Analysis." *Party Politics* 27 (5): 896–908. https://doi.org/10.1177/1354068820908023.

Carvalho, J., and D. Ruedin. 2020. "The Positions Mainstream Left Parties Adopt on Immigration: A Cross-Cutting Cleavage?." *Party Politics* 26 (4): 379–389. https://doi.org/10.1177/1354068818780533.

De Lange, S. L., and L. M. Mügge. 2015. "Gender and Right-Wing Populism in the Low Countries: Ideological Variations across Parties and Time." *Patterns of Prejudice* 49(1–2): 61–80. https://doi.org/10.1080/0031322X.2015.1014199

Galston, W. A. 2018. "The Populist Challenge to Liberal Democracy." *Journal of Democracy* 29 (2): 5–19.

Gidron, N. 2022. "Many Ways to Be Right: Cross-Pressured Voters in Western Europe." *British Journal of Political Science* 52 (1): 146–161. https://doi.org/10.1017/S0007123420000228.

Hawkins, K. A., R. E. Carlin, L. Littvay, and C. R. Kaltwasser, eds. 2018. *The Ideational Approach to Populism: Concept, Theory, and Analysis*. London: Routledge.

Hjorth, F., and M. V. Larsen. 2022. "When Does Accommodation Work? Electoral Effects of Mainstream Left Position Taking on Immigration." *British Journal of Political Science* 52 (2): 949–957.

Hobolt, S. B., and J. Tilley. 2016. "Fleeing the Centre: The Rise of Challenger Parties in the Aftermath of the Euro Crisis." *West European Politics* 39 (5): 971–991.

Holmes, S. 1993. *The Anatomy of Antiliberalism*. Cambridge, MA: Harvard University Press.

Hooghe, L., and G. Marks. 2018. "Cleavage Theory Meets Europe's Crises: Lipset, Rokkan, and the Transnational Cleavage." *Journal of European Public Policy* 25 (1): 109–135.

Holmes, S. 2021. "The Antiliberal Idea." In *Routledge Handbook of Illiberalism*, edited by A. Sajó, R. Uitz, and S. Holmes, 3–15. London: Routledge.

Huber, R. A., and C. H. Schimpf. 2016. "A Drunken Guest in Europe?." *Zeitschrift für vergleichende Politikwissenschaft* 10 (2): 103–129. https://doi.org/10.1007/s12286-016-0302-0.

Ignazi, P. 1992. "The Silent Counter-Revolution: Hypotheses on the Emergence of Extreme Right-Wing Parties in Europe." *European Journal of Political Research* 22 (1): 3–34. 10.1111/j.1475-6765.1992.tb00303.x.

Ivaldi, G., M. E. Lanzone, and D. Woods. 2017. "Varieties of Populism across a Left-Right Spectrum: The Case of the Front National, the Northern league, Podemos and Five Star Movement." *Swiss Political Science Review* 23 (4): 354–376. https://doi.org/10.1111/spsr.12278.

Ivarsflaten, E. 2008. "What Unites Right-Wing Populists in Western Europe? Re-Examining Grievance mobilization Models in Seven Successful Cases." *Comparative Political Studies* 41 (1): 3–23. https://doi.org/10.1177/0010414006294168.

Jolly, S., R. Bakker, L. Hooghe, G. Marks, J. Polk, J. Rovny, …, and M. A. Vachudova. 2022. "Chapel Hill Expert Survey Trend file, 1999–2019." *Electoral Studies*, 75:102420. https://doi.org/10.1016/j.electstud.2021.102420.

Juon, A., and D. Bochsler. 2020. "Hurricane or Fresh Breeze? Disentangling the Populist Effect on the Quality of Democracy." *European Political Science Review* 12 (3): 391–408. https://doi.org/10.1017/S1755773920000259.

Kaltwasser, C. R. 2012. "The Ambivalence of Populism: Threat and Corrective for Democracy." *Democratization* 19 (2): 184–208.

Krause, W., and H. Giebler 2020. "Shifting Welfare Policy Positions: The Impact of Radical Right Populist Party Success Beyond Migration Politics." *Representation*, 56 (3): 331–348. https://doi.org/10.1080/00344893.2019.1661871.

Kriesi, H., and J. Schulte-Cloos. 2020. "Support for Radical Parties in Western Europe: Structural Conflicts and Political Dynamics." *Electoral Studies* 65:102138. https://doi.org/10.1016/j.electstud.2020.102138.

Lindberg, S. I., N. Düpont, M. Higashijima, Y. B. Kavasoglu, K. L. Marquardt, M. Bernhard, …, and B. Seim. 2022. *Codebook Varieties of Party Identity and Organization (V–Party) V2*. Varieties of Democracy (V-Dem) Project. Sweden: Varieties of Democracy. https://doi.org/10.23696/vpartydsv2.

Lubbers, M., M. Gijsberts, and P. Scheepers. 2002. "Extreme Right-Wing Voting in Western Europe." *European Journal of Political Research* 41 (3): 345–378. https://doi.org/10.1111/1475-6765.00015.

Lührmann, A., and S. I. Lindberg. 2019. "A Third Wave of Autocratization Is Here: What Is New About it?." *Democratization* 26 (7): 1095–1113. https://doi.org/10.1080/13510347.2019.1582029.

Meijers, M. J. 2017. "Contagious Euroscepticism: The Impact of Eurosceptic Support on Mainstream Party Positions on European Integration." *Party Politics* 23 (4): 413–423. https://doi.org/10.1177/1354068815601787.

Meijers, M. J., and A. Zaslove. 2021. "Measuring Populism in Political Parties: Appraisal of a New Approach." *Comparative Political Studies* 54 (2): 372–407. https://doi.org/10.1177/0010414020938081.

Meléndez, C., and C. R. Kaltwasser. 2021. "Negative Partisanship towards the Populist Radical Right and Democratic Resilience in Western Europe." *Democratization* 28 (5): 949–969. https://doi.org/10.1080/13510347.2021.1883002.

Mouffe, C. 2005. *The Return of the Political*. London: Verso.

Mudde, C. 2004. "The Populist Zeitgeist." *Government and Opposition* 39 (4): 541–563. https://doi.org/10.1111/j.1477-7053.2004.00135.x.

Mudde, C. 2007. *Populist Radical Right Parties in Europe*. Cambridge: Cambridge University Press.

Mudde, C. 2013. "Three Decades of Populist Radical Right Parties in Western Europe: So What?." *European Journal of Political Research* 52 (1): 1–19. https://doi.org/10.1111/j.1475-6765.2012.02065.x.

Mudde, C. 2014. "Fighting the System? Populist Radical Right Parties and Party System Change." *Party Politics* 20 (2): 217–226. https://doi.org/10.1177/1354068813519968.

Mudde, C., and C. R. Kaltwasser. 2013. "Exclusionary vs. Inclusionary Populism: Comparing Contemporary Europe and Latin America." *Government and Opposition* 48 (2): 147–174. https://doi.org/10.1017/gov.2012.11.

Muis, J., and T. Immerzeel. 2017. "Causes and Consequences of the Rise of Populist Radical Right Parties and Movements in Europe." *Current Sociology* 65 (6): 909–930. https://doi.org/10.1177/0011392117717294.

Müller, J. W. 2016. *What Is Populism?*. University of Pennsylvania press.

Norris, P. 2020. "Measuring Populism Worldwide." *Party Politics* 26 (6): 697–717. https://doi.org/10.1177/1354068820927686.

Norris, P., and R. Inglehart. 2019. *Cultural Backlash: Trump, Brexit, and Authoritarian Populism*. Cambridge: Cambridge University Press.

Pappas, T. S. 2019. *Populism and Liberal Democracy: A Comparative and Theoretical Analysis*. Oxford: Oxford University Press.

Pemstein, D., K. L. Marquardt, E. Tzelgov, ..., J. von Römer. 2020. "The V-Dem Measurement Model: Latent Variable Analysis for Cross-National and Cross-Temporal Expert-Coded Data." Working Paper No. 21, 5th edition. University of Gothenburg, Varieties of Democracy Institute.

Pirro, A. L., and B. Stanley. 2022. "Forging, Bending, and Breaking: Enacting the 'Illiberal Playbook' in Hungary and Poland." *Perspectives on Politics* 20 (1): 86–101. https://doi.org/10.1017/S1537592721001924.

Riker, W. H. 1988. *Liberalism against Populism: A Confrontation between the Theory of Democracy and the Theory of Social Choice*. Wisconsin: Waveland Press.

Rooduijn, M. 2014. "The Mesmerising Message: The Diffusion of Populism in Public Debates in Western European Media." *Political Studies* 62 (4): 726–744. https://doi.org/10.1111/1467-9248.12074.

Rooduijn, M., and T. Akkerman. 2017. "Flank Attacks: Populism and Left-Right Radicalism in Western Europe." *Party Politics* 23 (3): 193–204. https://doi.org/10.1177/1354068815596514.

Rooduijn, M., S. Van Kessel, C. Froio, A. Pirro, S. De Lange, D. Halikiopoulou, and P. Taggart. 2019. "The PopuList: An Overview of Populist, Far Right, Far Left and Eurosceptic Parties in Europe." www.popu-list.org.

Rummens, S. 2017. "Populism as a Threat to Liberal Democracy." In *The Oxford Handbook of Populism*, edited by C. Rovira Kaltwasser, P. Taggart, P. Ochoa Espejo, and P. Ostiguy, 554–570. Oxford: Oxford University Press.

Ruth-Lovell, S. P., A. Lührmann, and S. Grahn. 2019. "Democracy and Populism: Testing a Contentious Relationship." Working Paper No. 91, University of Gothenburg, Varieties of Democracy Institute.

Rydgren, J. 2004. "Explaining the Emergence of Radical Right-Wing Populist Parties: The Case of Denmark." *West European Politics* 27 (3): 474–502. https://doi.org/10.1080/0140 238042000228103.

Schumacher, G., and K. Van Kersbergen. 2016. "Do Mainstream parties Adapt to the Welfare Chauvinism of Populist Parties?." *Party Politics* 22 (3): 300–312. https://doi.org/10.1177/1354068814549345.

Spierings, N., M. Lubbers, and A. Zaslove, 2017. "'Sexually Modern Nativist Voters': Do They Exist and Do They Vote for the Populist Radical Right?." *Gender and Education* 29 (2): 216–237. https://doi.org/10.1080/09540253.2016.1274383.

Spoon, J. J., and H. Klüver. 2020. "Responding to Far Right Challengers: Does Accommodation Pay Off?." *Journal of European Public Policy* 27 (2): 273–291. https://doi.org/10.1080/13501 763.2019.1701530.

Taggart, P. 2000. *Populism: Concepts in the Social Sciences*. Philadelphia: Open University Press.

Turnbull-Dugarte, S. J., J. Rama, and A. Santana. 2020. "The Baskerville's Dog Suddenly Started Barking: Voting for VOX in the 2019 Spanish General Elections." *Political Research Exchange* 2 (1): 1781543. https://doi.org/10.1080/2474736X.2020.1781543.

Urbinati, N. 2014. *Democracy Disfigured*. Cambridge, MA: Harvard University Press.

Vachudova, M. A. 2020. "Ethnopopulism and Democratic Backsliding in Central Europe." *East European Politics* 36 (3): 318–340 https://doi.org/10.1080/21599165.2020.1787163.

Zulianello, M. 2020. "Varieties of Populist Parties and Party Systems in Europe: From State-of-the-Art to the Application of a Novel Classification Scheme to 66 Parties in 33 Countries." *Government and Opposition* 55 (2): 327–347. https://doi.org/10.1017/gov.2019.21.

CHAPTER 4

On the Persistence of Radical Right Populism in Europe: The Role of Grievances and Emotions

Hans-Georg Betz

Introduction

In the most recent parliamentary elections in France, Marine Le Pen's Rassemblement national obtained 89 seats in the Assemblée nationale, an unprecedented result for a political formation still widely considered radical right. The only other time the party managed to gain a significant number of seats was in 1986. At the time, the party (Jean-Marie Le Pen's Front national) benefited from a change in the electoral rules, from a majoritarian to a proportional system.

A few months later, in Sweden, the Sverigedemokraterna recorded their highest result ever. With more than 20% of the vote, the party surpassed all other relevant parties save for the Sveriges socialdemokratiska arbetareparti (Social Democrats) Finally, in the September general elections in Italy, Fratelli d'Italia emerged as the clear winner, paving the way for a new center-right coalition government led by Giorgia Meloni. Both parties have their roots in postwar neo-fascism, although, by now, both parties have disavowed the past.

The three cases are hardly exceptional. Quite the contrary. The populist radical right, as these parties are referred to these days, in Europe has demonstrated remarkable tenacity and resilience, and this is in the face of, oftentimes profound, hostility on the part of the "political establishment." It is not without a certain irony that in a number of European countries today, the populist radical right has, for all practical purposes, become an intricate part of the political establishment. The Italian Lega is a prominent case in point, as is the Front/Rassemblement national in France.

To be sure, the populist radical right in Europe has experienced considerable fluctuations of their fortunes, in some cases ending in the disappearance of individual parties. This was the case, for instance, with the German Republikaner, Sweden's Ny Demokrati, the Swiss Autopartei, and the Dutch Lijst Pim Fortuyn/Lijst Vijf Fortuyn. At the same time, new parties emerged, and this happened even in countries such as Spain and Portugal that were, until recently, considered immune to the populist radical right temptation.

What accounts for the European radical right populism's staying power? At the time the first of these parties burst onto the political scene—in 1973 in Denmark, Mogens Glistrup's anti-tax Fremskridtspartiet came out of nowhere to gain 16% of the vote in that year's "landslide" election—they were easily dismissed as ephemeral political curiosities, as "flash" or protest parties, here today, gone tomorrow (Lane 2008, 172). And yet they never left. Even the COVID-19 pandemic largely failed to lethally harm them, as some analysts hoped. Neither has Russia's invasion of Ukraine, despite the close personal and/or ideological proximity of several populist leaders to Vladimir Putin (Jack 2022).

The burgeoning literature on radical right populism offers a range of propositions designed to explain the rise and success of parties adhering to this ideology. It has little to say about their remarkable staying power. To a significant extent, this literature betrays a disconcerting lack of historical sensitivity and understanding. Thus, for instance, there is a tendency to attribute the "rise" of radical right populism to the financial crisis (Guiso et al. 2022). This was certainly true for the German AfD (Alternative für Deutschland; in other cases, most prominently Spain and Portugal, not so much.

In what follows, I advance a tentative approach offering a plausible explanation for the continued appeal of these parties. This is all the more remarkable given the serious setbacks, defections, splits, and scandals (including corruption scandals) that have bedeviled most of them. And it is even more remarkable, given the fact that on the occasion they have managed to accede to the levers of power, that they have little to show in terms of concrete results. The Lega Nord is a prime point in case. The Lega was part of several center-right coalitions, headed by Berlusconi. For a number of years, it held the ministry for institutional reform and devolution. Yet, it never managed to turn into reality its core demand: namely, the radical transformation of the Italian state. Despite years in government on the side of Berlusconi, the dream of federalism remained as elusive as ever.

Mobilizing grievances and emotions

Central to the analysis that follows is the notion of grievances. As Matthew Flinders and Markus Hinterleitner have recently noted, populist politics is above all grievance politics. The authors define grievance politics as "the fuelling and funneling of negative emotions and various blame-based political strategies which explicitly challenge and confound many of the core principles and values that have traditionally underpinned conventional conceptions of party politics" (Flinders and Hinterleitner 2022, 1). Grievances are the result of the demands of individuals to public authorities being ignored and/or dismissed and, therefore, people remain unsatisfied within the established democratic framework.

If the unresponsiveness of public authorities is experienced as stemming from a fundamental lack of respect for and recognition of the concerns of ordinary people, there is an opening for what the sociologist Robert Jansen (2011, 82) has referred to as populist mobilization. Jansen defines populism as a political project that mobilizes ordinary people into contentious political action while "articulating an anti-elite, nationalist rhetoric that valorizes ordinary people." Jansen's definition raises an important point that is essential for the understanding of populism's appeal: populism bestows "value" to ordinary people and their views, anxieties, and concerns. Populists claim for themselves that they "hear your pain"—something the established political parties have too often neglected to do (O'Keefe and Becker 2017). Giving value to ordinary people, in turn, is an act of recognition, an acknowledgment that a person possesses "social 'validity,'" that she "counts," deserves dignity, and merits respect (Honneth and Margalit 2001, 115).

It seems that these days, recognition, dignity, and respect are in short supply, particularly when it comes to politics. Also, nowadays a significant number of citizens in Western-style liberal democracies believe that politicians do not care about people like them. Political disenchantment, cynicism, and distrust have been rampant for decades, providing ever new fertile ground for populist entrepreneurs (Corbett 2020). This distinguishes a grievance-based approach to populist mobilization from structural approaches, such as the "modernization loser" thesis. Liberal democracy, particularly in combination with macrostructural processes over which the individual has no control, such as globalization, produces an almost inexhaustible stream of grievances—some economic, others social, and still others cultural. Hardly surprising that those without a voice, as populist leaders from Jörg Haider to Jean-Marie to Marine Le Pen have incessantly insisted, have turned to political entrepreneurs who promote and market themselves as "tribunes of the people" (Le Pen 2019).

The prominent political theorist John McCormick has recently characterized populism as "modern, representative democracy's 'cry of pain.'" The pain results from "the insults and injuries caused by supposedly representative political systems that explicitly promise majorities the authority to govern, but that, in reality, do not facilitate popular rule in any substantive sense" (McCormick 2018, 4). Quite the opposite. As Nadia Urbinati (2011, 266), summarizing McCormick's central charge, has put it, in modern liberal democracies, representation and universal suffrage "are the symbols of an institutional disempowerment of the people with people's consent." Nadia Urbinati, by the way, is far from endorsing populism as a remedy for the defects of liberal democracy.

She does, however, provide a compelling explanation for the institutional disempowerment of the people—"the eternal philosophical prejudice against the competences in government of ordinary people" (Urbinati 2011, 160). Others would go even further, suggesting that this type of prejudice goes far beyond competencies in government. In fact, it reflects nothing short of a profound disdain and contempt for ordinary people, dismissed as immature, ignorant, narrow-minded, parochial, and xenophobic, if not outright racist (Dion 2015). On this view, contempt and disdain are expressions of the demophobia or what McCormick has characterized as "ochlophobia," which has informed the elite's attitude toward the masses for ages (D'Eramo 2013; McCormick 2019). History provides a wealth of evidence that sustains the notion that Horatius's famous quip "odi profanum vulgus et arceo"

(I hate the common masses and avoid them) resonates throughout the ages, until today (Isenberg 2016).

Pierre Rosanvallon has recently introduced a further aspect of elite contempt for those below: the "disdain of indifference." It finds its most poignant expression in treating the Other as if she were invisible, as if she "counted for nothing, did not exist," and was "useless and worthless" (Rosanvallon 2021, 25–26). Rendering the Other invisible is an act of misrecognition, which provokes a sense of powerlessness and shame in the Other. At the same time, it has become increasingly common, in movies, on TV, and in the media, to publicly denigrate ordinary people, make fun of their lives, and "treat them with thinly veiled contempt" (Berezin 2017, 333–334). In Britain, for instance, there has been a growing recognition of and sensitivity to the way ordinary people have been portrayed (Tyler 2008). The Brexit vote in Britain as well as the revolt of the gilets jaunes in France have shed further light on parts of the population that have remained largely invisible in the past (Alzingre 2018). The disdain of indifference has taken on new dimensions with the most recent technological revolution. Digitalization/artificial intelligence, automation, and robotization have rendered—and will continue to do so—some workers' skills obsolete while enhancing the skill premium for others, resulting in growing inequality while, in the process, generating new grievances on the part of those who feel redundant, structurally irrelevant, and useless and worthless.

Grievances provoke a whole range of strong emotions—anger, rage, resentment, and indignation. These emotions, in turn, offer myriad opportunities for populist mobilization (Sauer 2020; Rhodes-Purdy et al. 2021; Tietjen 2022). The indignados whose protest in the early 2010s shook Spain to the core are an important case in point. They laid the ground for the foundation of Podemos, Spain's prominent populist left party. Another important example is that of the above-mentioned gilet jaunes who recruited their participants especially from among citizens who perceived themselves as being excluded from the system and who no longer believed in the institution. As in the case of the indignados in Spain, their protest was to a large extent informed by anger, indignation, and rage, which infused the unprecedented populist wave that marked the first round of the 2022 presidential election.

Anger, resentment, indignation—what all of these emotions have in common is that they represent reactions to perceived moral injuries, injustices, and slights. They are informed by persistent feelings of being subject to insults, of being dismissed as irrelevant, useless, and worthless together with an urge to fight back, but being unable to do so: a combination of revengefulness, helplessness, and powerlessness. George Marcus and his colleagues (2019) have shown that among these emotions, anger is particularly conducive to populist mobilization. As Marcus (2021, 91) has noted in his other work, anger "serves as the watchdog of justice and, as such, is a foundational antecedent of populist movements." Anger results from the perception of unfairness and injustice, of having been wronged. This is associated with the belief that there is an external agent responsible for the wrong together with the notion that the external agent acted with full intention. It is at this point that anger turns into resentment. In common parlance, resentment tends to carry a negative connotation. This, however, is rather unfair. As Michelle Schwarze and John Scott (2015, 266) have recently argued, following Adam Smith's observation in his Theory of Moral Sentiments, "We need the perturbing passion of resentment to motivate our concern for injustice."

In most cases, grievance-inspired emotions result from individual experiences of moral injury and injustice; on occasion, they are elicited by collective experiences, which do not have an immediate bearing on the individual. A case in point is the nation-populist rhetoric of the British trade unions in the 1980s and early 1990s. What informed it was "feelings of shame, anger and rage" over Britain's economic decline, which was experienced as humiliating and shameful. "Once an independent nation and the workshop of the world, Britain was now seen as being little more than a 'dumping ground', 'a warehouse' or 'shop window' for other people's goods." And in true populist fashion, the unions "explicitly claimed to speak for the nation and to be representing 'the national interest' 'the true interests of the British people', 'the needs and concerns of the British people' and 'the collective common sense of Britain'" (Vogler 2000, 33). The result was an economic nationalist discourse that was strikingly similar to the one advanced by the promoters of Britain's exit from the European Union a few decades later. In both cases, the populist discourse was infused with a heavy dose of nostalgia, motivated by a strong desire to turn back the clock to a time when Britain was still in a position to control and determine its own destiny (Campanella and Dassù 2019).

What Gary Younge, in the pages of the *Guardian*, has characterized as "a melancholic longing for a glorious past," which he thought had underpinned the Brexit vote, is hardly peculiar to Britain. In fact, nostalgia is firmly entrenched in contemporary populist discourse. And for good reason. Nostalgia is generally defined as a longing for the past or, more precisely, for an idealized past. Originally, however, nostalgia referred to a yearning for home, what in German is known as *Heimweh*. When populism evokes nostalgia, it does so in both senses. As Tukka Yiä-Anttila (2017, 342) has argued, nostalgia derives much of its emotional momentum and appeal from conjuring up a sense of familiarity, which is "particularly compatible with the populist valorization of the experience of the common people. At the same time, nostalgia is closely associated with the experience of loss—the loss, for instance, of a familiar space, of a sense of community, of a way of life, of a position of privilege. These are losses that are experienced across the social spectrum, which might explain, to a certain extent at least, the relatively diverse appeal of Western Europe's populist radical right.

There is a third reason for the importance of nostalgia for the populist radical right. Populism is a particular form of identitarian politics (Betz and Johnson 2004). Emotions are essential for identity. As Ronald Grigor Suny has noted, national identities are "saturated with emotions that have been created through teaching, repetition and daily reproduction until they become common sense. The very rhetoric of nationalism reveals its affective base." National histories are replete with stories and tropes of heroic deeds and betrayals, victories and defeats, all of them "embedded in familiar emotions—anxiety, fear, insecurity and pride" (Suny 2005, 43). National communities are held together "by emotional ties as well as rational considerations; indeed, the two work together to solidify and reinforce group identification. Identification is basically an emotive tie" (1). Populist entrepreneurs have been well aware of the importance of these emotional ties. It is telling that after Brexit, Europe's populist radical right parties reorganized themselves under a common "Identity and Democracy" roof.

By now, there is widespread agreement that grievances are central to populist politics. More often than not, however, the discussion stops here, or stays at a rather general and abstract level. Flinders and Hinterleitner (2022, 5), for instance, mention "governments' failure to address societal problems such as rising levels of inequality"; Barry Eichengreen (2018, x) maintains that populism "is activated by the continuation of economic insecurity, threats to national identity, and an unresponsive political system; and a recent article on radical right voting in Europe states that "immigration-related grievances in democratically developed countries are one of the key drivers of far-right party support" (Erisen and Vasilopoulou 2022, 635). Little mention is made of what this means in concrete terms. Yet studies of populist mobilization across time and space provide a wealth of concrete examples of grievances that provoked populist revolt (Betz 2018). They suggest that grievances come in a wide range of guises resulting from a diverse set of causes. This is equally true for the emotions that grievances tend to engender. In most cases, the mix of anger and rage, anxiety and indignation underlying contemporary voter insurrection can be traced to one central cause: the government's apparent, callous disregard for the distress experienced by a large swath of ordinary people. The rise and entrenchment of populist radical right parties over the past decades in Europe and elsewhere have followed this very same logic. It would go beyond the scope of this chapter to account for each and every case of populist radical right mobilization. A selection of paradigmatic cases is sufficient to make the point.

The curse of the past: The German Republikaner

The Republikaner was founded in 1983 by two defectors from the Bavarian Christian Social Union (CSU) and Franz Schönhuber, a prominent journalist and host of a popular show on Bavarian television with the telling title *Jetzt red I* (Now It's My Turn to Speak). The show allowed ordinary citizens to confront Bavarian politicians with their questions and concerns. In 1981, Schönhuber published his wartime memoir entitled *Ich war dabei* (I Was Among Them) about his wartime adventures as a member of the Waffen-SS. After the book was published, Schönhuber lost his position with Bavarian television and was subsequently shown the cold shoulder by Munich's high society and Bavaria's political establishment. His joining the Republikaner was a decision motivated by personal grievances and resentment—an opportunity to exact revenge on those who he believed had wronged him (Betz 1990). His personal experience made him particularly sensitive to latent grievances and resentments among parts of the German public, particularly with regard to Germany's confrontation with its past. At the time, questions were raised as to whether or not it was time to "lay the past to rest" (what in German is known as *Schlussstrich*). After all, some 40 years had passed since the end of the war, and Germany had made considerable efforts to deal with its past. This led to a vivid debate about the "historization" of Germany's Nazi past, which proved to be highly polarizing (Broszat 1985; Diner 1987).

The Republikaner stood on the side of those who called for an end of reducing German history to the 12 years of the Nazi regime. And for good reason. Germany's Nazi past was one of the reasons for the division of the country. The 1980s marked a decade of profound change in Eastern and Central Europe, most prominently in Poland. Only in divided Germany, nothing seemed to move. Hardly surprising then that the Republikaner promoted themselves as staunch advocates of German unification. And then, there was the question of migration, which has always been a source of grievance. In Germany, this was a particularly delicate issue. The 1980s saw a growing inflow of ethnic Germans from the Soviet Union; in Germany, they were known as *Spätaussiedler* (late resettlers). Not everyone in Germany welcomed the new arrivals with open arms. In the late 1980s, more than 30% of German respondents in representative polls called for a drastic reduction in the number of resettlers. Their influx obviously provoked grievances among parts of the German population. There were suspicions that the newcomers were given privileges, such as housing, which were not always available to the "native" Germans. There was also the notion that Germany's strict migration rules were not applied to resettlers, even if their ethnic background was dubious. Ethno-nationalism prevented the Republikaner from exploiting these grievances.

The dramatic gains of the Republikaner in the 1980s, particularly in the affluent southern part of the country, however, cannot be reduced to nationalist sentiments. More often than not, it was socioeconomic grievances that propelled voters to support the new party. It did particularly well in working-class districts in big and medium-sized cities such as Munich, Nuremberg, and Augsburg. Gerd Paul, in a study from 1989, mentions issues that, once again, figure prominently in the current debate on radical right populism: the problem of "socially disadvantaged districts" with "old and, in part, low-quality apartments," disconnected from the vibrant parts of the city, which suffer from "poor infrastructure and social problems." To this one might add a shortage of social housing that was disadvantaging young couples without children. And reminiscent of what we are witnessing today, Paul points to fears of social decline, social deprivation, and status loss stemming from rapid technological change and "social modernization" as important factors influencing support for the Republikaner (Paul 1989, 545). Add to this the sentiment that the established political parties were "fixated on the saturated majority of the Two-Thirds society" while caring little about the concerns of "ordinary people" (Paul 1989, 548).

The rise of the Republikaner is a paradigmatic case of the motivational power of grievances and the emotions evoked by them—anxiety with respect to the future, fear, anger, resentment. All of them were engendered, on the one hand, by a diffuse sense of being ignored and treated unfairly by the political establishment and, on the other, by the notion that "the own people" should come first. It is hardly surprising that the Republikaner entered the campaign for the 1989 European election with the slogan "Die Republikaner—Deutschland zuerst" (The Republikaner—Germany First), a nativist trope suggesting that benefits should be reserved for native citizens (Betz 2019). At the same time, the Republikaner was among the first on the populist radical right to warn of the threat Islam posed to European culture (Röther 2019, 107).

The Republikaner certainly managed to appeal to a range of concerns prevalent among parts of the German public. In the end, however, they faded away as quickly as they had appeared, falling victim to quarrels and defections and, last but not least, to German unification, which deprived the party of its core demand.

Against Rome (and the South): The Lega Nord

In the most recent general elections in Italy, the Lega received a bit more than 8% of the vote. This was a far cry from the 34% the party had garnered in the European election of 2019. This was a severe blow to the Lega's strongman Matteo Salvini, who had turned the Lega from a regionalist populist party (the Lega Nord) into a nationwide party. The Lega's origins go back to the late 1980s, a time of increasing turmoil in Italian politics. What started out as a loose alliance of regional leagues soon turned itself into a political party, led by Umberto Bossi. The new party benefited greatly from the collapse of the established political parties in the early 1990s, which, for a time, left the Lega as a serious political contender in the northern part of the country. This was to a large extent because the Lega promoted itself very successfully as the voice of all the grievances that had been simmering among Northern Italians for decades—and which the established parties, and here particularly the Christian Democrats, had consistently ignored.

The Lega is the perfect expression of what Ilvo Diamanti (1996) has characterized as "il male del Nord" (the malaise of the north). In his work, Diamanti provides a wide range of insights into what motivates important segments of Northern Italian society to shift allegiance to the new party, Umberto Bossi's reputation as crude and offensive notwithstanding. In Diamanti's analysis, the sentiment of "frustration" appears over and over again. Northerners are frustrated about the rising tax burden, the inefficiency of the public administration, the excessive role of the state and partic-ularly the established parties in economic and social affairs, and the growing presence of migrants (Diamanti 1996, 61). Most of these grievances are materialist in nature, even if questions of identity and belonging do play a certain role (Diamanti 1993, 105).

There is a growing sense of "relative deprivation" resulting from the perception that the north "counts little" in national politics despite its preponderant economic weight. The reason is not hard to find. Starting sometime in the 1970s, the major political parties shifted their focus to the southern parts of the country, the Mezzogiorno, which the Lega considered "laggard and corrupt" and "a voracious sinkhole for northern taxes" (Montalbano 1993). Once again, the reason was simple: the south might have been relatively poor compared to the north, but it had a huge trove of voters. In other words, the main grievance on the part of Northern Italians was that, despite working hard to make a living, their taxes were stolen from them by a corrupt political class that used the funds to buy votes in the south and thus maintain themselves in power. Hence one of the Lega's most memorable slogans: "Roma ladrona, la Lega no perdona" (Rome the big thief, the Lega does not pardon). Add to this the age-old animosity toward the South, which stemmed from the fact that public administration posts in the north had increasingly been filled with Southerners; that the Mafia had spread to the north, targeting businesses for extorsion; and that for decades Northern capital had "imported" relatively cheap Southern labor. All of this resulted, as the Lega would put it, in a state of "Southern hegemony" to the detriment of the productive forces of the north. From this perspective, the rise of the Lega also marked an anti-Southern revolt. As Umberto Bossi once put it, the

Lombards had not defeated the Austrians "so that one hundred years later the southerners could come along to boss us around" (Biorcio 1997, 135–137).

All of these grievances provoked an emotional response in the north, resulting in a growing number of Northerners turning to the Lega. Studies focusing on the emergence and establishment of the Lega in northern regions find widespread rage among small entrepreneurs and professionals in the face of rising taxes as well as growing anxiety among ordinary workers in the face of their diminished "visibility." The latter is a function of the growing "marginality" of the working class as a result of technological innovation, reflected in their declining "political and cultural relevance" (Marzano 1998, 8). What unites small entrepreneurs, professionals, and ordinary workers is a strong "producerist" ethos, which divides society into "makers" and "takers"—an ethos that informs the Lega's crusade against "assistenzialismo" associated with the state and the south (Diamanti 1993, 111). In short, the Lega is the expression of a revolt of the "productive" north against the south, which the political class is charged with keeping in a state of permanent dependence. Hence the Lega's increasingly belligerent discourse, culminating in the threat of secession and the creation of an independent "Padania"— an empty threat, as it turns out, reflected in Matteo Salvini's decision to turn the Lega into a party with national ambitions, including the south. The strategy backfired. In the 2022 general elections, the Lega suffered significant losses, particularly in the north (Cangemi 2022).

Against arrogant neighbors (and Brussels): The Swiss People's Party

In 2003, during the campaign for that year's national election, the St. Gallen section of the Swiss People's Party (SVP) hung up a poster depicting the upper portion of a man with stereotypical Negroid features, including a ring through his nose. The caption read: "Wir Schweizer sind immer mehr die Neger!" (We the Swiss are more and more the negroes). And below: "Jetzt ist genug (Enough is enough). In the election, the SVP received 26.8% of the vote. The result marked the temporary culmination of a trend that had started in the mid-1990s, which saw the party, in less than a decade, more than double its electoral base to become Switzerland's largest political party. In the context of Switzerland's highly stable party system, this was nothing short of a revolution, particularly given the fact that the SVP had been a member of Switzerland's collective government coalition for decades, which made it an intricate part of the country's political establishment.

What accounts for the SVP's dramatic gains in the 1990s is, above all, the party's embrace of populism under the leadership of Christoph Blocher from the SVP's powerful Zurich section (Skenderovic 2007). In the process, the SVP appealed to a range of grievances, anxieties, and concerns, perfectly captured by the poster mentioned above. There are at least two ways to interpret its message. One is "they take us for imbeciles." The other, "We, the true Swiss, are increasingly being discriminated against and victimized." It is reasonable to assume that it is a combination of the two. And for good reason.

In the second half of the 1990s, Switzerland came under growing international scrutiny and pressure with respect to its behavior during World War II, particularly concerning financial transactions. The focus was both on "looted gold" that had ended up in Swiss banks and on numbered bank accounts maintained in Swiss institutions by persons who had perished during the Holocaust (see Vagts 1997). Things escalated when an American report (the so-called Eizenstat report) charged the Swiss with having collaborated with the Nazis while characterizing Swiss banks as "Nazi banks" (Wurz 2013). The charges had a significant impact on Swiss public opinion. There was a sense that Switzerland was being singled out, treated unfairly, and prejudicated.

It was at this point that Blocher stepped up to defend Switzerland's reputation and honor. In several major speeches, he argued that Switzerland had acted more than honorably during the war, given its delicate geographical location, and that the attacks against Switzerland were to a large extent an attempt on the part of Switzerland's left (characterized as "self-righteous, hypocrites and other moralists") to malign and bad-mouth the country (Blocher 1997). In short, Blocher managed to frame the issue in terms of misrecognition: Those accusing the Swiss of having acted dishonorably during the war refused to recognize the dire circumstances Switzerland confronted during that period as well as the efforts the Swiss had made, as well as the sacrifices they had made, to resist in the face of a substantial threat to the country.

This type of discourse jibed well with one of Blocher's central concerns—to prevent Switzerland from joining the process of European integration.

Once again, this was framed as an attempt on the part of left-wing, cosmopolitan elites to eradicate Swiss sovereignty and identity. Under the circumstances, it is hardly surprising that the party would adopt a radical anti-immigration program, targeting in particular the growing Muslim minority in the country. With this, the party responded to a number of migration-related grievances, such as crime and security ("crime has a name: excessive immigration"), the exploitation of the welfare state, and, in particular, the "creeping Islamization of the country." In this way, the party responded to diffuse fears and anxieties (reflected, for instance, in the referendum to ban the construction of minarets) of a growing number of "native-born" citizens who no longer felt at home in their own country. Add to this the growing concern about urban sprawl and the mushrooming of retail outlets; skyrocketing real estate prices and rents, particularly in the Zurich and Geneva regions; and an overburdened infrastructure. All these factors fueled support for the SVP.

True to form, the SVP framed all of these problems in nativist terms, blaming them on the "mass immigration" of the past decades, which the party, in turn, blamed on the "Linken und Netten" (the left and the nice ones). Riding a wave of anger and indignation among its supporters and potential supporters, the party provocatively asked: "Should Linke und Nette destroy Switzerland?"[1] To be sure, the upsurge in support for the SVP in the 1990s cannot be reduced to one single causal factor. Xenophobia has a long tradition in Switzerland, culminating in the ignominious treatment of German Jewish refugees being denied refuge in Switzerland. Responsible for the closing of Switzerland's borders to Jewish refugees was the head of the ministry of justice, who belonged to a party that, after the war, would turn into the SVP (Jost 2007). Central to this tradition is the exaltation of history, tradition, and particularly *Heimat*—the highly emotional attachment to one's home reflected in the party's appeal to nostalgia. Nostalgia for the days when the world was still intact; when men were still men and women kept out of politics; when Switzerland was still a Christian country, conflicts between Protestants and Catholics notwithstanding; when foreign laborers were sent home when they were no longer needed; and when Switzerland's rural tradition still largely defined its identity. A poster from 2019 depicting a chalet surrounded by trees with a pole flying the Swiss flag next to it is a

---

[1] https://www.svp.ch/wp-content/uploads/Inserat_Apfel_286x130_DE.pdf.

perfect example of this kind of emotional appeal. As is the caption that provocatively asks: "Attached to your home?"[2] The message is clear: those who are, better vote for SVP if they wish to stop the destruction of their *Heimat* (Hildebrand 2017).

The case of the SVP provides strong support for the argument that grievances and emotions play a significant role in the persistence and continued electoral success of radical right populism in Western Europe. This is even more true in Central and Eastern Europe. Postcommunist Central and Eastern Europe are awash in grievances—some of them recent, others going far back in history. Hungary is a prominent case in point. In the aftermath of World War I, Hungary lost a substantial part of its territory to new countries that emerged from the ashes of the Austro-Hungarian Empire. Ever since, "Trianon" (the treaty that redrew Hungary's borders), which holds a "hegemonic position in Hungarian social memory," has been a raw wound for Hungarians—and one that refuses to heal (Kovács 2016, 531). As such, it has provided fertile ground for grievance- and memory-based populist mobilization. In 2004, Hungary held a referendum on the question of extending citizenship to ethnic Hungarians living outside of Hungary's borders. Low turnout rendered the referendum results invalid but established Viktor Orbán's Fidesz, which had argued that the vote was an opportunity "to reunite a nation torn apart by Trianon" as the champion of Hungarian nostalgic nationalism.[3] A second aspect of this kind of nostalgia is the reference to religion, which is reflected in the conjuring up of the Crown of St. Stephen as a symbol of Hungary's Christian identity and national sovereignty (Chotiner 2021). It is this emotional appeal to a politics of victimization that, to a large extent, informs the populist radical right's hold on power in Hungary. It evokes instances of national humiliation to fuel anger and resentment. To a certain extent, as Ivan Krastev and Stephen Holmes have argued, this is also a fallout from the "politics of imitation of the West" that informed politics in Central and Eastern Europe following the collapse of the communist regimes. Imitation not only produced "feelings of inadequacy, inferiority, dependency, lost identity, and involuntary insincerity," it also came "to feel like a loss of sovereignty" (Krastev and Holmes 2018, 118).

---

2   https://www.facebook.com/SVPch/photos/a.180156395461646/1811680688975867/?type=3&theater.
3   https://balkaninsight.com/2019/11/25/how-hungarys-trianon-trauma-inflames-identity-politics/.

Post-Cold War traumata and elusive identities:
Central European populism

This has been particularly true in the eastern part of Germany. During the Cold War period, the German Democratic Republic promoted itself as a socialist model country without, however, challenging the guiding role of the Soviet Union. German reunification exposed a different reality. As it turned out, economically, technologically, and in terms of infrastructure, the eastern part of the country lagged decades behind the western part. At the same time, however, the Kohl government claimed that it would take no time for the east to catch up with the west. It has taken significantly longer, however. In 2013, the five eastern German Länder trailed the western ones by significant margins. Per capita GDP in Saxony and Thuringia, for instance, was some 30% lower than in Bavaria (Borger and Müller 2014, 2). These are the two Länder where the Alternative für Deutschland (AfD) has been the strongest in recent years. In the most recent general elections, the party received more than 26% of the vote in Saxony (compared to a bit more than 10% overall) while winning 10 out of 16 direct mandates.

A number of studies suggest that the AfD's prominence in the east is largely due to its ability to express, mobilize, and explain grievances as well as to cater to a range of emotions, such as anger and resentment. These grievances are less grounded in material deprivation than the result of a profound sense of misrecognition. Most important of all, there is the widespread perception that after more than three decades since unification, easterners are still considered second-class citizens. This is to a large extent the result of the experience of denigration and disparagement on the part of the west, which never truly recognized the achievements of ordinary east Germans working under conditions of constant shortages in the former GDR (Betz and Habersack 2019). At the same time, it is the product of the perception of not being taken seriously, of counting for nothing, of perhaps even being dismissed as useless. This is particularly true in structurally weak regions, or what a prominent study of eastern Thuringia refers to as the "internal periphery" (Schmalz et al. 2021). This holds particularly true for skilled workers. Once the backbone of the economy, they have a strong sense of not being valued, of not being recognized, of being treated unfairly (Dörre 2020). It is among (male) skilled workers in structurally weak regions in eastern

Germany that the AfD has been strongest. And this is solely for sociopsychological reasons: What the AfD has done, Dörre maintains, is "to make the invisible visible" (Monath 2020).

To be sure, over the past decades, the west did transfer large sums of money to the east. Yet, money is no remedy for humiliation, and it cannot compensate for the lack of recognition and for the degradation of a person's lifetime achievement (Ziener 2018). It is this sense of constant humiliation that provokes strong emotions. New terminologies, such as *Wutbürger* (irate citizen) and *Zornpolitik* (politics of rage), which have entered the common German parlance, reflect the growing importance of emotions in politics, both in eastern Germany and elsewhere in Europe. Suffice it to say that most of these emotions have a negative connotation. The AfD, with its "pay-attention-to-ordinary-people" message, has successfully surfed on this wave of grievances and negative emotions. At the same time, it has met demands for political representation that were long ignored and neglected by the established parties (Yoder 2020).

Conclusion

Some 40 years ago, Stuart Hall coined the term "authoritarian populism" in reference to Thatcherism. In a subsequent text, Hall (1985, 126) noted that Thatcherism was "a multi-faceted historical phenomenon, which it would be ludicrous to assume could be 'explained' along one dimension of analysis only." This applies equally to contemporary radical right populism. Prominent explanations, such as the "modernization loser" thesis or the notion that the populist radical right represents a "materialist" reaction to the advance of "postmaterialism," clarify some aspects of the phenomenon, but hardly all of it. As the cases outlined above illustrate, the causes of the rise of radical right populism in Europe as well as its staying power over time are variegated and complex, and depend, to a significant extent, on the individual context of the case.

There are, however, common traits that suggest that the analytical approach adopted in this chapter is a fruitful way to understand, to an extent, the nature of radical right populism in Europe. The in-depth engagement with individual cases of populist mobilization provides a wealth of empirical evidence illustrating the central importance of grievances and emotions for populist mobilization. Many of these grievances are associated with perceived slights, denigration, and contempt on the part of "the elite" vis-à-vis ordinary people. It is striking how often notions of dignity, respect, recognition, and visibility are evoked in the context of populist mobilization. This was the case, for instance, in the aftermath of Donald Trump's election in the United States, during the revolt of the gilets jaunes in France, and, as we have seen, in the establishment of the AfD in the eastern part of Germany. It is equally striking how often affects and emotions are being evoked, particularly in the context of nostalgia and "antagonistic remembering" (such as Trianon in Hungary). In fact, "emotions play an essential role" (Barna and Knap 2022) in antagonistic remembering.

One influential answer centers upon major crises, such as the financial crisis of 2008 and the Syrian "refugee crisis" a few years later (Rhodes-Purdy et al. 2021). The cases discussed above demonstrate, however, that crises are only one of the many different instances that can provoke grievances. Even relatively mundane events or seemingly minor political decisions can trigger an outburst of anger, rage, and indignation. The revolt of the gilets jaunes is a paradigmatic case in point (Alzingre 2018). In the most recent presidential election in Austria, the incumbent received a disappointingly narrow majority of the vote. Austrian observers interpreted the president's poor performance as a reflection of the general mood in the country. Never before, one of them commented in a prominent news magazine, "were frustration and rage so widespread, never before generalized suspicion as deeply engrained, never before the mood so explosive" (Linsinger 2022). Under the circumstances, radical right populism is likely to be here to stay, at least for the foreseeable future.

Bibliography

Alzingre, P. 2018. "'Gilets jaunes': la revanche des invisibles." *Les Echos*, December 3. https://www.lesechos.fr/idees-debats/cercle/opinion-gilets-jaunes-la-revanche-des-invisibles-204593 (Accessed May 13, 2023).

Barna, I., and Á. Knap. 2023. "Analysis of the Thematic Structure and Discursive Framing in Articles about Trianon and the Holocaust in the Online Hungarian Press Using LDA Topic Modelling." *Nationalities Papers*, Early View 51 (3): 603–621. https://doi.org/10.1017/nps.2021.67.

Berezin, M. 2017. "On the Construction Sites of history: Where Did Donald Trump Come from?." *American Journal of Cultural Sociology* 5 (3): 322–337. https://doi.org/10.1057/s41290-017-0045-7.

Betz, H.-G. 1990. "Politics of Resentment: Right-Wing Radicalism in West Germany." *Comparative Politics* 23 (1): 45–60. https://doi.org/10.2307/422304.

Betz, H.-G. 2019. "Facets of Nativism: A Heuristic Exploration." *Patterns of Prejudice* 53 (2): 111–135. https://doi.org/10.1080/0031322X.2019.1572276.

Betz. H.-G. 2018. "Populist Mobilization across Time and Space." In *The Ideational Approach to Populism: Concept, Theory, and Analysis*, edited by K. A. Hawkins, R. E. Carlin, L. Littvay, and C. R. Kaltwasser. London: Routledge.

Betz, H.-G., and F. Habersack. 2019. "Regional Nativism in East Germany. The Case of the AfD." In *The People and the Nation. Populism and Ethno-Territorial Politics in Europe*, edited by Reinhard Heinisch, Emanuele Massetti, and Oscar Mazzoleni, 110–35. London: Routledge.

Betz, H.-G., and C. Johnson. 2004. "Against the Current—Stemming the Tide: The Nostalgic Ideology of the Contemporary Radical Populist Right. *Journal of Political Ideologies* 9 (3): 311–327. https://doi.org/10.1080/1356931042000263546.

Biorcio, R. 1997. *La Padania promessa: La storia, le idée e la logica d'azione della Lega Nord*. Milan: Il Saggiatore.

Blocher, C. 1997. "Die Schweiz und der Zweite Weltkrieg: Eine Klarstellung." *Zurich-Oerlikon*, March 1. https://www.blocher.ch/wp-content/uploads/pdf_assorted/970301klarstellung.pdf (Accessed May 13, 2023).

Borger, K., and M. Müller. 2014. "In der Normalität angekommen—Deutschland 25 Jahre nach dem Mauerfall." *KFW Economic Research*, No. 73, September 30.

Broszat, M. 1985. "Plädoyer für eine Historisierung des Nationalsozialismus." *Merkur* 39 (May): 373–385.

Campanella, E., and M. Dassù. 2019. "Brexit and Nostalgia." *Survival* 61 (3): 103–111. https://doi.org/10.1080/00396338.2019.1614781.

Cangemi, A. 2022. "Cosa è il Comitato del Nord lanciato da Umberto Bossi e cosa sta succedendo nella Lega." fanpage.it, October 3. https://www.fanpage.it/politica/cosa-e-il-comitato-del-nord-lanciato-da-umberto-bossi-e-cosa-sta-succedendo-nella-lega/ (Accessed May 13, 2023).

Chotiner, I. 2021. "Why Conservatives Around the World Have Embraced Hungary's Viktor Orbán." *The New Yorker*, August 10. https://www.newyorker.com/news/q-and-a/why-conservatives-around-the-world-have-embraced-hungarys-viktor-orban (Accessed May 13, 2023).

Corbett, J. 2020. "The Deconsolidation of Democracy: Is It New and What Can Be Done About It?." *Political Studies Review* 18 (2): 178–188. https://doi.org/10.1177/1478929919864785.

D'Eramo, M. 2013. "Populism and the New Oligarchy." *New Left Review* 82 (July/August): 5–28.

Diamanti, I. 1993. "La Lega, imprenditore politico della crisi. Origini, crescita e successo delle leghe autonomiste in Italia." *Meridiana* 16:99–153.

Diamanti, I. 1996. *Il male del Nord: Lega, localismo, sécession*. Rome: Donzelli.

Diner, D. 1987. "Zwischen Aporie und Apologie—Über Grenzen der Historisierung des Nationalsozialismus." *Gewerkschaftliche Monatshefte* 3:153–159.

Dion, J. 2015. *Le mépris du peuple*. Paris: Éditions des liens qui libèrent.

Dörre, K. 2020. *In der Warteschlange: Arbeiterinnen und die radikale Rechte*. Münster: Westfälisches Dampfboot.

Eichengreen, B. 2018. *The Populist Temptation: Economic Grievance and Political Reaction in the Modern Era*. New York: Oxford University Press.

Erisen, C., and S. Vasilopoulou. 2022. "The Affective Model of Far-Right Vote in Europe: Anger, Political Trust, and Immigration." *Social Science Quarterly* 103 (3): 635–648. https://doi.org/10.1111/ssqu.13153.

Flinders, M., and M. Hinterleitner. 2022. "Party Politics vs. Grievance Politics: Competing Modes of Representative Democracy." *Society*, March 14:1–10. https://doi.org/10.1007/s12115-022-00686-z.

Guiso, L., M. Morelli, T. Sonno, and H. Herrera. 2022. "The Financial Drivers of Populism in Europe." Discussion Paper No. DP17332. Centre for Economic Policy Research, May 28. https://cepr.org/system/files/publication-files/139706-the_financial_drivers_of_populism_in_europe.pdf (Accessed May 13, 2023).

Hall, S. 1985. "Authoritarian Populism: A Reply." *New Left Review* May/June:115–124.

Hildebrand, M. 2017. *Rechtspopulismus und Hegemonie. Der Aufstieg der SVP und die diskursive Transformation der politischen Schweiz*. Bielefeld: Transcript Verlag.

Honneth, A., and A. Margalit. 2001. "Recognition." *Proceedings of the Aristotelian Society* (supplementary volumes) 75:111–139. https://www.jstor.org/stable/4107035

Isenberg, N. 2016. *White Trash: The 400-Year Untold History of Class in America*. New York: Viking.

Jack, V. 2022. "Putin's European Pals Have to Eat Their Words." *Politico*, February 26. https://www.politico.eu/article/vladimir-putin-european-pals-eat-their-words-marine-le-pen-eric-zemmour-matteo-salvini-milos-zeman-alex-salmond-gerhard-schroder-boris-johnson-jean-luc-melenchon-francois-fillon-viktor-orban/ (Accessed May 13, 2023).

Jansen, R. S. 2011. "Populist Mobilization: A New Theoretical Approach to Populism." *Sociological Theory* 29 (2): 75–96. http://www.jstor.org/stable/23076372.

Jost, H.-U. 2007. "Tradition und Modernität in der SVP." *Traverse: Zeitschrift für Geschichte=Revue d'histoire* 14 (1): 25–44.

Kovács, É. 2016. "Overcoming History through Trauma. The Hungarian Historikerstreit." *European Review* 24 (4): 523–534. https://doi.org/10.1017/S1062798716000065.

Krastev, I., and S. Holmes. 2018. "Imitation and Its Discontents." *Journal of Democracy* 29 (3): 117–128.

Lane, J.-E. 2008. *Comparative Politics: The Principal-Agent Perspective*. London: Routledge.

Le Pen, J.-M. 2019. *Tribun du peuple*. Paris: Éditions Muller.

Linsinger, E. 2022. "Die Zorn-Wahl: Alarmstufe rot für die Regierung." *Profil*, October 9. https://www.profil.at/meinung/die-zorn-wahl-alarmstufe-rot-fuer-regierung/402175416 (Accessed May 13, 2023).

Marcus, G. 2021. "The Rise of Populism: The Politics of justice, Anger, and Grievance." In *The Psychology of Populism: The Tribal Challenge to Liberal Democracy*, edited by J. P. Forgas, W. D. Crano, and K. Fiedler, 81–104. London: Routledge.

Marcus, G. E., N. A. Valentino, P. Vasilopoulos, and M. Foucault. 2019. "Applying the Theory of Affective Intelligence to Support for Authoritarian Policies and Parties." *Advances in Political Psychology* 40 (S1): 109–139. https://doi.org/10.1111/pops.12571.

Marzano, M. 1998. "Etnografia della Lega Nord. Participazione e linguaggio politico in quattro sezioni piemontesi." *Quaderni di Sociologia* 17:1–28.

McCormick, J. S. 2018. "Democracy, Plutocracy and the Populist Cry of Pain." Paper presented at John Cabot University Rome, Political Theory Colloquium, Rome, 8 October. https://chicago.academia.edu/JohnMcCormick (Accessed May 13, 2023).

McCormick, J. S. 2019. "The New Ochlophobia? Populism, Majority Rule, and Prospects for Democratic Republicanism." In *Republicanism and the Future of Democracy*, edited by Yiftah Elazar and Geneviève Rousselière,130–151. Cambridge: Cambridge University Press.

Monath, H. 2020. "Arbeiter und die radikale Rechte: 'Die AfD macht die Unsichtbaren sichtbar.'" *Der Tagesspiegel*, December 5. https://www.tagesspiegel.de/politik/die-afd-macht-die-unsichtbaren-sichtbar-6861760.html (Accessed May 13, 2023).

Montalbano, W. D. 1993. "ITALY: Who's the Bossi? He's Crude, but Fed-Up Voters Love Him." *Los Angeles Times*, October 1. https://www.latimes.com/archives/la-xpm-1993-10-01-mn-41041-story.html (Accessed May 13, 2023)

O'Keefe, C., and D. Becker, 2017. "Sen. Bernie Sanders on His 'Guide to Political Revolution.'" wbur, Radio Boston, August 28. https://www.wbur.org/radioboston/2017/08/28/bernie-sanders-revolution (Accessed May 13, 2023)

Paul, G. 1989. "Die 'Republikaner': Profile einer neuen Partei." *Gewerkschaftliche Monatshefte* 9:547–548.

Rhodes-Purdy, M., R. Navarre, and S. M. Utych, 2021. "Populist Psychology: Economics, Culture and Emotions." *Journal of Politics* 82 (4): 1559–1572. https://doi.org/10.1086/715168.

Rosanvallon, P. 2021. *Les Épreuves de la vie. Comprendre autrement les Français*. Paris: Seuil.

Röther, C. 2019. *Islamismus von außen: Religionswissenschaftliche Analyse der islamkritischen Szene in Deutschland*. Baden Baden: Ergon.

Sauer, B. 2020. "Authoritarian Right-Wing Populism as Masculinist Identity Politics. The Role of Affects." In *Right-Wing Populism and Gender—European Perspectives and Beyond*, edited by G. Dietze and J. Roth. Bielefeld: Transcript Verlag.

Schmalz, S., S. Hinz, I. Singe, and A. Hasenohr. 2021. *Abgehängt im Aufschwung: Demografie, Arbeit und rechter Protest in Ostdeutschland*. Frankfurt: Campus.

Schwarze, M. A., and J. T. Scott. 2015. «Spontaneous Disorder in Adam Smith's Theory of Moral Sentiments: Resentment, Injustice, and the Appeal to Providence." *Journal of Politics* 77 (2): 463–476. https://doi.org/10.1086/679750.

Skenderovic, D. 2007. "Immigration and the Radical Right in Switzerland: Ideology, Discourse and Opportunities." *Patterns of Prejudice* 14 (2): 155–176. https://doi.org/10.1080/00313220701265528.

Suny, R. G. 2005. "Why We Hate You: The Passions of National Identity and Ethnic Violence." Paper submitted to the Workshop in Mass Killing and Genocide, December 2-3. https://www.researchgate.net/publication/46438458_Why_We_Hate_You_The_Passions_of_National_Identity_and_Ethnic_Violence (Accessed May 23, 2023).

Tietjen, R. R. 2022. "The Affects of Populism." *Journal of the American Philosophical Association*, First View:1–19. https://doi.org/10.1017/apa.2021.56.

Tyler, I. 2008. "'Chav Mum Chav Scum': Class Disgust in Contemporary Britain." *Feminist Media Studies* 8 (1): 17–34. https://doi.org/10.1080/14680770701824779.

Urbinati, N. 2011. "Republicanism: Democratic or Popular." *Good Society* 20 (2): 157–169.

Vagts, D. F. 1997. "Switzerland, International Law and World War II." *American Journal of International Law* 91 (3): 466–475. https://doi.org/10.2307/2954183.

Vogler, C. 2000. "Social Identity and Emotion: The Meeting of Psychoanalysis and Sociology." *Sociological Review* 48 (1): 19–42. https://doi.org/10.1111/1467-954X.0020.

Wurz, J. 2013. "Rückblick auf die Kontroverse um die Holocaust-Gelder." swissinfo.ch, September 3. https://www.swissinfo.ch/ger/zwei-revisionen_rueckblick-auf-die-kontroverse-um-die-holocaust-gelder/36759886 (Accessed May 13, 2023).

Ylä-Anttila, T. 2017. "Familiarity as a Tool of Populism: Political Appropriation of Shared Experiences and the Case of Suvivirsi." *Acta Sociologica* 60 (4): 342–357. https://doi.org/10.1177/0001699316679490.

Yoder, J. 2020. "'Revenge of the East'? The AfD's Appeal in Eastern Germany and Mainstream Parties' Responses." *German Politics and Society* 38 (2): 35–58. https://doi.org/10.3167/gps.2020.380202.

Younge, G. 2018. "Britain's Imperial Fantasies Have Given Us Brexit." *The Guardian*, February 18, https://www.theguardian.com/commentisfree/2018/feb/03/imperial-fantasies-brexit-theresa-may (Accessed May 23, 2023).

Ziener, M. 2018. "Das lange Ringen um Anerkennung." *Deutschlandfunk*, October 2. https://www.deutschlandfunkkultur.de/ostdeutschland-das-lange-ringen-um-anerkennung-100.html (Accessed May 23, 2023).

Part II

Political Participation under Populism: Trends and Limits

CHAPTER 5

The Limits of Democratic Competition: Time-Series, Cross-Sectional Evidence of the Asymmetrical Impact of Polarization on Europeans' Political Attitudes and Behavior

Enrique Clari and Carlos García-Rivero

Introduction

Polarization and the authoritarian behavior of political elites have been identified as the key avenues through which democracies nowadays derail and ultimately die (Bermeo 2016; Levitsky and Ziblatt 2018). During the current "wave of autocratization" (Lührmann and Lindberg 2019), elected illiberal leaders take advantage of the divisive environment that polarization generates within society and thus manage to eviscerate democratic norms and institutions without being held accountable for their malfeasances (Graham and Svolik 2020; Svolik 2019). Europe, Hungary, and Poland are usually cited as quintessential examples of the almost inevitable process of democratic backsliding that unfolds once "severe" or "pernicious" polarization has become entrenched (McCoy and Somer 2019; McCoy et al. 2018).

In this chapter, we present original evidence pointing to another way in which polarization can lead to the deterioration of democracy. By analyzing time-series, cross-sectional (TSCS) data from all waves of the European

Social Survey (ESS), we show that polarization has an asymmetrical impact on liberal and authoritarian citizens. In particular, we find that liberal citizens become more disaffected with the system and less identified with political parties as polarization rises, whereas authoritarians tend to become more engaged and to feel better represented by the political elite. Luckily for the prospects of liberal democracy, we also find that liberals' "diffuse support" (Easton 1965) for the system remains unaltered—however, their withdrawal from the public sphere can ultimately leave ample room for the success of populist radical right parties (PRRPs) among an emboldened authoritarian electorate.

Our results thus shed new light on the causal mechanism linking political polarization, authoritarianism, and democratic backsliding. In particular, we argue that the rise of polarization can have a significant impact on the demand for illiberal policies as it reconnects authoritarian citizens with the system while repelling liberals. However, the magnitude of this phenomenon will ultimately depend on the particular situation of each country, most notably, on the share of authoritarian relative to liberal voters.

The rest of the chapter is structured as follows: in the next section, we review the literature on the relationship between political polarization and democratic backsliding as well as describe how our hypotheses fit into the growing research on the declining support for democracy. Then, we present the dataset and explain our empirical strategy to disentangle longitudinal and cross-sectional effects with the aid of multilevel models. In the third section, we describe some political trends across Europe and report the results from the models. In the last section, we summarize our key findings and connect them to the larger discussion about democratic deconsolidation and declining support for liberal values in postindustrial democracies.

Literature Review

Polarization is seen as a fundamental driver of democratic backsliding across the globe (Haggard and Kaufman 2021; Jee et al. 2021; Waldner and Lust 2018). In polarized societies, political competition degenerates into an unrestrained, hyper-partisan struggle between antagonistic groups that see each other as existential threats and are therefore prepared to throw themselves into the arms of an authoritarian leader as long as this keeps the "out-group" at bay. The vicious dynamic that ensues once "pernicious polarization" (McCoy and Somer 2019; McCoy et al. 2018) has become entrenched has been described in many countries where democratic institutions have recently eroded, most notably in the United States (e.g., Finkel et al. 2020; Iyengar et al. 2019) and in Central and Eastern Europe (e.g., Vachudova 2019; Enyedi 2016), but the same logic applies to all democratic settings.

In fact, there is ample empirical support—both comparative (e.g., Orhan 2022; Arbatli and Rosenberg 2021) and experimental (Fossati et al. 2022; Carey et al. 2020; Graham and Svolik 2020)—for the idea that polarization lowers democratic standards among the population and enables authoritarian leaders to violate norms without being held accountable. As an influential account puts it, "Under [political polarization], citizens and political actors alike have incentives to endorse non-democratic actions to gain or keep power, and to prevent or remove their opponents from power" (Somer et al. 2021, 2).

Still, the exact reasons why citizens in consolidated democracies turn into "passive by-standers" (Saikkonen and Christensen 2022) and fail to punish incumbents' transgressions are not always fully fleshed out. For instance, some authors lay special stress on the kind of "cynical" or "hypocritical" (Simonovits et al. 2022) partisan attachment that polarization generates and on the important instrumental dimension that strengthens support for democracy (Carey et al. 2022), while others appear to characterize it as a blameless strategy forced upon otherwise committed democrats. Which kind of polarized partisanship ultimately guides voters' decisions—whether a truly partisan, opportunistic, or merely preemptive attachment—remains an empirical question, but there seems to be little doubt about its detrimental effect on democracy.

Their valuable insights notwithstanding, a shortcoming of most of the studies we have just reviewed is that, in focusing on the immediate impact of polarization on electoral choice, they do not investigate how polarization may influence other relevant political attitudes at the individual level. Furthermore, since participants in most experimental designs are conceptualized as belonging to the rather homogeneous category of "ordinary citizens," we still have no data at all about the different impacts that polarization may have on different social groups.

This omission is particularly regrettable in light of the growing body of literature claiming that support for democracy is declining across liberal regimes (e.g., Foa et al. 2020). Explanations about this alleged trend abound: a well-known but highly contested hypothesis claims that younger citizens, who have always lived under democracy and consequently take their freedoms for granted, feel a greater attraction than their elders toward authoritarian discourses (Foa and Mounk 2016, 2017). In contrast, a fundamentally incompatible theory posits that, due to their feeling of estrangement with a postindustrial and cosmopolitan society in which they no longer feel at home, it is actually the older and middle-aged generations who are leading the current "cultural backlash" (Norris and Inglehart 2019) against progressive values.

But even if, as many others have claimed (e.g., Zilinsky 2019; Wuttke et al. 2022), there is no compelling evidence about the decline of democratic values in mature democracies, it is still worth analyzing to what extent polarization can generate different reactions among liberal and authoritarian citizens in societies, like those of Europe, where the cleavage between cosmopolitan, liberal values and nativist, illiberal attitudes has become a fundamental structuring factor of political competition.

To investigate the contextual effects of polarization on individual attitudes as well as the moderating role of authoritarianism, we formulate a set of hypotheses derived from the relevant literature. In particular, in line with the theory of "critical citizens" (Norris 1999, 2011), we should expect liberal individuals to oppose the polarizing strategies adopted both by particular social groups and by political parties, and to become more dissatisfied as the strident tone of polarized discourses threatens the stability of democratic norms and institutions. And so, we formulate Hypothesis 1a:

H1a: When polarization grows, liberals become less satisfied with the way democracy works.

Conversely, authoritarians should feel comfortable in an environment of polarization, especially if it is fostered by leaders of PRRPs and thus allows for the electoral success of such kind of parties (Harteveld et al. 2021b):

H1b: When polarization grows, authoritarians become more satisfied with the way democracy works.

In terms of "diffuse support" (Easton 1965) for democracy, we expect liberal citizens to hold on to their principles and not to lose their faith in them. If they are truly "critical citizens" (Norris 1999, 2011), then support for the system, which we measure in terms of political trust, should remain stable among liberals irrespective of the level of polarization. Therefore:

H2: When polarization grows, political trust does not fall among liberals.

Polarization has been said to "repoliticize" the electoral space and increase partisan affinity of individuals as a consequence. After all, a certain level of ideological polarization is necessary for voters to tell parties apart and to be able to make a choice between candidates (Downs 1957). Still, at the current moment, political polarization in Europe looks more like a sign of discursive decay than of ideological renovation, and since it usually translates into a populist rhetoric, we are more inclined to believe that, in terms of partisan affinity, polarization will only repel liberal individuals even more. So:

H3a: When polarization grows, liberals feel less identified with any particular political party.

On the other hand, authoritarians should feel attracted to this kind of relentless, aggressive rhetoric, especially, again, if it comes from PRRP leaders and it contains a people-centric, nativist outlook of democracy. Therefore:

H3b: When polarization grows, authoritarians feel more identified with a particular political party.

Moreover, we expect a greater political participation in times of polarization, both among authoritarians and among liberals even if Hypothesis 3a turns out to be supported by the evidence. The reason is that negative partisanship can be a mobilizing force as effective as a positive partisan attachment, and so all individuals should be more likely to vote as long as they feel that there is a meaningful choice to be made, be it in support of one's favorite candidate or simply to prevent that one's rival gains office. This logic also applies to authoritarianism, as research shows that authoritarianism "is not politically relevant in a vacuum but influences party contestation when events and elites activate it" (Engelhardt et al. 2021). And so:

H4: When polarization grows, political participation rises both among liberals and authoritarians.

Finally, the expected effect of polarization on mobilization can be further refined if we account for the recent rise of PRRPs across the globe, including the European continent. The correlation between authoritarian values and voting for PRRPs is well known (e.g., van Assche et al. 2019; Vasilopoulos and Lachat 2018), yet some authors note that this connection is particularly strong "under conditions of social and political fragmentation" (Dunn 2015, 377). Political polarization constitutes, indeed, a strong signal of "social and political fragmentation," and it is often used by PRRP leaders to fuel authoritarian sentiments (Harteveld et al. 2021b). Hence, our last two hypotheses are as follows:

H5a: Polarization has an overall positive impact on the success of PRRPs.
H5b: The positive effect of polarization on the probability of voting for PRRPs is especially strong among authoritarians.

Data and Methods

To study the effect of polarization on Europeans' political attitudes and behavior, we merge individual-level data from all nine rounds of the European Social Survey with aggregate, country-level polarization scores from the V-Dem dataset (Coppedge et al. 2021). Our final sample includes over 375,000 individual interviews that were conducted in 29 different European democracies through the years 2002–2018. However, not all countries participated in the project with the same consistency, or indeed in the same rounds (see Table 5A.1 in the Appendix for a summary of all countries included in the analysis, as well as the years in which they took part in the

ESS), so we follow the ESS's recommendation to include a weighting variable in our models (we use the item *"anweight"*).

Dependent variables

We measure political engagement, that is, positive evaluations about the system's effectiveness and representativeness (Dahlberg et al. 2015; Linde and Ekman 2003), through three different variables: (1) satisfaction with democracy (*"How satisfied are you with the way democracy works in your country?"*) (2) political trust (an additive index that includes confidence in *"the country's Parliament"* and in the *"legal system,"* see Table 5A.2 in the Appendix), and (3) partisan attachment (*"Is there a particular political party that you feel closer to than all the other parties?,"* 1=*Yes*, 0=*No*).

Political mobilization, in turn, is measured in terms of effective electoral participation (*"Did you vote in the last general elections celebrated in your country?,"* 1=*Yes*, 0=*No*). In addition, we code a dummy variable capturing the vote for PRRPs compared to having voted for a different party (1=*Voted for a PRRP*, 0=*Voted for a different party*). To decide which parties to classify as PRRP, we relied on the Popu-List dataset (Rooduijn et al. 2019) and selected only those labeled both as "populist" and as "radical right" (the full list of parties falling under the PRRP category in our sample can be found in Table 5A.3 in the Appendix)

Independent variables

To gauge authoritarian values, we use the "conservation" factor derivable from Schwartz's (1992, 2012) universal human values scale, which is included in all ESS rounds. Conservation is a latent construct based on three fundamental, interrelated values—security, conformity, and tradition—that "emphasize order, self-restriction, preservation of the past, and resistance to change" (Schwartz 2012, 8). Building on Schwartz's theory, we add together individual scores from five separate items to build our authoritarianism scale. In these items, respondents were asked to evaluate how similar they were relative to the description of a fictitious person exhibiting such kind of values (the exact wording of all items can be found in Table 5A.2 in the Appendix). Schwartz's and other similar scales have successfully been used in the field of political psychology to capture a particular authoritarian contempt for pluralist, tolerant values that are most visible in those circumstances when one's desire for "social conformity" stands in conflict with the value of "personal autonomy" (Feldman 2003).

Regarding polarization, there is no standard way of measuring it in the "pernicious" sense we have given to the concept (indicators of "affective" and "ideological" polarization would not do the job). Therefore, we rely on V-Dem's (Coppedge et al. 2021) *v2cacamps* item, which covers all country-year observations in our sample and contains experts' evaluations of the question *"Is society polarized into antagonistic, political camps?."*[1] Possible responses range from 0 (*"Not at all"*) to 4 (*"Yes, to a large extent. Supporters of opposing political camps generally interact in a hostile manner"*) and these values were later codified as z-scores.

In addition, all our models control for a number of individual and contextual potential confounders, such as birth cohort (0=*Interwar*, 1=*Baby Boom*, 2=*Generation X*, 3=*Millennial*, 4=*Generation Z*), gender (0=*Female*, 1=*Male*), occupation (1=*Manual workers*, 2=*Employees*, 3=*Liberal professionals and managers*), educational level (1=*Less than lower secondary*, 2=*Lower secondary*, 3=*Upper secondary*, 4=*Postsecondary*, 5=*Tertiary*), domicile (0=*Urban*, 1=*Rural*), ideological self-placement (0=*Extreme left* to 10=*Extreme right*), satisfaction with the household's current income (four levels from *"Very difficult to cope"* to *"Living comfortably"*), satisfaction with the state of the country's economy (0=*"Extremely dissatisfied"* to 10=*"Extremely satisfied"*), level of democracy (V-Dem's liberal democracy index ranging from 0 to 1), quality of government (Teorell et al. 2021), vote share of anti-pluralist parties (based on V-Party's (Düpont et al. 2021) anti-pluralism index[2] and weighted accordingly), unemployment rate (World Bank), and logged GDP per capita (World Bank).

Finally, as the outcome variables "vote" and "vote for PRRPs" refer to vote recall rather than vote intention, we have lagged their contextual predictors in order to control for reverse causation. In particular, we have decided to use a

---

[1] The clarifying note reads: "Here we refer to the extent to which political differences affect social relationships beyond political discussions. Societies are highly polarized if supporters of opposing political camps are reluctant to engage in friendly interactions, for example, in family functions, civic associations, their free time activities and workplaces."

[2] "Anti-pluralism" is defined as a party's "[lack of] commitment to democratic norms prior to election."

The Limits of Democratic Competition

4-year lag in an attempt to capture the whole electoral cycle—although we have lost a large number of individual observations as a result (see Table 5.1 below).

Table 5.1 Descriptive summary

Variable	N	Mean	Std. Dev.	Min	Pctl. 25	Pctl. 75	Max
Dependent variables							
Satisfaction with democracy	365,538	0.528	0.249	0	0.4	0.7	1
Political trust	375,122	0.481	0.238	0	0.3	0.65	1
Feel close to party	371,031						
No	188,427	50.8%					
Yes	182,604	49.2%					
Voted in last general elections	346,822						
No	78,094	22.5%					
Yes	268,728	77.5%					
Voted for a PRRP	215,499						
No	196,631	91.2%					
Yes	18,868	8.8%					
Individual predictors							
Generation	377,954						
Interwar	81,700	21.6%					
Baby Boom	123,599	32.7%					
Generation X	93,243	24.7%					
Millennial	72,129	19.1%					
Generation Z	7,283	1.9%					
Gender	379,108						
Female	202,607	53.4%					
Male	176,501	46.6%					
Occupation	326,601						
Manual worker	107,632	33%					

(Continued)

Variable	N	Mean	Std. Dev.	Min	Pctl. 25	Pctl. 75	Max
Employee	139,002	42.6%					
Director/liberal professional	79,967	24.5%					
Education	377,221						
Less than lower secondary	46,718	12.4%					
Lower secondary	70,764	18.8%					
Upper secondary	144,939	38.4%					
Postsecondary	16,109	4.3%					
Tertiary	98,691	26.2%					
Rural domicile	378,495						
No	119,578	31.6%					
Yes	258,917	68.4%					
Left-right self-placement	330,193	0.509	0.218	0	0.4	0.6	1
Feeling about present income	371,900						
Very difficult to cope	24,638	6.6%					
Difficult on present income	65,515	17.6%					
Coping on present income	169,493	45.6%					
Living comfortably	112,254	30.2%					
Satisfaction with the economy	370,713	0.463	0.251	0	0.3	0.7	1
Authoritarianism	367,548	0.671	0.174	0	0.56	0.8	1
Country-year predictors							
Political polarization	376,361	0.374	0.211	0	0.218	0.525	1
Liberal democracy	379,433	0.822	0.146	0	0.8	0.901	1
Quality of government	379,433	0.64	0.251	0	0.429	0.857	1
Anti-pluralist parties	379,433	0.135	0.17	0	0.033	0.174	1
Unemployment	379,433	0.248	0.166	0	0.127	0.328	1
GDP p/c (log)	379,433	0.601	0.217	0	0.436	0.744	1

Note: All continuous variables have been normalized to range from 0 to 1.

Source: European Social Survey.

MODEL

Our dataset has a TSCS structure, which calls for the use of multilevel models as a way of accounting for the clustering of the data (see Table 5.2). In comparative surveys such as these, individual responses at level 1 are nested within country-year observations at level 2, and these in turn are nested within country observations at level 3, which poses the additional challenge of differentiating the longitudinal from cross-country contextual effects. In fact, ignoring this issue would be particularly problematic in our case, since the hypotheses we have formulated about the impact of polarization on individual attitudes refer both to contextual effects and cross-level interactions.

Consequently, we follow Fairbrother's (2014) method to decompose and identify the "within" (WE) and "between" effects (BE) of our predictors, that is, the effects on the outcome variable derived from contextual changes over time within countries themselves as opposed to the results attributable to time-invariant differences across countries. Furthermore, we use Giesselmann and Schmidt-Catran's (2019) approach to obtain a purely "within" estimator for our cross-level interactions, which consists of including two additional versions of the interaction term in the model based on

Table 5.2 Variance at each level in the three-level hierarchical structure

	Satisfaction democracy (%)	Political trust (%)	Feeling close to a party (%)	Voted in last elections (%)	Voted for a PRRP (%)
Individual	76.9	72.5	94.7	93	26.6
Country-year	3.9	3.2	0.7	0.5	24
Country	19.2	24.3	4.6	6.5	49.4
Total clust.	23.1	27.5	5.3	7	73.4

Note: Values derived from null models with random intercepts at the country-year and country levels.

Source: European Social Survey.

the mean values of the two interacting variables.[3] Finally, all our models add a random slope for each individual variable in the interaction term, since failing to do so "constitutes a specification error that will often have severe consequences for statistical inference about the coefficient of the cross-level interaction term ... and about the main effect of the lower-level predictor involved in the interaction" (Heisig and Schaeffer 2019, 2).

Results

Figure 5.1 shows, for each country, the change over time in its average authoritarianism and polarization scores. The lines thus represent mean scores for both variables in each country-year observation relative to a country's overall mean. In other words, whenever a line rises above the "country-mean" marker, that value should be interpreted as a country-year observation in which authoritarianism (or polarization) was higher than the country's overall mean across all rounds. In contrast, values below the marker stand for lower-than-average scores in a given year.

So, what does Figure 5.1 tell us? Regarding authoritarianism, there is little within-country change, which is in line with the common assumption that values and personality traits are quite stable through time (Schwartz 1992)—although there is also evidence showing that contextual and individual factors can induce within-person changes (e.g., Bardi and Goodwdin 2011, Tormos et al. 2017), especially among young individuals (Vecchione et al. 2020, 2016). But perhaps most interestingly, we also see that in a handful of countries—including "consolidated" democracies, such as Austria, Switzerland, Denmark, and Sweden—authoritarianism has grown in the last years, and in some of them it stands at an all-time high even today.

As far as polarization is concerned, the trend is much clearer: during the last five years, polarization has risen to its highest levels in most European countries and there is no single country in which, between 2014 and 2018, it

---

3   The interaction term is thus entered three times in the model: the first version interacts the demeaned values of both variables and its estimate is the one that can be interpreted as a "within" effect. The two additional versions—*demeaned contextual predictor * mean individual predictor* and *mean contextual predictor * demeaned individual predictor*—are meant to absorb the remaining "between" variance that could plague the purely "within" estimate if they were not included in the model.

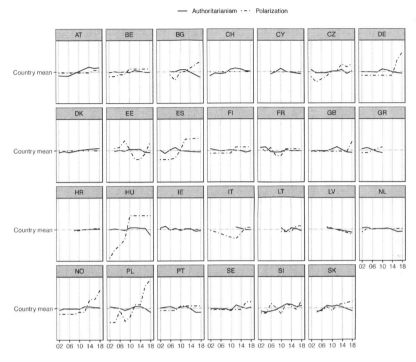

Figure 5.1 Within-country trends in authoritarianism and polarization

Source: Popu-List (Rooduijn et al. 2019).

Note: Unweighted scores. Trends for Luxembourg and Iceland are not included due to missing values.

was lower than average compared to the period prior to the financial crisis.[4] Still, cross-country differences are bigger here than in the case of authoritarianism, and so there is a considerable fraction of the European continent where polarization has remained quite stable through time. Likewise, we should not forget that Figure 5.2 portrays only within-country trends, and so it would be incorrect to conclude that polarization in, say, Germany, Spain, or Norway is now as high as it is in backsliding countries like Hungary and Poland.

---

4 The only exception here is Latvia, but mean values for this country correspond with only two observations (see Table 5A.1 in the Appendix), and its highest value actually comes from the ESS wave conducted in 2008.

Turning now to the results from our models, Table 5.3 summarizes the estimated effect of authoritarianism and polarization on individual political attitudes and behavior. As a preliminary step, let us first take a look at their relationship at the individual level. In terms of *engagement*, the first row of estimates in Table 5.3 shows that, controlling for the influence of time and a whole set of other individual and contextual factors, European authoritarians were significantly more satisfied with the way democracy worked throughout the 2002–2018 period than liberals were, and they also had slightly greater confidence in the regime's institutions. However, authoritarians felt somewhat less close to a particular party than liberals did (although the effect is nonsignificant), which may be due to the electoral irrelevance of most PRRPs until quite recent times. Overall, then, authoritarianism is not associated with any anti-system proclivities and hence should not be confused with other factors driving support for PRRPs, such as populist attitudes (e.g., Castanho-Silva et al. 2020; Schulz et al. 2018; Akkerman et al. 2014).

Table 5.3 Summary of results

	Sat. dem.	Pol. trust	Close party	Voted	Voted PRRP
	Est.	Est.	O.R.	O.R.	O.R.
Authoritarianism	**0.52**···	**0.03**··	0.94	0.89	**2.47**···
Polarization (WE)	8.61	**1.34**·	0.33	0.00ª	109742481.63
Polarization (BE)	-0.33	0.02	1.42	0.86	**965.09**·
Polarization (WE)*Authoritarianism	**1.89**·	0.05	**4.37**·	1.01	**25.17**º
Polarization (BE)*Authoritarianism	0.01	0.03	**2.29**···	**2.61**···	0.72
Individual-level controls	✓	✓	✓	✓	✓
Country-year-level controls	✓	✓	✓	✓	✓
Time control	✓	✓	✓	✓	✓

(*Continued*)

	Sat. dem.	Pol. trust	Close party	Voted	Voted PRRP
N (individual)	266,823	269,468	266,317	193,966	133,554
N (country-year)	196	196	196	144	142
N (country)	28	28	28	26	26

Note: Values shown are beta coefficients and odds-ratios. All models include random intercepts by country-year and country observations and a random slope for the authoritarianism predictor. ^{a} $p<0.1$ * $p<0.05$ ** $p<0.01$ *** $p<0.001$.

Source: European Social Survey.

This is not to say, however, that authoritarians endorse the same democratic values attributable to liberal citizens. On the contrary, authoritarians' greater satisfaction with the way democracy works is probably driven by instrumental evaluations of the system's performance rather than by judgments of its normative superiority. Likewise, it would be wrong to believe that authoritarians' greater political trust equates to greater levels of "diffuse support" (Easton 1965) for the principles and institutions of democracy. Instead, it probably reflects the authoritarian predisposition to not challenge existing hierarchies and to favor regime stability.

Regarding *mobilization*, authoritarians are less likely to vote than liberal citizens (although the effect is nonsignificant), but when they do vote, they are in turn much likelier to choose a PRRP. In fact, authoritarians are on average almost two and half times more likely to vote for a PRRP compared to the rest of the electorate, which further calls into question their allegiance to democratic values.

When it comes to polarization, "within" estimates reveal that its growth is positively associated with satisfaction and political trust, but it reduces individual partisan identification. Likewise, a rise in polarization lowers the overall probability of voting compared to that of abstaining, but crucially, polarization has a very strong effect on the likelihood of voting for a PRRP, which it fuels dramatically. In terms of "between effects," countries in which polarization was, on average, higher than the European mean throughout the entire time period, tend to have lower levels of satisfaction with democracy, slightly larger levels of political trust, greater partisan attachment, lower electoral participation rates, and much higher levels of support for PRRPs.

Overall, however, many of the estimates of polarization's contextual effect are nonsignificant, and thus we find no support for Hypothesis 4 ("When polarization grows, political participation rises both among liberals and authoritarians") and only slight evidence backing up Hypothesis 5a ("Polarization has an overall positive impact on the success of PRRPs").

At this point, the reader may be tempted to interpret the lack of statistical significance of some of our predictors as an actual lack of evidence for the rest of our hypotheses, but note that the mediating role which we have predicted the liberal-authoritarian values would play on polarization precisely calls for this kind of results: after all, nonsignificant estimates for society, in general, can conceal significant relationships among different groups *within* society, such as liberal and authoritarian citizens.[5] To test this possibility, we now turn to the results from the interaction variables.

For a better interpretation of the estimates, Figures 5.2 and 5.3 plot predicted values and probabilities among authoritarians (respondents scoring in the top decile of the country-centered authoritarianism scale) and liberals (respondents scoring in the bottom decile) separately. The figures portray both "within" and "between" contextual effects since their joint visualization may yield additional insights.

The first column in Figure 5.2 shows the results for the variable on *satisfaction with the way democracy works*. We find that greater polarization makes liberals less satisfied but authoritarians more satisfied. In fact, satisfaction levels among liberals match only those of authoritarians in times of very low polarization (two standard deviations below a country's mean), while growing polarization further widens the gap between both groups. This finding supports both Hypothesis 1a ("When polarization grows, liberals become less satisfied with the way democracy works") and Hypothesis 1b ("When polarization grows, authoritarians become more satisfied with the way democracy works"). It appears, however, that the relationship does not hold cross-sectionally, since countries where polarization is higher than

---

[5] Of course, an additional reason why our contextual predictors may sometimes fall short of statistical significance could be that they simply lack enough variance, that is, polarization may not change enough within countries over time or, on average, across countries in order for the predictor to be significant. A quick look at the longitudinal and cross-sectional variance in polarization scores (extracted from null models, not shown) suggests that this problem may indeed be plaguing the within-effects estimates, since only 7.9% of the variance takes place within countries, whereas most of it (92.1%) is attributable to differences across countries.

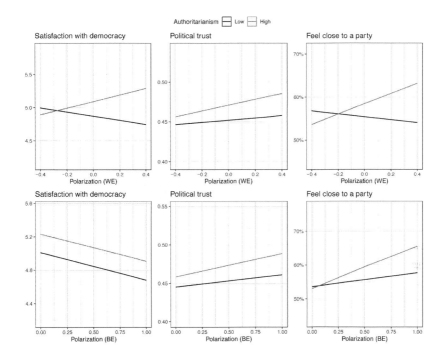

Figure 5.2 Effect of polarization on engagement conditional on authoritarianism
Source: Popu-List (Rooduijn et al. 2019).

average also have lower average levels of satisfaction—although the between-effects are not significant.

Turning now to *political trust*, the middle column shows that authoritarians become slightly more trusting than liberals—whose levels of political trust also increase—as polarization rises, but neither the within-effects nor the between-effects are statistically significant, which means that polarization does not impact authoritarians and liberals differently. What we do find, however, is that levels of political trust among liberals remain unaltered when polarization rises, which corroborates the intuition behind Hypothesis 2 ("When polarization grows, political trust does not fall among liberals") that truly "critical" citizens will support democratic institutions unconditionally, even when the hard times come.

In terms of *partisan identification*, the third column suggests that authoritarians become more identified with a particular party when polarization grows, whereas exactly the opposite happens among liberals. In fact, as shown by the between-effects coefficient, liberals living in countries where polarization was higher than average feel significantly less attached to a given party than authoritarians. Thus, Hypothesis 3a ("When polarization grows, liberals feel less identified with any particular political party") and Hypothesis 3b ("When polarization grows, authoritarians feel more identified with a particular political party") are corroborated, which effectively means that polarization has the simultaneous effect of alienating liberals from and connecting authoritarians with the system.

As regards political mobilization (Figure 5.3), the within interaction term is nonsignificant, so polarization appears to have the same effect on liberals and authoritarians—that is, it slightly reduces their likelihood of vot-

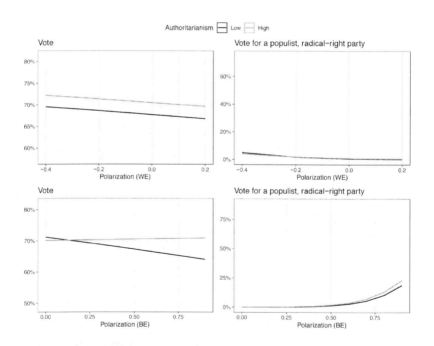

Figure 5.3 Effect of polarization on mobilization conditional on authoritarianism
Source: Popu-List (Rooduijn et al. 2019).

ing. We should note, however, that, on average, liberals are significantly less likely to vote than authoritarians in those countries where polarization is higher, which could indicate that polarization ultimately demobilizes liberal citizens and makes them "withdraw" from the public sphere.

Finally, when it comes to the probability of voting for a PRRP, our results contradict Hypothesis 5b ("The positive effect of polarization on the probability of voting for PRRPs is especially strong among authoritarians"), since authoritarians are in fact less likely—albeit nonsignificantly so—to vote for a PRRP as polarization rises. Liberals, however, become significantly less likely to vote for a PRRP when polarization grows, perhaps due to their reaction against illiberal incumbents or to their realization of the real threat posed by PRRPs to democratic institutions. However, this democratic countermobilization effect seems to disappear when polarization levels surpass a certain threshold, and, in countries with high polarization, the gap between authoritarians and liberals in terms of support for PRRPs actually fades away.

Overall, our results provide arguments for both the optimist and the pessimist. On the one hand, liberal citizens are sensitive to the rise of polarization and they manage to voice their discontent with the way politics is going without falling prey to unbridled cynicism. On the other, authoritarians seem to feel quite comfortable in a context of polarization, and they even

Table 5.4 Summary of hypotheses, results, and their possible effect on democracy

	Expected effect of an increase in polarization	Result	Democracy
H1a	Liberals become more dissatisfied	✓	+
H1b	Authoritarians become more satisfied	✓	−
H2	Liberals' trust remains stable	✓	+
H3a	Liberals become less identified with a party	✓	unclear
H3b	Authoritarians become more identified with a party	✓	−
H4	Overall, electoral participation grows	unclear	unclear
H5a	Overall, the probability of voting for a PRRP grows	✓	−
H5b	Authoritarians become more likely to vote for a PRRP	×	−

Source: European Social Survey.

become more attached to political parties, especially—and here comes the pessimist's caveat—to PRRPs.

Discussion

To sum up our results, we have found that polarization has a strong and asymmetrical impact on the political attitudes and behavior of citizens across European democracies. Relying on different measures of engagement and mobilization and controlling for longitudinal and cross-sectional confounders, we have shown that authoritarian individuals become more satisfied with the system and feel better represented when polarization rises, whereas exactly the opposite happens among liberal individuals: they grow more disenchanted with the system's performance and alienated from their representatives. In fact, once polarization surpasses a certain threshold, it may even have the effect of depressing electoral participation among liberals. Fortunately, though, liberals remain supportive of democratic principles and institutions irrespective of the level of polarization.

The implications of our findings are wide-ranging. On the one hand, we have gone beyond studies linking polarization to hyper-partisanship and uncovered another way in which it can fuel democratic backsliding: we have argued that, as polarization rises, liberals tend to withdraw from political life and to demobilize, while authoritarians feel just as comfortable or even more than before. Given that the authoritarians are much likelier to vote for PRRPs than liberal individuals, the asymmetrical effect of polarization can ultimately generate a context in which liberals leave an emboldened sector of authoritarian voters unchecked.

On the other, we have indirectly contributed to the "populism-as-a-corrector versus populism-as-a-threat" debate by showing that the kind of polarizing discourse used by populist leaders to "perform crisis" (Moffitt 2015) does not have a neutral impact on society. Actually, it appears to rise the spirits of authoritarians while making the rest of the population more disaffected, and hence populism cannot be seen as an innocuous political movement.

Still, our analysis faced a number of limitations: first, our scale of authoritarianism refers to universal human values and, therefore, contains no strictly political content. We believe this to be an advantage (since it guarantees that the independent variable is truly *independent* from other political factors), but readers could just as well object that we have been talking about reactionary or ultra-conservative individuals instead of "real" authoritarians.

Second, despite our best efforts to work with a reliable indicator of polarization at the aggregate level, we have to admit that the concept remains elusive and hard to quantify. Some researchers use data from party manifestos and social surveys to craft measures of, respectively, ideological and affective polarization, but we think that the "pernicious" kind of polarization that our argument alludes to is best captured by V-Dem's item.

Finally, we have been cautious not to claim that our results constitute conclusive evidence of a *causal* connection between polarization and the engagement and mobilization of individual citizens. Yet, the fact that our output from multilevel, random effects models fits pretty well with the predictions from previous literature on the psychological consequences of polarization and the political attitudes of authoritarian citizens makes us confident enough about their validity.

APPENDIX

Table 5A.1 Participation in the European Social Survey by country and year

Country	2002	2004	2006	2008	2010	2012	2014	2016	2018
AUT	✓	✓	✓				✓	✓	✓
BEL	✓	✓	✓	✓	✓	✓	✓	✓	✓
BGR			✓	✓	✓	✓			✓
CHE	✓	✓	✓	✓	✓	✓	✓	✓	✓
CYP			✓	✓	✓	✓			✓
CZE	✓	✓	✓	✓	✓	✓	✓	✓	✓
DEU	✓	✓	✓	✓	✓	✓	✓	✓	✓
DNK	✓	✓	✓	✓	✓	✓	✓		✓
EST		✓	✓	✓	✓	✓	✓	✓	✓
ESP	✓	✓	✓	✓	✓	✓		✓	✓
FIN	✓	✓	✓	✓	✓	✓	✓	✓	✓
FRA	✓	✓	✓	✓	✓	✓	✓	✓	✓
GBR	✓	✓	✓	✓	✓	✓	✓	✓	✓

(Continued)

GRC	✓	✓		✓	✓				
HRV				✓	✓				✓
HUN	✓	✓	✓	✓	✓	✓	✓	✓	✓
IRL	✓	✓	✓	✓	✓	✓	✓	✓	✓
ISL		✓				✓		✓	✓
ITA	✓					✓		✓	✓
LTU				✓		✓	✓	✓	✓
LUX	✓	✓							
LVA				✓					✓
NLD	✓	✓	✓	✓	✓	✓	✓	✓	✓
NOR	✓	✓	✓	✓	✓	✓	✓	✓	✓
POL	✓	✓	✓	✓	✓	✓	✓	✓	✓
PRT	✓	✓	✓	✓	✓	✓	✓	✓	✓
SWE	✓	✓	✓	✓	✓	✓	✓	✓	✓
SVN	✓	✓	✓	✓	✓	✓	✓	✓	✓
SVK		✓	✓	✓	✓	✓			✓

Source: European Social Survey.

Table 5A.2 Wording of items in index variables

Authoritarianism	"Tell me how much each person is or is not like you ..." (1–6)
Item 1	*Wants to live in secure surroundings and to avoid anything that might endanger safety.*
Item 2	*Believes people should do what they are told and follow rules at all times, even when no one is watching.*
Item 3	*Wants that government ensures safety against all threats and the state to be strong so it can defend its citizens.*
Item 4	*Thinks that it is important to behave properly and avoid doing anything people would say is wrong.*
Item 5	*Thinks that tradition is important and tries to follow traditions and customs handed down by religion or family.*
Political trust	"Please tell me how much you personally trust each of the institutions ..." (0–10)
Item 1	*[Country's] Parliament.*
Item 2	*The legal system.*

Source: European Social Survey.

Table 5A.3 Populist radical right parties by country

Country	Party name
AUT	BZÖ, FPÖ
BEL	Front National, Parti Populaire, VB
BGR	Attack, NFSB
CHE	Freiheits-Partei, SVP, Ticino League
CYP	—
CZE	Svoboda a přímá demokracie, Úsvit přímé demokracie
DEU	AfD
DNK	DF, Fremskridtspartiet
EST	EKRE
ESP	Vox
FIN	True Finns
FRA	Debout la France, FN
GBR	UKIP
GRC	LAOS
HRV	HDSSB
HUN	Fidesz, Jobbik, KDNP
IRL	—
ISL	—
ITA	Fratelli d'Italia, Lega Nord
LTU	JL
LUX	—
LVA	—
NLD	Forum voor Democratie, PVV
NOR	FrP
POL	Kukiz, League of Polish Families, LPR, PiS
PRT	—
SWE	SD
SVN	SDS, SNS
SVK	SNS, SR

Source: Popu-List.org.

Bibliography

Akkerman, A., C. Mudde, and A. Zaslove. 2014. "How Populist Are the People? Measuring Populist Attitudes in Voters." *Comparative Political Studies* 47 (9): 1324–1353.

Arbatli, E., and D. Rosenberg. 2021. "United We Stand, Divided We Rule: How Political Polarization Erodes Democracy." *Democratization* 28 (2): 285–307.

Bardi, A., and R. Goodwin. 2011. "The Dual Route to Value Change: Individual Processes and Cultural Moderators." *Journal of Cross-Cultural Psychology* 42 (2): 271–287.

Bermeo, N. 2016. "On Democratic Backsliding." *Journal of Democracy* 27 (1): 5–19.

Carey, J., K. Clayton, G. Helmke, B. Nyhan, M. Sanders, and S. Stokes. 2020. "Who Will Defend Democracy? Evaluating Tradeoffs in Candidate Support among Partisan Donors and Voters." *Journal of Elections, Public Opinion and Parties* 32 (1): 230–245.

Castanho Silva, B., S. Jungkunz, M. Helbling, and L. Littvay. 2020. "An Empirical Comparison of Seven Populist Attitudes Scales." *Political Research Quarterly* 73 (2): 409–424.

Coppedge, M., J. Gerring, C. H. Knutsen, S. I. Lindberg, J. Teorell, N. Alizada, and D. Ziblatt. et al. 2021. *V-Dem Codebook v11.1*. Varieties of Democracy (V-Dem) Project. Sweden: Varieties of Democracy.

Dahlberg, S., J. Linde, and S. Holmberg. 2015. "Democratic Discontent in Old and New Democracies: Assessing the Importance of Democratic Input and Governmental Output." *Political Studies* 63:18–37.

Downs, A. (1957). "An Economic Theory of Political Action in a Democracy." *Journal of Political Economy* 65 (2): 135–150.

Dunn, K. 2015. "Preference for Radical Right-Wing Populist Parties among Exclusive-Nationalists and Authoritarians." *Party Politics* 21 (3): 367–380.

Düpont, N., B. Kavasoglu, A. Lührmann, and O. J. Reuter. 2021. "Party Organizations Around the Globe. Introducing the Varieties of Party Identity and Organization Dataset (V-Party)." Working Paper No. 124. University of Gothenburg, Varieties of Democracy Institute.

Easton, D. 1965. *A Systems Analysis of Political Life*. New Jersey: John Wiley.

Engelhardt, A. M., S. Feldman, and M. J. Hetherington. 2021. "Advancing the Measurement of Authoritarianism." *Political Behavior*, 1–24.

Enyedi, Z. 2016. "Populist Polarization and Party System Institutionalization: The Role of Party Politics in De-Democratization." *Problems of Post-Communism* 63 (4): 210–220.

Fairbrother, M. 2014. "Two Multilevel Modeling Techniques for Analyzing Comparative Longitudinal Survey Datasets." *Political Science Research and Methods* 2 (1): 119–140.

Feldman, S. 2003. "Enforcing Social Conformity: A Theory of Authoritarianism." *Political Psychology* 24 (1): 41–74.

Finkel, E. J., C. A. Bail, M. Cikara, P. H. Ditto, S. Iyengar, S. Klar, and J. N. Druckman. 2020. "Political Sectarianism in America." *Science* 370 (6516): 533–536.

Foa, R. S., and Y. Mounk. 2016. "The Danger of Deconsolidation: The Democratic Disconnect." *Journal of Democracy* 27 (3): 5–17.

Foa, R. S., and Y. Mounk. 2017. "The Signs of Deconsolidation." *Journal of Democracy* 28 (1): 5–15.

Foa, R., A. Klaasen, M. Slade, and A. Collins Rand. 2020. "The Global Satisfaction with Democracy Report 2020." University of Cambridge, Centre for the Future of Democracy.

Fossati, D., B. Muhtadi, and E. Warburton. 2021. "Why Democrats Abandon Democracy: Evidence from Four Survey Experiments." *Party Politics* 28 (3): 554–566. https://doi.org/10.1177/1354068821992488.

Giesselmann, M., and A. W. Schmidt-Catran. 2019. "Getting the within Estimator of Cross-Level Interactions in Multilevel Models with Pooled Cross-Sections: Why Country Dummies (Sometimes) Do Not Do the Job." *Sociological Methodology* 49 (1): 190–219.

Graham, M. H., and M. W. Svolik. 2020. "Democracy in America? Partisanship, Polarization, and the Robustness of Support for Democracy in the United States." *American Political Science Review* 114 (2): 392–409.

Haggard, S., and R. Kaufman. 2021. *Backsliding: Democratic Regress in the Contemporary World*. Cambridge: Cambridge University Press.

Harteveld, E., A. Kokkonen, J. Linde, and S. Dahlberg. 2021a. "A Tough Trade-Off? The Asymmetrical Impact of Populist Radical Right Inclusion on Satisfaction with Democracy and Government." *European Political Science Review* 13 (1): 113–133.

Harteveld, E., P. Mendoza, and M. Rooduijn. 2021b. "Affective Polarization and the Populist Radical Right: Creating the Hating?." *Government and Opposition*, 1–25.

Heisig, J. P., and M. Schaeffer. 2019. "Why You Should Always Include a Random Slope for the Lower-Level Variable Involved in a Cross-Level Interaction." *European Sociological Review* 35 (2): 258–279.

Iyengar, S., Y. Lelkes, M. Levendusky, N. Malhotra, and S. J. Westwood. 2019. "The Origins and Consequences of Affective Polarization in the United States." *Annual Review of Political Science* 22:129–146.

Jee, H., H. Lueders, and R. Myrick. 2021. "Towards a Unified approach to Research on Democratic Backsliding." *Democratization*, 1–14.

Levitsky, S., and D. Ziblatt. 2018. *How Democracies Die*. New York: Broadway Books.

Linde, J., and J. Ekman. 2003. "Satisfaction with Democracy: A Note on a Frequently Used Indicator in comparative Politics." *European Journal of Political Research* 42 (3): 391–408.

Lührmann, A., and S. I. Lindberg. 2019. "A Third Wave of Autocratization Is Here: What Is New about It?." *Democratization* 26 (7): 1095–1113.

McCoy, J., and M. Somer. 2019. "Toward a Theory of Pernicious Polarization and How It Harms Democracies: Comparative Evidence and Possible Remedies." *Annals of the American Academy of Political and Social Science* 681 (1): 234–271.

McCoy, J., T. Rahman, and M. Somer. 2018. "Polarization and the Global Crisis of Democracy: Common Patterns, Dynamics, and Pernicious Consequences for Democratic Polities." *American Behavioral Scientist* 62 (1): 16–42.

Moffitt, B. 2015. "How to Perform Crisis: A Model for Understanding the Key Role of Crisis in Contemporary Populism." *Government and Opposition* 50 (2): 189–217.

Norris, P., ed. 1999. *Critical Citizens: Global Support for Democratic Government*. Oxford: Oxford University Press.

Norris, P. 2011. *Democratic Deficit: Critical Citizens Revisited*. Cambridge: Cambridge University Press.

Norris, P., and R. Inglehart. 2019. *Cultural Backlash: Trump, Brexit, and Authoritarian Populism*. Cambridge: Cambridge University Press.

Orhan, Y. E. 2022. "The Relationship between Affective Polarization and Democratic Backsliding: Comparative Evidence." *Democratization*, 1–22.

Rooduijn, M., S. Van Kessel, C. Froio, A. Pirro, S. De Lange, D. Halikiopoulou, and P. Taggart. 2019. "The PopuList: An Overview of Populist, Far Right, Far Left and Eurosceptic Parties in Europe." www.popu-list.org.

Saikkonen, I., and H. S. Christensen. 2022. "Guardians of Democracy or Passive Bystanders? A Conjoint Experiment on Elite Transgressions of Democratic Norms." *Political Research Quarterly* March. https://doi.org/10.1177/10659129211073592.

Schulz, A., P. Müller, C. Schemer, D. S. Wirz, M. Wettstein, and W. Wirth. 2018. "Measuring Populist Attitudes on Three Dimensions." *International Journal of Public Opinion Research* 30 (2): 316–326.

Schwartz, S. H. 1992. "Universals in the Content and Structure of Values: Theoretical Advances and Empirical Tests in 20 Countries." In *Advances in Experimental Social Psychology*, vol. 25, edited by B. Gawronski, 1–65. Cambridge, MA: Academic Press.

Schwartz, S. H. 2012. "An Overview of the Schwartz Theory of Basic Values." *Online Readings in Psychology and Culture* 2 (1): 2307–2319.

Simonovits, G., J. McCoy, and L. Littvay. 2022. "Democratic Hypocrisy and Out-group Threat: Explaining Citizen Support for Democratic Erosion." *Journal of Politics* 84 (3).

Somer, M., J. L. McCoy, and R. E. Luke. 2021. "Pernicious Polarization, Autocratization and Opposition Strategies." *Democratization* 28 (5): 929–948.

Svolik, M. W. 2019. "Polarization versus Democracy." *Journal of Democracy* 30 (3): 20–32.

Teorell, J., A. Sundström, S. Holmberg, B. Rothstein, N. Alvarado Pachon, and C. M. Dalli. 2021. "The Quality of Government Standard Dataset, Version Jan 21." University of Gothenburg, The Quality of Government Institute. http://www. qog. pol. gu. se doi, 10.

Tormos, R., C. M. Vauclair, and H. Dobewall. 2017. "Does Contextual Change Affect Basic Human Values? A Dynamic Comparative Multilevel Analysis across 32 European Countries." *Journal of Cross-Cultural Psychology* 48 (4): 490–510.

Vachudova, M. A. 2019. "From Competition to Polarization in Central Europe: How Populists Change Party Systems and the European Union." *Polity* 51 (4): 689–706.

van Assche, J., K. Dhont, and T. F. Pettigrew. 2019. The Social-Psychological Bases of Far-Right Support in Europe and the United States. *Journal of Community and Applied Social Psychology* 29 (5): 385–401.

Vasilopoulos, P., and Lachat, R. 2018. "Authoritarianism and Political Choice in France." *Acta Politica* 53 (4): 612–634.

Vecchione, M., S. Schwartz, G. Alessandri, A. K. Döring, V. Castellani, and M. G. Caprara. 2016. "Stability and Change of Basic Personal Values in Early Adulthood: An 8-Year Longitudinal Study." *Journal of Research in Personality* 63:111–122.

Vecchione, M., S. H. Schwartz, E. Davidov, J. Cieciuch, G. Alessandri, and G. Marsicano. 2020. "Stability and Change of Basic Personal Values in Early Adolescence: A 2-year Longitudinal Study." *Journal of Personality* 88 (3): 447–463.

Waldner, D., and E. Lust. 2018. "Unwelcome Change: Coming to Terms with Democratic Backsliding." *Annual Review of Political Science* 21:93–113.

Wuttke, A., K. Gavras, and H. Schoen. 2022. "Have Europeans Grown Tired of Democracy? New Evidence from Eighteen Consolidated Democracies, 1981–2018." *British Journal of Political Science* 52 (1): 416–428.

Zilinsky, J. 2019. "Democratic Deconsolidation Revisited: Young Europeans Are not Dissatisfied with Democracy." *Research & Politics* 6 (1): 2053168018814332.

CHAPTER 6

Populist Voter Profiles in Different Electoral Calls: Lessons from Spain[1]

Javier Antón-Merino, Sergio Pérez-Castaños, and Marta Méndez-Juez

INTRODUCTION

We live in a time of great change and uncertainty, in which societies are becoming increasingly polarized and institutions are proving less effective in responding to the demands of their citizens. In this political and social context, populist radical right parties (PRRPs) have taken advantage of a great opportunity to position themselves as indispensable partners of conservative governments through effective communication strategies based on the appeal of a primary conception of politics (Prodobnik et al. 2019). One of the current challenges in political science is to analyze the reasons that have led to the electoral success of these formations (Prodobnik et al. 2019; Durrheim et al. 2018; Staerklé and Green 2018; Kishishita 2018; Mudde and Rovira Kaltwasser 2018; Hameleers 2018) as well as the real chances of these parties achieving continuity over time and being acceptable partners in government.

Moreover, the fact that in politically composite states there are different levels of administration and government makes it particularly relevant to check whether the profile of the electorate is similar in all cases or, depending on the electoral arenas, not. This differentiation across levels is the case of the Spanish electoral context and, specifically, in the analysis of Vox as a PRRP.

---

[1] This chapter is part of the work of project BU060G19, thanks to funding obtained through the competitive program of the Junta de Castilla y León.

To this end, throughout the chapter, we will analyze whether there are differences in the electorate depending on the electoral arena under study.

This chapter has six sections. The following section will provide a theoretical review of the most recent academic literature to define those variables of analysis that are of greatest interest in the study of the populist radical right. Subsequently, a brief exploratory analysis will be made of the presence of Vox as a new political actor through a review of its electoral results. Next, Vox voter profiles will be established based on previous studies, and, in the following section, a logistic regression analysis will be carried out. This will seek to test the electoral characteristics of Vox voters to identify the extent to which there is an "average voter profile" for this party, regardless of the electoral arena in which it is competing. Finally, some brief conclusions will be drawn.

Radical Right Populism

In recent years, we have witnessed a new phenomenon in Europe: the rise of populism. But what do we mean by populism?[2] This term is perhaps one of the most controversial to analyze, as it encompasses a wide variety of imprecise phenomena (Mudde 2017). Populism is seen by Rivero (Chapter 2) as a parasitic ideology of democracy and as an endemism that is characteristic of democracy only. There are two basic assumptions in the populist understanding of democracy. The first one is that democracy is, literally, "the government in the name of the people." The second basic assumption of populism as an ideology is that all societies are divided into two closed and antagonistic groups: the people and the oligarchy.

The electoral success of PRRPs is due to multiple factors, depending on social and political context, that have generated a variety of approaches: theories that talk about economic inequality (Rama and Cordero 2018; Inglehart and Norris 2019); ones that focus on cultural reaction (Inglehart and Norris 2016); and those that highlight identity conflict (De Lange and

---

2   Only the key elements of these types of parties are identified here, as this issue has been extensively covered in Part I of this book.

Mugge 2015; Inglehart and Norris 2019; De Cleen and Stavrakakis 2017; Antón and Hernández-Carr 2016).

In the case of Vox, Anduiza (2018) asks whether it is "populist," as the content of its discourse poses difficulties in considering it as one.[3] However, he acknowledges that Vox has four fundamental characteristics that help categorize it as this type of party and that, in addition, connect with three currents that explain its growth.

Vox is characterized, first, by the insertion of the element of national unity as opposed to territorial dispersion by focusing its discourse on the rejection of regionalist and peripheral nationalist formations. Second, their "cultural reaction" is represented by a rejection of policies linked to equality—in areas such as feminism, equal marriage, and abortion. Third, their criminalization of "the different"—the immigrant—is a discourse based on marked nativism related to this same current. Last, Vox's discourse makes intensive use of aggressive language that denotes authoritarianism in both form and substance.

On the one hand, Ferreira (2019) argues that Vox fulfills the conditions to be considered a radical right party. However, the populist element is secondary in its discourse and program to the detriment of others such as nationalism.[4] It also differs from other European radical right parties in its clear neoliberal economic positioning and in its conservative attitude toward moral issues.

On the other hand, Mendes and Dennison (2020) argue that their electoral success may be due to a political context that highlights issues such as immigration or the territorial organization of the state, and even political disaffection. In addition to this explanatory factor, Vox's "normalization" and high profile in the media—in contrast to that obtained by other PRRPs in Spain—is a determining factor in its growth.

In short, this review of recent studies confirms that Vox fits the prototype of the PRRP that already exists in Europe. Thus, we construct our empirical measurement model on the basis of the concept of populism outlined at the beginning of this section by focusing on the explanatory variables that will

---

3   In Chapter 10, a similar discussion can be found on whether the elements of populist discourse are present on Vox's speeches.
4   In this line, a similar conclusion drawn both in the case of Vox and Chega (in Portugal) in Chapter 10.

be detailed in the section on the profile of the electorate and, subsequently, in the research methodology.

Vox as a paradigm in a multilevel electoral context

It can be established that the context of the Great Recession (2007–2013[5]) has been the best scenario for the entrenchment of PRRPs in a large part of Europe (Rama and Cordero 2018). The austerity policies carried out by governments of all ideological stripes, due to the severe impact of the crisis on the economy, provoked a certain sense of disaffection among citizens, leading to the flourishing of movements that sought to delegitimize these policies (Antón and Hernández-Carr 2016). This trend has explained the rise of some formations such as the National Front in France and Donald Trump's electoral success in the United States, which have been able to channel the anger of the popular and working classes that are most affected by the recession.

However, in the Spanish case, the strengthening and rise of the populist radical right Vox has not occurred in this context (Mendes and Dennison 2020). Although its genesis does take place in the Great Recession, insofar as it was founded in 2013, it did not manage to capitalize on citizens' disenchantment with the austerity measures. This discontent, however, will be captured by two other newly created formations in Spain: *Podemos* (the populist left party) and, later, *Ciudadanos* (the liberal party) (Ramiro and Gómez 2017).

However, it was until the vote of no confidence that ousted the conservative government that Vox reached historic highs in the electoral polls (Michavila 2019). This capitalization of the vote of discontent with the democratic system has its paradigm in the rise of movements of revolt against democracy (Zembylas 2021) as in the case of Poland, Hungary, or, more recently, with the incident of the assault on the Capitol on January 6, 2021, in the United States. In this way, the effects of the Great Recession were not so relevant in the process of Vox's consolidation, with political disaffection being one of the main ingredients for the electoral success that was to come (Turnbull-Dugarte et al. 2020).

---

5 Although this period is between 2007 and 2009, it is worth noting that it was not until 2013 that the world economy began to show signs of recovery and, therefore, marks the end of the Great Recession.

The December 2018 Andalusian regional elections marked the beginning of an electoral cycle highlighted by the entry of Vox representatives into the legislative chambers of different levels of government in Spain. These elections represented the end of the idea of "Iberian exceptionality" (Alonso and Rovira Kaltwasser 2015), which saw these types of parties in Spain achieve only poor results when compared to those in other parts of Europe. Subsequently, from 2018 to date, Vox has managed to have a presence in the European Parliament, Congress, Senate, 11 autonomous legislative bodies,[6] the assemblies of the Autonomous Cities of Ceuta and Melilla, and a multitude of municipalities.

As noted in the introduction, studying Spain in the electoral cycle that has just ended is a unique opportunity to see, in a short space of time, how the profile of the Vox voter has changed. Vox has faced over 15 different elections in four different electoral arenas, and this allows us to carry out a comparative analysis of the determining factors of political behavior, which will be detailed in the next section.

A few months after the Andalusian elections, general elections were held in April 2019, in which the citizens of the Valencian Community were also called to the polls to elect their regional representatives. In both elections, Vox exceeded 10% of the vote and was the fifth political force in terms of the number of representatives. For its part, the Spanish Socialist Workers' Party (PSOE) was the most voted-for party both in the Valencian Community and in Spain as a whole, but while in the former an agreement between left-wing parties led to the socialists retaining the presidency, at the national level, none of the candidates obtained sufficient support to form a government. This triggered a new election in November 2019, which was preceded by local, European, and 12 regional elections in May of the same year.

In the case of the May 2019 elections, the PSOE was the most voted-for political force in the European and municipal elections, as well as in 10 of the 12 autonomous communities where elections were held. For its part, the Partido Popular (hereafter, PP) was able to form a government with Ciudadanos (hereafter, Cs) in Castilla y León, the Community of Madrid, and the Region of Murcia. In the latter two regions, as in Andalusia, Vox

---

6   Vox has no representation in the autonomous communities of the Canary Islands, Castile-La Mancha, Extremadura, Galicia, La Rioja, and Navarre.

was key to the success of the regional government. These elections marked a setback in the electoral aspirations of Spain's PRRP formation that, despite the diversity of results, achieved only 6% of the vote in the European elections.[7] This setback was even more pronounced in the municipal elections, where, due to the party's weak territorial organizational structure, Vox failed to reach 4% of the vote in Spain as a whole.

In the November 2019 general elections that followed, PSOE managed to revalidate its majority and, this time, formed a coalition government with Podemos, with the support of nationalist and minority parties in the investiture. But these elections also brought about major changes in the balance of power in the right-wing bloc: the collapse of Cs (which lost 47 seats and went from being the third force, in terms of the number of votes, to fifth) caused a sharp rise in both the total number of votes and the number of seats for the PP and Vox. The latter became the third largest political force in Parliament, with 52 seats and more than 15% of the vote.

The first elections following the start of the COVID-19 pandemic were the Galician and Basque regional elections. In Galicia, the PP revalidated its absolute majority, ensuring that Vox did not obtain representation. In the Basque Country, the Basque Nationalist Party (PNV) was once again the most voted-for party, and Vox obtained only one seat in Parliament. Finally, the electoral cycle closed with the February 2021 regional elections in Catalonia and the early elections in the Community of Madrid in May 2021. In the former, the socialists were the most voted-for party, but the Catalan nationalist parties once again agreed to form a government. Vox obtained over 7.5% of the vote, winning 11 seats. In the Community of Madrid, the PP gained an ample majority, with 65 out of 136 being elected as members of Parliament. Despite this, the PP needed the support of Vox representatives, with 13 seats and over 9% of the vote, to be able to preside over the community.

After verifying the electoral evolution of this party and, above all, its growing strength due to its electoral impact, it is now time to turn to studies on its electorate. This will help us identify key variables that will allow a comparison between electoral arenas.

---

[7] European elections have been described by several authors as "second order elections," characterized by: lower voter turnout, better electoral prospects for small and new political parties, a higher percentage of invalid votes and poor electoral outcomes for governing parties (Reif and Schmitt 1980, 9).

Profile of Vox voters

In the case PRRPs, Rama and Cordero (2018) observe that, in countries less affected by the economic crisis, those who vote for these parties tend to be older, less educated, and belong to lower social classes, while in the most affected countries, they tend to be younger and better educated. In addition, Antón and Hernández-Carr (2016) found that the factors that really generate electoral support for these political formations are xenophobia and an anti-elite discourse. Further, Iglesias-Pascual et al. (2021) have noted the importance of aspects such as territorial scale (Turnbull-Dugarte 2019), administrative levels, and the distribution of the population in rural or urban areas (David et al. 2018; Rydgren and Ruth 2013) while analyzing the voter profile of this type of party.

Further, focusing their discourse on cultural issues, Boscán et al. (2018), Bernhard and Kriesi (2019), and Castro and Mo Groba (2020) link religion with the possibility of voting for these formations.[8]

Moreover, it is observed that PRRPs contribute to voter mobilization and generate greater interest in electoral campaigns (Żuk and Żuk 2020). García Hípola and Pérez Castaños (2021) argue that Vox's strategy is to use negative publicity or employ their resources to attack and to wear down opponents while still providing information.

Finally, some authors point out that populist radical right voters are more receptive to the mobilizing impact of an identity framework. Fernández Riquelme (2020), for example, argues that Vox takes advantage of a perlocutionary effect to win citizens' votes by activating what he describes as an "exclusionary nationalist sentiment."

Alonso and Rovira Kaltwasser (2015) find that Spain has been a breeding ground for the emergence of a PRRP. However, the existence of a major national axis (center-periphery) makes it difficult to construct a clear national "we," and the PP's success in attracting voters on the right have previously made it hard for parties like Vox to gain a foothold. Along the same lines, Barrio (2020) and Climent and Montaner (2021) point out that the limited success of populist political options in Spain has been due to the prevalence

---

[8] Authors also tend to refer to other lines of analysis to study electoral behavior toward these parties, such as their position on issues related to immigration or gender equality (Immerzeel et al. 2013; Donà 2020). But these issues will not be considered as a measure in this chapter as there are no variables in our dataset to assess them.

of left-right and center-periphery cleavages, which prevent the classic populist "people-elite" dichotomy from emerging.

However, thanks to the rise of Vox, a number of studies have been conducted in recent years (Barrio 2019; Michavila 2019) that have provided a more nuanced description of its voters. Thus, the most general profile, which coincides in several works, depicts a male voter, with a conservative ideology, living in urban areas, and of the Spanish average age or younger (Barrio 2019; Turnbull-Dugarte et al. 2020). Furthermore, this party's electorate has a marked Spanish nationalist character and when the territorial organization of the state also comes into play, it tends to position itself in favor of a politically centralized state (Barrio 2019; Turnbull-Dugarte 2019). In other factors such as education, we find disparities depending on the type of election analyzed, given that Barrio (2019) finds people with higher levels of education in regional elections while Turnbull-Dugarte et al. (2020) find people with lower education in national elections.

Finally, Turnbull-Dugarte et al. (2020) and Ferreira (2019) find that these voters tend to be highly dissatisfied with the political situation as they perceive politicians in negative terms. These authors also argue that this perception clearly stems from the Catalan conflict and that this triggers a response in the form of a strong Spanish identity, as a reaction to the "threat" of independence; in other words, the primacy of the Catalan conflict in public debate has made the fight against regional independence the main hallmark of this political formation (Mendes and Dennison 2022).

In addition to these sociodemographic variables, several authors have highlighted the clear anti-immigration and anti-feminist character of the formation (Michavila 2019). Likewise, these values regarding gender, territorial organization, nativism, and sovereignty have been portrayed as those that go directly against the fundamental values of the European Union (Gould 2019).

When comparing the Vox voter and the voter of other populist radical right parties in Europe, Rama and Santana (2020) conclude that the Vox electorate is younger, male, and more right-wing than average, and it is found among the moderately wealthy classes, students, those who consider the economic or political situation to be bad, and those who feel more Spanish and want greater territorial centralization. In this sense, Gould (2019) also argues that both Vox in Spain and Alternative for Germany rely on a fictitious narrative of national identity when appealing for votes.

Objectives and methods

Having set out the conditioning factors that identify the reasons for the success of PRRPs in Europe in general, and Spain in particular, we now proceed to analyze Vox's voter profile in four different electoral arenas: European, national, regional, and local. The aim is to check whether, following the example of the Spanish case and, specifically, the analysis of Vox, there are differences in the electorate depending on the electoral arena in which they compete.

In this sense, the profile is expected to vary depending on the electoral arena. Thus, we anticipate finding a similar trend to those put forward by other authors regarding both national and regional elections, while there might be changes in both local and European elections. This is largely explained by the theories of second-order elections (Reif and Schmitt 1980), which already indicated that minority formations or those with less specific weight—even anti-system—may be favored by electoral rules and/or the protest vote.

However, the fact that we are talking about elections of a different order is not the only justification for an analysis of the different electoral arenas and Vox's voters. As explained before, the studies carried out to date have found a multitude of differences among voters, both across countries and, in the specific case of Vox, across elections. Thus, depending on how the economic crisis has affected different countries, the success of PRRPs has been one or the other (Rama and Cordero 2018). The same can be presumed to be true in the Spanish regions, where, depending on whether they have been hit by the recession, Vox's success would have varied.

The second element to consider is the differences depending on the structure and habitat of the countries (Turnbull-Dugarte 2019). In this sense, once again, in the Spanish regions, there are differences not only based on their more rural or urban character but also differences in terms of their capacity for political execution and action—competencies resulting from decentralization—that can lead to differences in the vote. The third of the elements to be taken into consideration and which justifies the possibility of finding differences between levels of government pertains to national identity (Fernández Riquelme 2020). In theory, the voters of these formations have a homogeneous idea of their country, and, in the case of Spain, this identity varies in strength and duality depending on the region analyzed or the type of election at stake.

Finally, previous research has detected the existence of a change in Vox's electorate profile between the different elections held since 2018 (Turnbull-Dugarte et al. 2020). Thus, thanks to the analysis of different electoral arenas, it will be possible to verify whether these differences have indeed occurred both over time and simultaneously. This is because, in electoral terms, Vox's strength, owing to the results it obtained in the 2019 elections, has been very uneven not only between communities but also in the different municipalities in which it presented candidacies as well as in the European and national elections (Michavila 2019).

To test our objective and hypothesis, we use individual survey data from the Centro de Investigaciones Sociológicas de España (hereafter, CIS[9]). We use eight different post-electoral surveys conducted by this institution in elections of any kind. Of these, two have been treated individually, based on three different analyses; namely, study number 3269 analyzed the November 2019 general elections, and study number 3253 carried out its analysis for the local and European elections, which took place simultaneously by the end of May 2019. Finally, in order to analyze the sub-national arena, six asynchronous studies have been added: study number 3236, corresponding to the 2018 regional elections in Andalusia, which begin the electoral cycle ending in 2021 with the elections in Catalonia and Madrid; number 3253,[10] of 13 autonomous communities held between April (Valencia Community) and May 2019; numbers 3293 and 3294, for the regional elections held in 2020 in the Basque Country and Galicia, respectively; number 3306, for the 2021 regional elections in Catalonia; and finally, number 3328, for the 2021 elections in the Community of Madrid.

To carry out the regional study we use the strategy of cross-sectional data aggregation or cross-sections, which is typically employed to increase the number of observations in the same universe and, usually, also to contrast longitudinal effects (Wooldridge 2011). Thus, for the European and municipal levels, we counted 9,191 cases, for the national level 4,804 cases, and for the regional level 25,453 cases. Due to the low presence of declared Vox voters, all the databases have been weighted based on the aggregate electoral result

---

9   The CIS is a public institution that carries out social analyses through surveys on a variety of topics and, owing to the fact that it is a public center, all the data it collects are openly available (for more information, see http://www.cis.es).

10 They all share the same number as the survey regarding all three levels was conducted simultaneously, with different sections regarding each election.

obtained in the corresponding elections. In the case of regional elections that did not take place simultaneously, the average of all regions was used.

Despite the existence of different questions in each of the studies, we have been able to extract a series of indicators that are present across the board. Table 6.1 describes the variables that have been introduced in the different models and how they are categorized to understand the analysis that follows.

Table 6.1 Independent variables in the model

Variable name	Variable meaning	Coding for the analysis[a]
Sex	Sex	D: (1) man; (0) woman
Age	Age	S: (18) min.; (98) max.
Studies	Higher level of studies reached	S: (1) no studies; (4) university
Habitat size	Size of the town living in	S: (1) <2.000 inhabs.; (7) > 1.000.000 inhabs.
Employment	Employment situation	Fictional variables D: working (0), unemployed (1), retired (1), and others (1)
Social class	Social class	Fictional variables D: middle class (0); lower class (1); higher class (1)
Political sit.	Valuation of the political situation in the municipality/region/country/European Union	S: (0) >dissatisfaction; (4) >satisfaction
Religious	Religiousness	D: (1) religious; (0) nonreligious
Ideology	Ideological position	S: (0) rad. left; (10) rad. right
National id.	National identity position	S: (1) only Spanish; (5) only regional
Camp. interest	Interest in following the electoral campaign	S (1) None; (5) Many
Decentralization[b]	Preferences for a more decentralized country	S: (1) >centralism; (5) >decentralism

Source: Own elaboration.

Note:

[a] [S:] indicates scale; [D:] indicates dichotomic variable.

[b] This variable is not available on the national election dataset.

As can be seen, all the variables—with the sole exception of the one referring to decentralization, which was not asked about in the national study—are present in the four electoral arenas that will be measured here. To be able to compare the electorates, the dependent variable will always be the same, in dichotomous format, where the Vox voter has the value one (1) and the remaining voters, zero (0). With this type of variable, a logistic regression analysis (GLM) will be carried out, following the logit model, and combining both scale and dichotomous independent variables.

Data analysis

Thanks to the theoretical analysis derived from previous studies, and described earlier, it is clear what can be expected when it comes to identifying Vox's voter profile. Thus, we will proceed to test, with the variables included in Table 6.1, the four differentiated voter models for each of the electoral arenas.

After having carried out the relevant controls, Figure 6.1 shows the models of each of the analyzed electoral arenas through their coefficients. The graphical representation allows us to visually observe whether—or not—there are differences in terms of the profile of the Vox voter between elections.

Before breaking down each of the electoral arenas, it is worth highlighting the explanatory capacity of each model. Thus, the European model has a Nagelkerke R^2 of 0.67; the national model has an R^2 of 0.424; the regional one has an R of 0.635; and the local model has an R of 0.659. In this sense, all the analyses have outstanding explanatory power, and hence we can affirm their ability to generate differences in the voter's profiles by arenas, owing to their comparison.

Once the explanatory capacity of each model has been established, we will begin to analyze the different graphs of coefficients in Figure 6.1, starting with the electoral arena at a higher level—the European level—and ending with that closest to the citizenry—the local level. The layout of the graphs enables us to visually check how the different independent variables are statistically significant or not and whether the probability of voting for the party under analysis increases or decreases in each case as well as in a comparative perspective.

Populist Voter Profiles in Different Electoral Calls

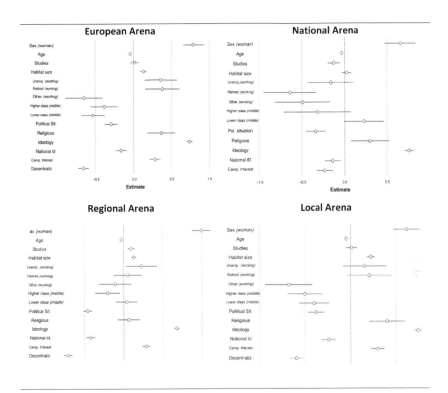

Figure 6.1 Model summary in different electoral arenas
Source: Own elaboration with data from CIS.

Thus, in the case of the European electoral arena, we can observe how being male and young increases the probability of voting for this type of party. In a positive way, we can also see the effect of habitat size—the larger the municipality, the greater the probability of voting for Vox. With respect to the dichotomous dummy variables that address employment status, we can see how the probability of voting for Vox increases if a person is unemployed or retired when compared to those who are working. However, this tendency is reversed when we talk about other different employment situations compared to workers. In terms of social class, as the graph shows, the probability of support for this political formation decreases when a citizen is upper or lower class, as the middle class is more likely to vote for the PRRP formation. Regarding the political context, the likelihood of supporting this formation decreases if a potential voter thinks the prevailing situation is better. However, it increases for people who consider themselves religious and for those more to the right on the ideological scale. The probabilities also increase for those who show a stronger Spanish national identity. In terms of interest in the electoral campaign, we find that people with a greater interest are more likely to vote for Vox, while, finally, those in favor of greater decentralization are less likely to vote for this formation.

Moving the focus to the national elections, we observe how the level of statistical significance of many variables disappears in this model. Gender and age continue to be significant, both in the same direction as in the previous analysis, with men and younger people more likely to vote for this party. In this case, the variable "studies" is also added, which denotes a higher probability of voting for this party when one has a lower level of studies. In terms of employment status, people who are retired or in other situations are less likely to vote for this populist formation. Social class again works in the same way, but this time only in the relationship between the middle class and lower class, with people being less likely to vote for Vox if they self-identify as belonging to the latter. The remaining variables, all significant, work exactly as in the previous model, drawing a profile of a right-wing religious person who considers the political situation to be negative and who feels more Spanish than with a dual or regional subjective national identity. It is worth highlighting that interest in the electoral campaign changes sign in this case when compared to the European arena—the greater the interest shown by someone, the less likely it is that they would vote for Vox.

The third of the electoral spaces to be analyzed is regional. In this case, we once again find similar trends to the previous two. Thus, the sex and age variables are statistically significant, with the probability of voting for Vox increasing among men and decreasing as we move up the age scale. As in the case of the European elections, the size of the municipality is again relevant and has a positive influence—the larger the municipality, the greater the probability of voting for Vox. In terms of employment status, the unemployed seem to be more likely than the employed to vote for Vox—an element that was also present in the European arena. The upper social class again shows a lower probability of voting for Vox than the average—as in the European case. The remaining variables work in a similar way to those already analyzed, showing a clear similarity between the European and national case, that is: assessment of a positive political situation influences negatively; ideology positively as we move to the right; subjective national identity negatively as we move toward a dual or solely regional sentiment; interest in the campaign positively; and decentralization negatively as more decentralizing options are provided. In this case, unlike in the two previous analyses, religiosity is not shown to be statistically significant. This autonomous region model shows a substantial difference when compared to the two previous analyses (as discussed below): namely, in the case of the explanatory capacity of the "studies" variable. This variable acquires statistical significance in this model, indicating that the probability of voting for Vox increases as the level of education rises, thus changing the effect from the national arena and showing our first main difference.

The last of the models under analysis is the municipal one. This study found that gender, age, and size of habitat act identically to the European and regional models; for their part, in the case of employment status, it is workers who seem to be more likely to vote for Vox than those who are in another situation not described in the model—unemployed and retired people do not report statistically significant results. Focusing now on social class, we observe that the middle class is more likely to vote for Vox than the upper and lower classes, to the extent that the direction of the values is negative. The remaining variables, all of which are significant, work in the same way as in the previous cases—that is, the probabilities increase as one becomes more religious, more right-wing on the ideological scale, and follows the electoral campaign with greater interest, and decrease as one's assessment of the political situation improves and as one moves toward a dual or solely regional identity and toward more decentralizing positions in terms of the territorial organization of the state.

In view of the different electoral scenarios in Spain in recent years, it is worth recapitulating the variables that profile the Vox voter in each electoral space. Table 6.2 shows the differences in each case, indicating each of the variables and the effect they have.

As can be seen, in the four electoral contexts, the probability of voting for Vox is higher among men and decreases with increasing age. As the variables shown in Table 6.1 are distributed, this gives us a profile of a young male, which is in line with the findings of Barrio (2019) and Turnbull et al. (2020).

Table 6.2 Summarization of voter profile by electoral scenario

Element	European	National	Regional	Local
Sex	Male	Male	Male	Male
Age	Younger	Younger	Younger	Younger
Studies		Lower	Higher	
Habitat	Bigger		Bigger	Bigger
Employment	Unempl./Retired Workers > Others	Workers	Unempl.	Workers
Social class	Middle vs. L/H	Middle vs. L	Middle vs. H	Middle vs. L/H
Political Sit.	Negative	Negative	Negative	Negative
Religiousness	Religious	Religious	-	Religious
Ideology	Right	Right	Right	Right
National ID.	Spanish	Spanish	Spanish	Spanish
Camp. interest	Interested	Not interested	Interested	Interested
Decentr.	Centraliz.		Centraliz.	Centraliz.

Source: Own elaboration.

We also find other elements common to the four arenas, such as ideology (Alonso and Rovira Kaltwasser 2015); assessment of the political situation (Ferreira 2019); subjective national identity; and attitudes toward decentralization (Barrio 2019; Turnbull-Dugarte 2019). One of these variables has a positive influence, and three others have a negative influence. The one with a positive influence is ideology, indicating that, in all cases, as one moves to the right on the ideological axis, the probability of voting for Vox increases. The three negative variables, indicating that when moving along the corresponding scales, the probability of voting for Vox decreases, correspond to the following: subjective national identity—the probabilities are lower as we move toward dual positions (combining Spanish sentiment with regional sentiment in different ways) and only of their region; the political situation—the better the assessment, the lower the probabilities; and, finally, decentralization—as we consider that Spain should be more decentralized, the probabilities decrease.

The influence of level of education does not have statistical significance in two of the four electoral arenas; however, in the case of the national elections, it shows a negative influence, with the probability of voting for Vox being lower among the most educated (Barrio 2019), while in the regional elections, the analysis shows the opposite result, with the most educated opting for this party (Rama and Cordero 2018). Regarding the size of the habitat, in all cases except at the national level, we find that the influence is positive, meaning that residents in larger municipalities are more likely to vote for this party. This might be explained by the fact that Vox is yet to have a strong structure at the local level, given that its emergence has been top-down, starting at the national level and moving down to the regions and municipalities.

Religiosity, on the other hand, shows positive values in all cases except at the regional level, where it is not statistically significant. This, according to the coding of the variable, denotes a greater probability of opting for this formation in the case of the voter self-identifying as Catholic, a finding which is in line with the postulates of Castro and Mo Groba (2020).

In terms of the social class of its voters, the middle class is the most likely to vote for Vox in all arenas. In some cases, such as in the European or local context, the likelihood is higher for the middle class than the other two classes; at the national level, it is only the lower class, while at the regional level, only the upper class. This is a counter-theoretical effect to Rama and Santana's (2020) finding that there is a higher probability of voting for Vox among the upper classes. The effect of employment status also fluctuates unevenly, with differences between the European and regional cases, on the one hand, and the national and local cases, on the other. The former is more likely to vote for Vox among the unemployed, while the latter is among workers.

The only case in which we find divergences between what happens in the different arenas is in voters' interest in following the electoral campaign (Żuk and Żuk 2020). In this sense, following the election campaign with greater interest leads to an increased likelihood of voting for the party under study. This is true in the European, regional, and local arenas, but the opposite at the national level. This might be because, as explained in the context of this chapter, 2019 was an intense electoral period, with two general elections coinciding in a span of seven months in addition to several regional, local, and European elections.

Taken together, the analysis reveals that demographics of the Vox voter to be a young, middle-class man. He is more likely to live in medium-sized or large municipalities. Moreover, he feels Spanish is ideologically right-wing, and is also in favor of a more centralized country. Finally, being a person of religious faith is also part of the profile of this electorate.

Conclusion

The main aim of this chapter was to test whether the different electoral arenas modified the profile of the populist radical right electorate in the case of Spain and, in particular, through Vox voters. In this sense, although the working hypothesis was about the possibility of finding differences linked to second-order choice theories, the results of the GLM models have shown us that there are no such differences—in line with the premonitory nature of the electoral context—and the study levels show variation only in two out of the four arenas.

With minor exceptions, the profile of the Vox voter in the different electoral arenas analyzed is similar. In general terms, the probability of voting for Vox increases among males, young people, those residing in larger municipalities, religious people, those with a low opinion of the political situation, those who are interested in the electoral campaign, those who consider themselves right-wing, with a predominantly Spanish national identity, and those who prefer a centralized territorial organization of the state. This absence of differences—with the exception of the variable referring to the level of education—may in many cases be due to the quasi-simultaneous nature of the elections, with several of them taking place at the same time, which may have resulted in a tendency toward a "nationalization of the vote" that will have to be verified with the analysis of subsequent processes.

However, as we have observed when analyzing the electoral context, the percentages of representation obtained by Vox in the last four years have differed according to the arenas in which the elections have been held. The explanation for this may be due to the party's lack of structure and penetration in the first analyzed elections, rather than the existence of a different voter profile from one election to the next. For example, in the municipal elections of May 2019, in which Vox obtained a very poor percentage of votes due to aspects that may have more to do with the structure of the party itself (very basic and with few candidates) or with the loyalty of the vote in rural areas of the country than with the fact that there are substantial differences between the profile of this voter and that of other types of elections.

A few years ago, everything indicated that Vox was destined to be a protest party, but the data show that it is here to stay. The regional elections in Castilla y León in February 2022—outside the cycle under study here—mark a turning point in the analysis of the party and its voters, as the party is not only seen as an acceptable governmental partner but as part of the government itself, in a similar way to the Austrian FPÖ—the last party of this type to govern a European region.

Bibliography

Alonso, S., and C. Rovira Kaltwasser. 2015. "Spain: No Country for the Populist Right?." *South European Society and Politics* 20 (1): 21–45. https://doi.org/10.1080/13608746.2014.985448.

Anduiza, E. 2018. "El discurso de Vox." *Agenda Pública*. http://agendapublica.elpais.com/el-discurso-de-vox/ (Accessed September 16, 2020).

Antón, J., and A. Hernández-Carr. 2016. "El crecimiento electoral de la derecha radical populista en Europa: parámetros ideológicos y motivaciones sociales." *Política y Sociedad* 53 (1): 17–28.

Barrio, A. 2019. *Vox, la fin de l'exception espagnole*. Paris: Fondation pour L'innovation Politique.

Barrio, A. 2020. "El débil arraigo del populismo en España." *Debats* 1 (134): 233–246.

Bernhard, L., and H. Kriesi. 2019. "Populism in Election Times: A Comparative Analysis of 11 Countries in Western Europe." *West European Politics* 42 (6): 1188–1208.

Boscán, G., I. Llamazares, and N. Wiesehomeier. 2018. "Populist Attitudes, Policy Preferences, and Party Systems in Spain, France, and Italy." *Revista Internacional de Sociología* 76 (4): e110. https://doi.org/10.3989/ris.2018.76.4.18.001.

Castro, P., and D. Mo Groba. 2020. "El issue de la inmigración en los votantes de VOX en las Elecciones Generales de noviembre de 2019." *Revista de Investigaciones Políticas y Sociológicas* 19 (1): 39–58

Climent, V., and M. Montaner. 2021. "Los partidos populistas de extrema derecha en España: Un análisis sociológico comparado." *Izquierdas* 49:910–931.

David, Q., J-B. Pilet, and G. Van Hamme. 2018. "Scale Matters in Contextual Analysis of Extreme Right Voting and Political Attitudes." *Kyklos* 71 (4): 509–536.

De Cleen, L. B., and Y. Stavrakakis. 2017. "Distinctions and Articulations: A Discourse Theoretical Framework for the Study of Populism and Nationalism." *Javnost—The Public, Journal of the European Institute for Communication and Culture* 24 (4): 301–319.

de Lange, S. L., and Mügge, L. M. 2015. "Gender and Right-Wing Populism in the Low Countries: Ideological Variations across Parties and Time." *Patterns of Prejudice* 49 (1–2): 61–80.

Donà, A. 2020. "What's Gender Got to Do with Populism?." *European Journal of Women's Studies* 27 (3): 285–292.

Durrheim, K., M. Okuyan, M. Sinayobye, E. García-Sánchez, A. Pereira, J. S. Portice, T. Gur, O. Wiener-Blotner, and T. F. Keil. 2018. "How Racism Discourse Can Mobilize Right-Wing

Populism: The Construction of Identity and Alliance in Reactions to UKIP's Brexit 'Breaking Point' Campaign." *Journal of Community and Applied Social Psychology* 26 (6): 385–405. https://doi.org/10.1002/casp.2347.
Fernández Riquelme, P. 2020. "Identidad y nostalgia: el discurso de VOX a través de tres eslóganes." *Sabir. International Bulletin of Applied Linguistics*, 1–2:77–114.
Ferreira, C. 2019. "VOX como representante de la derecha radical en España: un estudio sobre su ideología." *Revista Española de Ciencia Política*, 51:73–98.
García Hípola, G., and S. Pérez Castaños. 2021. "Las emociones como estrategia de comunicación en las elecciones europeas de 2019: VOX." *Más Poder Local* 43:20–27.
Gould, R. 2019. "Vox España and Alternative für Deutschland: Propagating the Crisis of National Identity." *Genealogy* 3 (4): 64. https://doi.org/10.3390/genealogy3040064.
Hameleers, M. 2018. "Start Spreading the News: A Comparative Experiment on the Effects of Populist Communication on Political Engagement in Sixteen European Countries." *International Journal of Press/Politics* 23 (4): 517–538. https://doi.org/10.1177%2F1940161218786786.
Immerzeel, T., E. Jaspers, and M. Lubbers. 2013. "Religion as Catalyst or Restraint of Radical Right Voting?." *West European Politics* 36 (5): 946–968. https://doi.org/10.1080/01402382.2013.797235.
Inglehart, R., and P. Norris. 2016. "Trump, Brexit, and the Rise of Populism: Economic Have-Nots and Cultural Backlash." Faculty Research Working Paper Series No. 25, Harvard Kennedy School.
Inglehart, R., and P. Norris. 2019. *Cultural Backlash. Trump, Brexit, and Authoritarian Populism*. New York: Cambridge University Press.
Iglesias-Pascual, R., V. Paloma, and I. Benítez. 2021. "The Role of Contextual Factors in the Electoral Resurgence of Extreme Right-Wing Forces in Spain: The Case of Andalusia." *Political Geography* 86:102356.
Kishishita, D. 2018. "Emergence of Populism under Ambiguity." *International Tax and Public Finance* 25:1559–1562.
Mendes, M., and J. Dennison. 2022. "Explaining the Emergence of the Radical Right in Spain and Portugal: Salience, Stigma and Supply." *West European Politics* 44 (11): 752–775. https://doi.org/10.1080/01402382.2020.1777504.
Michavila, N. 2019. "'De dónde salen sus 400.000 votos': Perfil sociológico del votante de Vox." In *La sorpresa Vox*, edited by J. Müller, 28–41. Barcelona: Deusto.
Mudde, C. 2017. "Populism: An Ideational Approach." In *The Oxford Handbook of Populism*, edited by C. Rovira Kaltwasser, P. Taggart, P. Ochoa, and P. Ostiguy, 27–47. Oxford: Oxford University Press.
Mudde, C., and C. Rovira Kaltwasser. 2018. "Studying Populism in Comparative Perspective: Reflections on the Contemporary and Future Research Agenda." *Comparative Political Studies* 51 (13): 1667–1693. https://doi.org/10.1177%2F0010414018789490.
Prodobnik, B., K. I. Skreblin, M. Koprcina, and H. E. Stanley. 2019. "Emergence of the Unified Right- and Left-Wing Populism—When Radical Societal Changes Become More Important Than Ideology." *Physica A: Statistical Mechanics and Its Applications* 517:459–474.
Rama, J., and G. Cordero. 2018. "Who Are the Losers of the Economic Crisis? Explaining the Vote for Right-Wing Populist Parties in Europe after the Great Recession." *Revista Española de Ciencia Política* 48:13–43.

Rama, J., and A. Santana. 2020. "In the Name of the People: Left Populists versus Right Populists." *European Politics and Society* 21 (1): 17–35.

Ramiro, L., and R. Gómez. 2017. "Radical-Left Populism during the Great Recession: Podemos and Its Competition with the Established Radical Left." *Political Studies* 65 (S1): 108–126.

Reif, K. and H. Schmitt. 1980. "Nine Second-Order National elections—A Conceptual Framework for the Analysis of European Elections Results." *European Journal of Political Research* 8:3–44. https://doi.org/10.1111/j.1475-6765.1980.tb00737.x.

Rydgren, J., and P. Ruth. 2013. "Contextual Explanations of Radical Right-Wing Support in Sweden: Socioeconomic Marginalization, Group Threat, and the Halo Effect." *Ethnic and Racial Studies* 36 (4): 711–728. https://doi.org/10.1080/01419870.2011.623786.

Staerklé, C., and E. Green. 2018. "Right-Wing Populism as a Social Representation: A Comparison across Four European Countries." *Community & Applied Social Psychology* 28:430–445. https://doi.org/10.1080/01419870.2011.623786.

Turnbull-Dugarte, S. 2019. "Explaining the End of Spanish Exceptionalism and Electoral Support for Vox." *Research & Politics* 6 (2): 1–8. https://doi.org/10.1177/2053168019851680.

Turnbull-Dugarte, S., J. Rama, and A. Santana. 2020. "The Baskerville's Dog suddenly Started Barking: Voting for VOX in the 2019 Spanish General Elections." *Political Research Exchange* 2 (1). https://doi.org/10.1080/2474736X.2020.1781543.

Wooldridge, J. M. 2011. *Introducción a la Econometría. Un enfoque Moderno*. México D.F.: Cengage Learning.

Zembylas, M. 2021. *Affect and the Rise of Right-Wing Populism: Pedagogies for the Renewal of Democratic Education*. New York: Cambridge University Press.

Żuk, P., and P. Żuk. 2020. "'Euro-Gomorrah and Homopropaganda': The Culture of Fear and 'Rainbow Scare' in the Narrative of Right-Wing Populists Media in Poland as Part of the Election Campaign to the European Parliament in 2019." *Discourse, Context & Media* 33:1–11. https://doi.org/10.1016/j.dcm.2019.100364.

CHAPTER 7

Ideological Congruence between Populist Right Parliamentary Elites and Their Voters: An Analysis of Poland, Sweden, and Germany

Carlos García-Rivero and Hennie Kotzè

INTRODUCTION

Ideological congruence is central to theories of representation and is linked to citizens' satisfaction with the political system (Ezrow and Xezonakis 2011). Moreover, political congruence is one of the most relevant strategies to assess the performance of political parties (Arnold and Franklin 2012; Belchior 2013).

Basically, ideological congruence examines the degree to which the preferences of the representatives echo those of citizens, on the assumption that political parties and citizens have bonds that are reflected in the degree of coincidence on political, social, cultural, or economic issues (Schmitt and Thomassen 1999; Powell 2004). In fact, congruence with their voters is a prerequisite for the success of political parties (Rabinowitz and MacDonald 1989).

Similarities in public policy goals between voters and their representatives are fundamental to the so-called selection model of representation (Mansbridge 2009) or the "responsible party model" (RPM) (Kitschelt and Wilkinson 2007). A basic assumption behind these models of representation is that citizens vote for parties promoting and defending policy options close to their own ideological preferences. In essence, for these models, democratic representation is a process in which parties offer policy alternatives to the electorate, and the electorate compares them with their own preferences. Finally, the citizenry will vote for the party whose policy offer is closest to their own preferences (Klingemann et al. 2017). This process is the essence of party-voter congruence.

According to Kitschelt and Rehm (2011, 23), when "established parties fail to represent preference configurations for which there is a demand in the electorate, sooner or later new political entrepreneurs may spot the market niche and successfully enter the political fray." This supply-and-demand dynamic explains the entry of both new parties into Parliaments, such as the green parties in many European Parliaments in the 1980s, and more recently those of the populist radical right parties (PRRPs) in the latest elections.

Tellingly, although ideological congruence is a central component of representation and has been studied amply in general, much less is known about congruence between populist right parties and their voters specifically. In fact, an indicator of the possible consolidation in the current party systems in Europe lies in the level of political congruence between party leaders and voters—in other words, the match between the demand side (the electorate) and the supply side (party leaders).

Although these parties consolidated in the electoral realm in the period between 2019 and the present, they flourished during the 2008–2012 economic crisis, even though they had already enjoyed some parliamentary representation before the crisis (Mudde 2004). A basic strategy to attract voters to the PRRPs is the claim that established political party representatives are no longer responsive to the voters' demands, whereas these parties offer to close the gap between the people and the political establishment, providing voters with public policy alternatives (Mudde and Kaltwasser 2012). Hence a comparative analysis of the electoral basis of such parties before and after the cited crisis seems crucial to properly understand the current situation and probabilities of further consolidation.

Against this background, this chapter analyzes the ideological congruence between voters and radical right parliamentarians before and after the 2008–2012 economic crisis in three European countries (Poland, Sweden, and Germany). These three countries faced the economic crisis in different ways; they have distinct cultural, social, and economic backgrounds; and all of them have radical right parties in their Parliaments.

Ideological congruence between party representatives and voters

Ideological congruence refers to the notion of ideology, but what is ideology? Many attempts have been made to define this concept since the term was coined in 1796 (de Tracy 1801). Basically, ideology is "an organization of opinions, attitudes and values—a way of thinking about man and society. We may speak of an individual's ideology with respect to different areas of social life; politics, economics, religion, minority groups, and so forth" (Adorno et al. 1950, 2). Ideologies are "patterned clusters of normatively imbued ideas and concepts, including particular representations of power relations. They are conceptual maps that help people navigate the complexity of their social universe and carry claims to social truth" (James 2015, 92–93). In short, ideologies "share four basic characteristics: i) they provide a systemic representation; ii) they guide a person's evaluations; iii) they provide a plan for action; and iv) they should be logically consistent" (García-Rivero and Kotzè 2019, 3).

Among the many proposed methods to organize and classify political ideologies is the left-right spectrum, which is the principal method of classifying political positions, values, attitudes, and political parties. The left usually highlights ideas such as equality, freedom, liberties, progress, or reform, and the right accentuates reaction, tradition, authority, hierarchy, and nationalism. Hence, the left-right self-placement is a "summary" of someone's ideology (Inglehart and Klingemann 1976). Although it relies very simplistically on a single-dimensional measure, the left-right spectrum still exposes an individual's position on the most relevant social, political, cultural, and economic issues and emerges as a heuristic device assisting the citizenry to simplify the complexity of ideologies into a one-dimensional space. The self-placement on the spectrum indicates an orientation to evaluate political options and parties, and hence to make political choices. The ideological orientation of a person is transferred onto a left-right scale facilitating his/her social and political orientation and communications *as long as* both citizens and representatives share the same understanding of its meaning.

The left-right self-placement responds to three main issues: economic issues, moral issues, and partisanship issues. First, (1) economic issues assume that the left-right scale reflects the attitude of the person regarding the relation between the economy and the state, social inequality, and the like; (2) moral issues refer to the identities upon which individuals base their sense of morality; and (3), as far as partisanship issues are concerned, they indicate that self-positioning on the scale is also the result of an identification with, or choosing to vote for, a certain political party, and consequently that the outcome of elections is based on the perceived values of the parties (Freire and Belchior 2011).

The component related to the economy is the most obvious: left-leaning voters strive more for egalitarian societies and the redistribution of goods and services (Gunther and Kuan 2007). The second component, morality, assumes that citizens' position on the scale reflects that they accept or reject certain behaviors in specific areas involving moral issues (i.e., abortion or homosexuality) (Hellwig 2008). Finally, the third component is related to voting for a political party. It refers to self-placing on the left-right scale in similar positions to that of the party leaders.

Overall, the higher the party-voter ideological congruence, the closer the (economic and moral) values of the voter and of the party representative will be. From this, it follows that "the study of the levels of left-right congruence between electors and representatives is crucial to understand the quality of political representation. The greater the level of left-right congruence between voters and representatives, the greater the probability [that] voters' issue preferences are well represented in parliament" (Freire and Belchior 2015, 3). Hence, an authoritative analysis of left-right self-placement cannot be completed until the comparison of citizens and party representatives has been incorporated into the analysis.

However, although there has been abundant analysis of left-right self-placement, the level of congruence between voters and party representatives has been left comparatively unattended in most analyses.[1] In this regard, unfortunately, some researchers have encountered important differences between members of the Parliament and voters. In fact, "for much of the academic, political and communications elite, left-right represents ideological content as well as political cues. For the public [the left-right scale] defines the structure of party space within which the voting choice

---

[1] Let alone the radical right party voter-representative congruence.

is made" (Arian and Shamir 1983, 157). Nie and Andersen (1974, 542) also delved into the issue of elite-mass differences and affirmed that it is possible to "find consistency and inter-correlation among elites' responses on several issues ... [However,] there is little or no interdependence ... in mass attitudes." This is, they continue, because the public lacks the "educational background, the contextual knowledge and the capacity to deal with abstract concepts" (542).

Barnes (1971) concluded that the values of the citizens were very similar to the opinions of the elites in his study on Italy. In fact, "the elite hold in an exaggerated form the opinions of the mass" (Barnes 1971, 171). On the other hand, Belchior (2010, 139) concluded that the idea that MPs represent the electorate's ideologies is far from reality, at least in Europe. Actually, "the institution of competitive elections has not proved itself to be a sufficiently efficient instrument to maintain the governing elites' responsiveness to the public, especially outside election periods." Freire and Belchior (2015, 29) and Sánchez-Ferrer (2018) found few similarities in their study on Portugal and Spain respectively, with similar results reached by Meyer and Wagner (2018). More recently, García Rivero and Kotzé (2019) also found that voter-representative ideological congruence is far from reality. To summarize, supply and demand do not match. However, these studies have focused on all parties in general and not on specific ones. This means that the analysis of populist party-voter congruence is scantier.

However, PRRPs rise as a challenge to conventional parties by stating that the traditional political representatives are not responsive to the values and preferences of ordinary citizens (Taggart 2000; Mudde 2004). Populists offer the renaissance of the popular will by claiming to reduce the distance between the representatives and the citizenry, formulating positions on issues ignored by conventional political parties (Mudde and Kaltwasser 2012). Hence, ideological congruence between populist representatives and their supporters is expected to be higher than average. Stated differently, the claim is that populists tend to correct the congruence gap between voters and parties. If populist parties managed to fill this gap, they are expected to consolidate over time. If not, their presence in the electoral realm might be more ephemeral. This chapter aims to analyze whether this is the case, albeit over a relatively short time span, in three European countries: Poland, Sweden, and Germany.

Method and Data

This section explains the method used, issues selected, data employed, and statistical techniques applied. Although there is a wide variety of methods, data, and issues available, we believe that the ones used below fairly convey the core values of the populist right parties and the voter-representative ideological congruence. The most common technique proposed is assessing the similarity between citizens' attitudes and representatives' positions relying on statistical techniques that measure the level of proximity between these two dimensions (Golder and Stramski 2010; Lupu et al. 2017; García-Rivero and Kotze 2019, among many others) following two main clusters of issues: economic and cultural.

To assess PRRP-voter ideological congruence, data on party positions and voter preferences on relevant policy issues are required. To estimate the positions of party elites, especially parliamentary representatives, one of the most straightforward approaches is to use survey data for party representatives as a proxy for party positions. However, sometimes researchers are constrained by a lack of data for many populist right party representatives (Backlung and Jungar 2019). A second commonly used method to ascertain party positions is through Manifesto Data Collection (Volkens et al. 2013), which is based on the analysis of electoral manifestos of political parties. However, there is no unanimity about how correctly these data reflect party positions on economic, moral, or political issues (Benoit and Laver 2006; Ruedin and Morales 2012). A third approach is to have voters estimate the positions of parties on a left-right scale (Van der Eijk and Franklin 1991; Blais and Bodet 2006). However, not all surveys include such a question and hence still reflect the perception of voters and not the actual views of party representatives. Finally, there is also a method that relies on party data from expert surveys (Benoit and Laver 2006). However, this is not necessarily the vision of the party as such, but of the experts and, thus, does not necessarily represent the values of party leaders.

In this study, we follow the first approach using survey data based on two datasets[2] per country: one for political elites (parliamentarians) and one for

---

2   The data used are the World Values Surveys and the Political Elite (parliamentarians) surveys conducted in 2006 and 2013. The World Values Survey can be accessed at http://www.worldvaluessurvey.org/wvs.jsp and technical information on the 2006 political elite survey can be consulted in Van Beek (2010, 309–310). The 2013 elite survey followed the same methodology. See also Table 7A.1.

the public. In the datasets, ideological self-identification was measured by the standard left-right self-placement. The wording was the same in all five surveys (see Table 7A.1). We then used regression analyses including variables measuring economic, moral, and partisanship factors to explore the patterns. We first present descriptive data (Tables 7.1 and 7.2), and then we run a regression (Tables 7.3, 7.4, and 7.5) including independent variables in three models: the first incorporating the traditional economic factors, the second introducing moral issues, and the third introducing party-related factors. Finally, we compare the results of left-right self-placement to voter patterns using a logistic binary regression (Table 7.6).

Issues

Briefly, empirical research has shown that populist party voters primarily cast their ballots for the radical right to be represented in terms of a combination of neoliberal (Kitschelt 1997, 2012) and socioculturally authoritarian policies (extension of rights and liberties on issues such as abortion and sexual freedom as well as tolerance toward immigrants and Muslims), rejection of the European Union and support for alternatives (nondemocratic) forms of government (De Lange 2007; Bakker et al. 2015; Rovny 2013; Zhirkov 2014; Backlung and Jungar 2019).

It is important to note that the extent to which these populist parties will manage to remain electorally successful, following their initial breakthrough, will depend heavily on factors such as organization and leadership (van Kessel 2013) and, of course, on ideological congruence—essentially a match between offer and demand (Backlung and Jungar 2019).

Taking into account the above description, the explanatory variables are divided into three different blocks: economic, cultural, and sociopolitical. Both elite and public surveys had identical items with the same possible values as responses. Independent variables have been selected in terms of their analytic validity, availability, and comparability. The exact items are indicated below (see Table 7A.1 in Appendix for more details).

(1) **Economic block**, which includes support for *inequality within society* measured with the variable "Incomes should be made more equal vs. we need larger income differences as incentives for individual effort"; the level of sup-

port for *individual responsibility*, measured with the variable "Private vs. government responsibility for provision of basics and goods"; the support for *private ownership* with the variable "Private ownership of business and industry should be increased vs. government ownership of business and industry should be increased."

(2) **Cultural block**, which includes moral values: First, level of *intolerance*, which is an index comprising the following variables: rejection of *immigrants* as neighbors, rejection of *people of different race* as neighbors, and the rejection of people of *different religions* as neighbors. Second, the block also includes the extension of *liberties*, which is an index composed of acceptance of *homosexuality*, *abortion*, and the *practice of prostitution* (Poteat and Mereish 2012; Jungar and Edenborg 2018)

(3) **Sociopolitical block**, which incorporates *support for democracy* and *support for military rule as a form of government* and *confidence in the European Union* (Marks et al. 2007; Hooghe et al. 2002).

CASES AND PARTIES

Data were gathered in Poland, Sweden, and Germany. These three countries were chosen as they each dealt with the economic crisis in a different way;[3] are different politically, culturally, and economically; and yet have PRRPs in their Parliaments. Hence, their selection allows us to test whether there are common characteristics in ideological congruence despite the countries being very different.

Respondents are divided by *partisanship*, which is based on the party that the citizens would vote for if there were to be an election the day after the survey was conducted in the citizens' survey; for the elites, this was the party of the parliamentarian. The exact wording is, for the public: "If there were a national election tomorrow, for which party on this list would you vote"; and for elites, the party endorsement at the Parliament of the party representative, when the survey was conducted in each Parliament. The parties have been recoded into populist left, moderate left, moderate right, and populist right (own categorization based on Keating and McCrone 2013; March 2011; Millard 2009; Szczerbiak 2018; Agius 2007; Steltemeier 2009; Nedelcu 2015; Franzmann and Kaiser 2006; Lindbom 2008; Conrad 2020; Pytlas 2020; Castle and Taras 2019; and Hellström et al. 2012).

---

3 See Table 7A.1 in the Appendix for detailed information and sources.

The parties represented were as follows:

- *Populist left* including Die Linke;
- *Moderate left* including Social Democratic Party of Germany, Grünen, Left and Democrats coalition LiD, Sojusz Lewicy Demokratycznej, Socjaldemokracja Polska, Ruch Poparcia Palikota, Miljöpartiet, Swedish Arbetareparti;
- *Moderate right* including Free Democratic Party, Christian Democratic Union of Germany, Christian Social Union, Polish Peasants Party, Free Voters (Bavaria), Polish Solidarity, Swedish Centerpartiet, Folkpartiet liberalerna; Kristdemokraterna, Swedish Moderaterna;
- *Populist right* including Alternative für Deutschland, Prawo i Sprawiedliwość (PiS), Samoobrona Rzeczpospolitej (SRP), Liga Polskish Rodzin, and Sverigedemokraterna.

There is, finally, an item that controls *for time* (first wave, 2007 and second wave, 2013), just before the economic crisis and when the worst of the economic crisis had passed. This item was used to incorporate the impact of the economic crisis into the analysis. Let us be clear: using different items in surveys specifically designed for measuring left-right self-placement may possibly measure this ideological construct in a more accurate way. Nevertheless, the proposed approach with the available selected items is in any case very important in the left-right scale, especially in the analysis of populist right parties, and it allows us to compare different countries with each other, at the mass and elite levels both before and after the financial crisis.

To summarize, the main aim is to analyze: (1) the basis of left-right self-placement as an indicator of major cultural, economic, and political issues; (2) whether there is any discernible difference between elites and the public (i.e., ideological congruence); (4) whether the financial crisis has had an impact on the factors that propel left-right self-placement (analysis before the crisis in 2007 and after the most severe impact of the crisis in 2013); and (4) whether the core values of liberties and intolerance explain ideological self-placement *both* at the general public *and* elite (parliamentarians) levels in the radical right part of the left-right spectrum.

As Kitschelt and Rehm (2011, 23), argue, when established parties do not represent the electoral demands of voters, sooner or later new political parties will appear in the market to replace them. This is the basic functioning of the supply and demand system that explains the success and demise of new parties in the past. In a similar vein, if there is no ideological congruence, then this explains the probable fading away of the same populist parties in the future.

Hypotheses

If the core representation feature of populism is responsiveness (Pitkin 1967), then a high level of ideological congruence can be expected among voters and their representatives in the radical right parties. In fact, one of the identity markers of populist parties is congruence with its supporters, situated on the radical right end of the political spectrum (Lefkofridi and Casado-Asensio 2013). Based on this argument, we posit the following hypotheses:

> *H1: There will be a higher level of congruence on the radical right spectrum between voters and representatives than on the moderate side.*

When there are multiple uncorrelated dimensions of political conflict, there is a risk that voters cannot cast their ballot for a party that represents them on all issues (Thomassen 2012). In this case, voters are likely to prefer the party that represents them on the policy issue(s) they find most important or salient (Giger and Lefkofridi 2014).

Moreover, capitalizing on a favorable opportunity momentum (economic crisis), PRRPs have attempted to establish cultural values as the party's flagship dimension and, hence, we expect a high level of congruence on the issues of liberties and tolerance. So, we then posit:

> *H2: There will be a higher degree of congruence on the radical right of the spectrum in the core values system (liberties and tolerance) than in any other segment of the left-right spectrum.*

This implies that voters vote for the populist radical right primarily to be represented on such unique policy positions, while other policies are of secondary concern. Then, not only is there congruence, but the vote itself is also based on the core value system, consequently:

H3: A radical policy stance on "core values" mainly propel voters to vote for radical right parties.

Data and technique

This study approaches the issue of public-elite differences on the basis of two datasets per country: one for political elites (parliamentarians) and one for the public. In the datasets, ideological self-identification was measured by the standard left-right self-placement (see Table 7A.1). The wording was the same in all five surveys. We then used regression analyses including variables measuring economic, moral, and sociopolitical issues with a division of partisanship ex ante to explore the patterns. In the regressions, we include the variables block-wise in four models: the first model incorporates the traditional economic factors, the second model introduces moral issues, the third presents country differences, and a fourth model controls for time.

Analysis

Tables 7.1 and 7.2 present a descriptive vision of the differences comparing elites and the general public both before and after the economic crisis in all explanatory variables. Table 7.1 shows figures of the basic indicators of populism: liberty, intolerance, confidence in the European Union, support for military rule, support for democracy, and left-right self-placement. There is also a comparison between voters and party leaders before and after the economic crisis of 2008–2012. Mainly, the populist right (both voters and elites) rank lower on liberties and rights extension both before and after the economic crisis, and they rank higher on intolerance (index of rejection of homosexuality, prostitution, and abortion). The economic crisis also seems to have left an imprint on the level of confidence in the European Union. The populist right as well as the populist left show the lowest level of confidence in the European Union. After the economic crisis, this level declines even further on the side of the populist right both at the elite and citizen levels. The level of support for democracy is also lower on the side of the populist right at both the elite and voter levels.

Interestingly, voters of radical right parties tend to endorse military rule more than their representatives do. On the whole, the economic crisis has left an imprint on the level of confidence in the European Union among populist right voters and representatives. The level of confidence falls after the economic crisis in both sectors. Finally, populist right voters and representatives show higher levels of support for military rule both before and after the economic crisis.

Overall, there seems to be a fairly high level of congruence between party representatives and voters but is this congruence similar among all groups?

Populists are expected to maintain a higher level of connection to society. Consequently, differences between the party leader and voters should be lower in the populist right parties than in others. This is presented in Table 7.2, which shows the gap between voters and representatives with the same indicators as presented in Table 7.1. Interestingly, the issue of granting rights and liberties (both before and after the economic crisis) is where the difference between leaders and voters is overall lowest among voters and representatives of the populist right, showing that there is a high level of consistency between "offer" and "demand" in terms of limitation of rights and in the level of intolerance on the radical right end of the spectrum. The measure of confidence in the European Union is also among the lowest among the populist right parties.

We now turn to an analysis of the basis of left-right self-placement. Tables 7.3, 7.4, and 7.5 present the results. The dependent variable is regressed on the battery of economic, cultural, and political items used in the descriptive part of the analysis above. Data are introduced block-wise to compare the blocks and to ascertain which block is more relevant when explaining left-right self-placement (percentage of explained variance of each block).

The first model includes economic issues; the second one incorporates liberties and intolerance issues and support for military rule; the third one incorporates differences between countries; and, finally, the fourth block includes the before-and-after crisis effect. Table 7.3 presents the results for all voters and representatives; Table 7.4 shows the analysis exclusively for voters and representatives of the radical right and the radical left, whereas Table 7.5 does it for moderates (left and right ones).

Overall (Table 7.3) figures indicate that, in general, both for the parliamentary elite and voters, the left-right spectrum is based on economic issues *and* on the extension of rights and values. The percentage of explained variance of model 1 is similar to the contribution of model 2. When the left-right self-placement is analyzed separately for moderates (left and right represen-

Table 7.1 Positions of party representatives and voters before and after the economic crisis

	Liberty	Intolerance	Confidence in EU	Democracy support	Left-right scale	Military rule support
Before crisis						
Populist left elite	26.00	0.00	2.00	4.00	2.36	1.00
Populist left citizen	16.85	0.16	2.00	3.50	3.38	1.23
Moderate left elite	21.23	0.06	2.68	3.90	3.76	1.01
Moderate left citizen	16.82	0.22	2.26	3.55	4.04	1.28
Moderate right elite	18.68	0.08	2.79	3.96	6.52	1.08
Moderate right citizen	15.04	0.18	2.35	3.52	5.78	1.43
Populist right elite	8.27	0.39	2.48	3.28	7.08	1.31
Populist right citizen	6.78	0.44	2.35	3.03	6.66	1.97
After crisis						
Populist left elite	24.31	0.06	2.19	4.00	1.88	1.00
Populist left citizen	14.41	0.50	2.07	3.45	3.60	1.24
Moderate left elite	20.69	0.03	2.72	3.87	3.49	1.04
Moderate left citizen	14.49	0.37	2.32	3.44	4.41	1.51
Moderate right elite	19.26	0.07	2.74	3.90	6.39	1.05
Moderate right citizen	14.58	0.28	2.46	3.52	5.54	1.48

(*Continued*)

Ideological Congruence

Populist right elite	7.14	0.22	1.94	3.50	8.45	1.11
Populist right citizen	8.49	0.33	2.10	3.01	7.05	2.07

Note: Entries represent the means of each variable.

Table 7.2 Congruence differences of party leaders and party voters before and after the economic crisis

	Liberty	Intolerance	Confidence in EU	Democracy support	Left-right scale	Military rule support
Before crisis						
Populist left	9.15	-.16	.00	.50	-1.02	-0.23
Moderate left	4.41	-.15	.42	.35	-.28	-0.27
Moderate right	3.64	-.11	.43	.44	.74	-0.35
Populist right	1.49	-.05	.13	.25	.42	-0.66
After crisis						
Populist left	9.90	-.43	.12	.55	-1.72	-0.24
Moderate left	6.20	-.33	.41	.43	-.92	-0.47
Moderate right	4.68	-.21	.28	.38	.85	-0.43
Populist right	-1.35	-.1	-.16	.49	1.40	-0.95

Note: Entries represent the distance between voters' and representatives' responses.

tatives and voters) and radicals (populist left and right), however, the results are different. Tables 7.4 and 7.5 present the results. Moderates' left-right self-placement (Table 7.4), that is both voters and representatives, is better explained by economic issues whereas, on the other hand, extremists' self-placement (Table 7.5), both voters and representatives, is far better explained

Table 7.3 Ideological congruence

	Elite								Voter						
	Model 1		Model 2		Model 3		Model 4		Model 1		Model 2		Model 3		Model 4
	B	S.E.	B	S.E.	B	S.E.	B	S.E.	B	S.E.	B	S.E.	B	S.E.	B	S.E.
Constant	6.2*	1.4	13.1*	5.7	10.1	5.5	8.6	5.5	5.2***	1.3	5.9***	1.7	5.2***	1.8	5.4	2.1
Economic issues																
Equality vs. differences in income	.27*	.15	.04	.1	-.04	.1	-.04	.1	.21***	.1	.18***	.1	.2***	.1	.2***	.1
Private vs. gov. ownership companies	-.26*	.15	-.04	.1	-.01	.1	-.02	.1	-.17***	.1	-.2***	.1	-.2***	.1	-.18***	.1
Private vs. gov. responsibility for provision	.15	.17	.03	.1	.01	.1	.02	.1	-.1***	.1	-.12***	.1	-.12***	.1	-.12***	.03
Rights and values																
Intolerance			.03	.3	.03	.2	.03	.3			.04*	.04	.02	.03	.02	.1
Liberty			-.85***	.02	-.63***	.03	-.55***	.1			-.13***	.01	-.12***	.1	-.12***	.03
Military rule support			-.03	1.4	-.01	1.3	-.01	1.3			.05**	.05	.07***	.1	.1***	.1
Country differences																
Germany					-.28		-.27*	.7					.1***	.1	.1***	
Poland					.06		.13	.7					.01	.1	.01	
Time																
After crisis							.09	.3							.01	
R^2	.39		.573		.61		.613		.109		.135		.142		.142	
R^2 Adj	.39		.566		.603		.605		.108		.134		.14		.14	

Note: B is the standardized regression coefficient. S.E. is the standard error *significant at the .05 level; ** significant at the .005 level and

Table 7.4 Ideological congruence (only extremists)

	Elite								Voter							
	Model 1		Model 2		Model 3		Model 4		Model 1		Model 2		Model 3		Model 4	
	B	S.E.	B.	S.E.	B.	S.E.	B.	S.E.	B	S.E.	B	S.E.	B	S.E.	B	S.E.
Constant	6.2***	1.5	13.1*	5.7	10.7	5.5	8.6	5.6	4.2***	.35	5.5***	.42	.3***	.51	6.3***	.6
Economic issues																
Equality vs. differences in income	.27*	.15	.04	.1	-.04	.1	-.04	.09	.3***	.03	.18***	.03	.04	.03	.05	.02
Private vs. gov. ownership companies	-.26*	.15	-.04	.1	-.01	.1	-.03	.08	.03	.03	-.03	.03	-.07	.03	-.06*	.02
Private vs. gov. responsibility for provision	.15	.17	.03	.1	.01	.1	.02	.08	.02	.03	-.02	.03	.02	.02	.02	.02
Rights and values																
Intolerance			.03	.3	.03	.2	.04	.27			.08**	.1	.08***	.1	.08**	.1
Liberty			-.85***	.02	-.63***	.03	-.55***	.04			-.29***	.01	-.13***	.01	-.13***	.01
Military rule support			-.03	1.4	-.01	1.3	-.01	1.3			.13***	.1	.01*	.1	-.01	.01
Country differences																
Germany					-.28*	.79	-.27*	.78					-.48***	.33	-.44***	.37
Poland					.06	.67	.13	.72					0	.373	.04	.3
Time																
After crisis							.1	.35							.07*	.1
R^2	.294		.823		.842		.849		.075		.188		.319		.323	
R^2 Adj	.266		.809		.825		.829		.072		.182		.312		.315	

Note: B is the standardized regression coefficient. S.E. is the standard error * significant at the .05 level; ** significant at the .005 level and *** significant at the .001 level. Dependent variable: L-R self-placement.

161

Table 7.5 Ideological congruence (only moderates)

	Elite								Voter						
	Model 1		Model 2		Model 3		Model 4		Model 1		Model 2		Model 3		Model 4
	B	S.E.	B	S.E.	B	S.E.	B	S.E.	B	S.E.	B	S.E.	B	S.E.	B	S.E.
Constant	3.3***	.31	9.2***	4.1	9.4***	1.2	9.2***	1.2	5.3***	1.3	5.9***	1.7	5.5***	.18	5.5***	.21
Economic issues																
Equality vs. differences in income	.34***	.03	.32***	.03	.28***	.03	.3***	.03	.21***	.04	.2***	.01	.2***	.01	.2***	.01
Private vs. gov. ownership companies	-.26***	.03	-.27***	.03	-.26***	.03	-.27***	.03	-.2***	.05	-.2***	.1	-.18***	.01	-.18***	.01
Private vs. gov. responsibility for provision	.3***	.04	.28***	.03	.31***	.03	.31***	.03	-.1***	.03	-.12***	.1	-.12***	.01	-.12***	.01
Rights and values																
Intolerance			.01	.2	.02	.2	.02	.2			.04*	.05	.02	.05	.02	.05
Liberty			-.17***	.01	-.19***	2.1	-.19***	.01			-.13***	.04	-.12***	.05	-.12***	.01
Military rule support			-.15***	.2	.11***	.14	.11***	.2			.1*	.04	.07***	.07	.1***	.03
Country differences																
Germany					-.13***	.14	-.13***	.14					.1***	.1	.1***	.1
Poland					-.1*	.16	-.08*	.16					.01	.1	.01	.1
Time																
After crisis							.06*	.12							.01	
R^2	.549		.593		.605		.608		.109		.135		.142		.142	
R^2 Adj	.546		.587		.598		.601		.108		.134		.14		.14	

Note: B is the standardized regression coefficient. S.E. is the standard error * significant at the .05 level; ** significant at the .005 level and *** by values (political rights and tolerance) than by economic issues. This is the case for both voters and parliamentarians.

Finally, Table 7.6 shows figures for "vote" for populist right parties (general public survey). The most relevant issues are values (intolerance and liberty), confidence in the EU, and support for military rule as evidenced by the percentages of explained variance. Percentage explained variance of model 2 is twice that of model 1 (economic issues). Results also indicate that there are no large differences among countries as explained variance does not increase considerably when countries are included in model 3.

Table 7.6 Vote for populist parties

	Model 1		Model 2		Model 3		Model 4	
	Exp(B)	S.E.	Exp(B)	S.E.	Exp(B)	S.E.	Exp(B)	S.E.
Constant	.01***	.2	.15***	.29	.28***	.36	.7	.39
Economic issues								
Equality vs. differences in income as incentives	1.2***	.02	1.1***	.02	.99	.02	.98	.02
Private vs. government ownership of business	1.2***	.02	1.1***	.02	1.0	.02	1.0	.02
Private vs. government responsibility for provision	1.1***	.02	1.0	.02	.99	.02	.99	.02
Extension of rights and values								
Liberty			.87***	.01	.92***	.01	.93***	.01
Intolerance			1.0*	.06	1.4***	.08	1.3***	.08
Military rule support			1.7***	.06	1.3***	.07	1.3***	.07
Confidence in the EU			.7***	.07	.6***	.07	.6***	.08

(Continued)

	Model 1	Model 2	Model 3	Model 4
Country differences[a]				
Germany			.24*** .3	.3*** .28
Poland			10.5*** .2	11.5*** .19
Time				
After crisis				.508*** .11
Nagelkerke-R²	.11	.31	.47	.48
% Correct 1-value (overall) prediction	3.7 (85.6)	21 (86.4)	39.4 (87.5)	45.8 (89)

Note: Dependent variable: Vote for Populist right party.

[a] Category reference: Sweden. Exp(B): exponential value of logistic coefficient; S.E.: standard error * significant at the 0.05 level; ** significant at the 0.005 level and *** significant at the 0.001 level.

Conclusion

Ideological congruence is central to political representation and is linked to the level of citizens' satisfaction with the polity. It is also one of the basic strategies to analyze party performance. Mostly, ideological congruence represents the degree to which the preferences of party leaders are similar to those of the citizens they represent. Bonds between political parties and voters will be manifested in the degree of overlap on relevant issues between party leaders and voters.

There have been many studies on the rise of populist parties, but few of them have focused on the ideological congruence of voters and their representatives, and, of the few we know of, none analyzes the party voter-party leader congruence in terms of the public opinion of both the voters and party representatives. Moreover, although some growth in the support for populist parties was noticeable early in the twentieth century around Europe, their breakthrough was mainly after the 2008–2012 economic crisis.

In this chapter, we analyzed the populist party voter-representative congruence in three selected countries in Europe before and after the economic crisis and our findings are as below:

- There is evidence of strong ideological congruence between populist right party voters and their party representatives;
- In the *core value system* (liberties and intolerance), the level of congruence of parliamentarians and voters of populist right parties is even more evident and much more pronounced compared to other parties;
- Significantly, this core value system is also the main factor propelling the populist right vote.

Overall, it seems that populist parties have shown growth in Europe and, presumably, will take the lead in right-wing politics, at least in the three European countries that were included in this study. To generalize, most probably, their more recent electoral successes all over Europe will not be ephemeral.

APPENDIX

Table 7A.1 Information on survey sample, variables, and countries

Countries	Party representatives survey sample (*N*)	Party voters survey sample (*N*)	GDP loss during economic crisis (2007–2014) (%)[a]	Unemployment increase during economic crisis (2007–2014) (%)[b]	Populist right parties in Parliament (%)[c] 2007	2015	2022
Germany	192	2,450	-3.6	-3.7	0	0	14
Poland	145	735	-6.3	1.9	36	60	53
Sweden	202	1,140	-11.8	1.7	0	0	18

Variables	Label				Values		
Self-placement Left-right	Left-right scale: views of respondent				1–10		
Inequality index including							
Inequality	Incomes should be made more equal vs. we need larger income differences as incentives for individual effort				1–10		
Individual Responsibility	Private vs. government responsibility for provision of basics and goods				1–10		
Private vs. public ownership	Private ownership of business and industry should be increased vs. government ownership of business and industry should be increased				1–10		
Tolerance: Index including Rejection of:							
Immigrants	Having as neighbors: Immigrants				0–1		

166

People of different race	Having as neighbors: People of a different race	0–1
People of different religion	Having as neighbors: People of a different religion	0–1
Liberties: Index including Acceptance of:		
Homosexuality	Justification of homosexuality	1–10
Abortion	Justification of abortion	1–10
Prostitution	Justification of prostitution	1–10
Confidence in the EU	Confidence in organizations: European Union	1–4
Support for democracy	Political system: Having a democratic political system	1–4
Support for military rule	Political system: Having the army rule	1–4

Note: [a] See Kotzé and García-Rivero (2017, Table 1).
[b] World Bank Data.
[c] Interparliamentary Union.

Bibliography

Adorno T., E. Frenkel-Brunswik, D. J. Levinson, and S. R. Nevitt. 1950. *The Authoritarian Personality*. New York: Harper.

Agius, C. 2007. "Sweden's 2006 Parliamentary Election and After: Contesting or Consolidating the Swedish Model?." *Parliamentary Affairs* 60 (4): 585–600. https://doi.org/10.1093/pa/gsm041.

Arian, A., and M. Shamir. 1983. "The Primarily Political Function of the Left-Right Continuum." *Comparative Politics* 15 (1): 139–158. https://doi.org/10.2307/421673.

Arnold, C., and M. N. Franklin. 2012. "Introduction: Issue Congruence and Political Responsiveness." *West European Politics* 35 (6): 1217–1225. https://doi.org/10.1080/01402382.2012.713741.

Backlung, A., and A. C. Jungar. 2019. "Populist Radical Right Party-Voter Policy Representation in Western Europe." *Representation* 55 (4): 393–413. https://doi.org/10.1080/00344893.2019.1674911.

Bakker, R., C. de Vries, E. Edwards, L. Hooghe, S. Jolly, G. Marks, J. Polk, J. Rovny, M. Steenbergen, and M. A. Vachudova. 2015. "Measuring party positions in Europe: The Chapel Hill Expert Survey Trend File, 1999–2010." *Party Politics* 21 (1): 143–152. https://doi.org/10.1177/1354068812462931.

Barnes, S. H. 1971. "Left, Right and the Italian Voter." *Comparative Politics* 2 (2): 157–175.

Belchior A. M. 2010. "Ideological Congruence among European Political Parties." *Journal of Legislative Studies* 16 (1): 124–142. https://doi.org/10.1080/13572330903542191.

Belchior A. M. 2013. "Explaining left-Right Party Congruence across European Party Systems: A Test of Micro-, Meso-, and Macro-Level Models." *Comparative Political Studies* 46 (3): 352–386. https://doi.org/10.1177/0010414012453695.

Benoit, K., and M. Laver. 2006. *Party Policy in Modern Democracies*. London: Routledge.

Blais, A., and M. A. Bodet. 2006. "Does Proportional Representation Foster Closer Congruence between Citizens and Policy Makers?." *Comparative Political Studies* 39 (10): 1243–1262. https://doi.org/10.1177/0010414005284374.

Castle, M., and R. Taras. 2019. *Democracy in Poland*: New York: Routledge.

Conrad, M. 2020. "From the Eurozone Debt Crisis to the Alternative for Germany." *Frontiers in Political Science* 27 (August). https://doi.org/10.3389/fpos.2020.00004

De Lange, S. 2007. "A New Winning Formula? The Programmatic Appeal of the Radical Right." *Party Politics* 13 (4): 411–435. https://doi.org/10.1177/1354068807075943.

De Tracy, D. 1801. *Project Les Éléments d'idéologie*. Paris: Courcier.

Ezrow L., and G. Xezonakis. 2011. "Citizen Satisfaction with Democracy and Parties' Policy Offerings." *Comparative Political Studies* 44 (9): 1152–1178. https://doi.org/10.1177/0010414011405461.

Franzmann, S., and A. Kaiser. 2006. "Locating Political Parties in Policy Space: A Reanalysis of Party Manifesto Data." *Party Politics* 12 (2): 163–188. https://doi.org/10.1177/1354068806061336.

Freire, A., and A. Belchior. 2011. "What Left and Right Means to Portuguese Citizens." *Comparative European Politics* 9:145–167. http://dx.doi.org/10.1057/cep.2009.14.

Freire, A., and A. M. Belchior. 2015. "Ideological Representation in Portugal: Congruence between Deputies and Voters in Terms of Their Left-Right Placement and Its Substantive

Meaning." In *Political Representation in Portugal: The Years of the Socialist Majority, 2005–2009*, edited by A. Freile and J. M. Leire Vegas, chapter 5. Lisbon: Escrytos.

Garcia Rivero, C., and H. Kotzè. 2019. "The Value and Partisanship Basis of Left-Right Placement after the Financial Crisis." *Comparative Sociology* 18 (5–6): 567–594. https://doi.org/10.1163/15691330-12341511.

Giger, N., and Z. Lefkofridi. 2014. "Salience-Based Congruence Between Parties & Their Voters: The Swiss Case." *Swiss Political Science Review* 20:287–304. https://doi.org/10.1111/spsr.12069.

Golder, M., and J. Stramski. 2010. "Ideological Congruence and Electoral Institutions." *American Journal of Political Science* 53 (1): 90–106. https://doi.org/10.14201/rlop.22648.

Gunther R., and H. Kuan. 2007. "Value Cleavages and Partisan Conflict." In *Democracy, Intermediation, and Voting on Four Continents*, edited by R. Gunther, J. R. Montero, and H. J. Puhle. Oxford: Oxford University Press.

Hellström, A., T. Nilsson, and P. Stoltz. 2012. "Nationalism vs. Nationalism: The Challenge of the Sweden Democrats in the Swedish Public Debate." *Government and Opposition* 47 (2): 186–205. https://doi.org/10.1111/j.1477-7053.2011.01357.x.

Hellwig, T. 2008. "Explaining the Salience of Left-Right Ideology in Postindustrial Democracies: The Role of Structural Economic Change." *European Journal of Political Research* 47:687–709. https://doi.org/10.1111/j.1475-6765.2008.00778.x.

Hooghe, L., G. Marks, and C. J. Wilson. 2002. "Does Left/Right Structure Party Positions on European Integration?." *Comparative Political Studies* 35 (8): 965–989. https://doi.org/10.1177/001041402236310.

Inglehart R., and H. D. Klingemann. 1976. "Ideology and Values." In *Political Action: Mass Participation in Five Western Democracies*, edited by S. H. Barnes and M. Kasse, 203–280. Beverley Hills, CA: Sage.

James, P. 2015. *Urban Sustainability in Theory and Practice: Circles of Sustainability*. New York: Routledge.

Jungar, A.-C., and E. Edenborg. 2018. "Homonationalism in the Nordic Region: PRR Parties and LGBTQ Rights." Paper presented at the XXV IPSA World Congress, July 23, Brisbane.

Keating, M., and D. McCrone, eds. 2013. *The Crisis of Social Democracy in Europe*. Edinburgh, UK: Edinburgh University Press.

Kitschelt, H. 1997. *The Radical Right in Western Europe: A Comparative Analysis*. Ann Arbor: University of Michigan Press.

Kitschelt, H. 2012. "Social Class and the Radical Right: Conceptualizing Political Preference Formation and Partisan Choice." In *Class Politics and the Radical Right*, edited by J. Rydgren, 224–251. London: Routledge.

Kitschelt, H., and P. Rehm. 2011. "Party Alignments: Change and Continuity." Paper presented at the Conference on the Future of Democratic Capitalism. University of Zurich, Zurich, June 16–18.

Kitschelt, H., and S. I. Wilkinson. 2007. "Citizen–Politician Linkages: An Introduction." In *Patrons, Clients, and Policies*, edited by H. Kitschelt and S. I. Wilkinson, 1–49. Cambridge: Cambridge University Press.

Klingemann, H. D., D. Gancheva, and B. Wessels. 2017. "Ideological Congruence: Choice, Visibility and Clarity." In *Parties, Governments and Elites: The Comparative Study of Democracy*, edited by P. Harfst, I. Kubbe, and T. Poguntke, 53–72. Wiesbaden: Springer.

Kotze, H., and C. Garcia-Rivero. 2017. "Institutions, Crises, and Political Confidence in Seven Contemporary Democracies. An Elite–Mass Analysis." *Journal of Public Affairs* 17:e1642.

Lefkofridi, Z., and J. Casado-Asensio. 2013. "European Vox Radicis: Representation and Policy Congruence on the Extremes." *Comparative European Politics* 11 (1): 93–118. https://doi.org/10.1057/cep.2012.1.

Lindbom, A. 2008. "The Swedish Conservative Party and the Welfare State: Institutional Change and Adapting Preferences." *Government and Opposition*, 43 (4): 539–560. https://doi.org/10.1111/j.1477-7053.2008.00268.x.

Lupu, N., L. Selios, and Z. Warner. 2017. "A New Measure of Congruence: The Earth Mover's Distance." *Political Analysis* 25 (1): 95–113. https://doi.org/10.1017/pan.2017.2.

Mansbridge, J. 2009. "'Selection Model' of Political Representation." *Journal of Political Philosophy* 7 (4): 369–398. https://doi.org/10.1111/j.1467-9760.2009.00337.x.

Marks, G., L. Hooghe, M. Steenbergen, and R. Bakke. 2007. "Crossvalidating Data on Party Positioning on European Integration." *Electoral Studies* 26 (1): 23–38. https://doi.org/10.1016/j.electstud.2006.03.007.

Meyer, T. M., and M. Wagner. 2020. "Perceptions of Parties' Left-Right Positions: The Impact of Salience Strategies." *Party Politics* 26 (5): 664–674.

Millard, F. 2009. "Poland: Parties without a Party System, 1991–2008." *Politics & Policy* 37:781–798. https://doi.org/10.1111/j.1747-1346.2009.00198.x

March, L. 2011. *Radical Left Parties in Europe*. London: Routledge.

Mudde, C. 2004. "The Populist Zeitgeist." *Government and Opposition* 39 (4): 542–563. https://doi.org/10.1111/j.1477-7053.2004.00135.x.

Mudde, C., and C. R. Kaltwasser. 2012. *Populism in Europe and the Americas: Threat or Corrective for Democracy?*. Cambridge: Cambridge University Press

Nedelcu, H. 2015. "Anti-Establishment Radical Parties in the 21st Century Europe." PhD dissertation, Carleton University, Ottawa, Ontario.

Nie, N., and K. Andersen. 1974. "Mass Belief System Revisited: Political Change and Attitude Structure." *Journal of Politics* 36:540–572.

Pitkin, H. F. 1967. *The Concept of Representation*. Berkeley: University of California Press.

Poteat, V. P., and E. H. Mereish. 2012. "Ideology, Prejudice, and Attitudes toward Sexual Minority Social Policies and Organizations: Sexual Minority Social Policies and Organizations." *Political Psychology* 33 (2): 211–224. https://doi.org/10.1111/j.1467-9221.2012.00871.x.

Powell, B. G. 2004. "Political Representation in Comparative Politics." *Annual Review of Political Science* 7:273–296. https://doi.org/10.1146/annurev-polisci-050718-032814.

Pytlas, B. 2020. "Party Organisation of PiS in Poland: Between Electoral Rhetoric and Absolutist Practice." *Politics and Governance* 9 (4): 340–353. https://doi.org/10.17645/pag.v9i4.4479.

Rabinowitz, G., and S. Macdonald. 1989. "A Directional Theory of Issue Voting." *American Political Science Review* 83 (1): 93–121. https://doi.org/10.2307/1956436.

Roberts, G. K. 2016. *German Electoral Politics*. Manchester: Manchester University Press.

Rovny, J. 2013. "Where Do Radical Right Parties Stand? Position Blurring in Multidimensional Competition." *European Political Science Review* 5 (1): 1–26. https://doi.org/10.1017/S1755773911000282.

Ruedin, D., and L. Morales. 2012. "Obtaining Party Positions on Immigration from Party Manifestos." Paper presented at the Elections, Public Opinion and Parties (EPOP) Conference, Oxford, UK, September 7.

Schmitt, H., and J. J. A. Thomassen. 1999. *Political Representation and Legitimacy in the European Union*. Oxford: Oxford University Press.

Steltemeier, R. 2009. "On the Way Back into Government? The Free Democratic Party Gearing Up for the 2009 Elections." *German Politics and Society* 27 (2): 63–75.

Szczerbiak, A. 2018. "What Prospects for the Polish Left?." *Social Europe*. https://socialeurope.eu/what-are-the-prospects-for-the-polish-left (Accessed May 20, 2022).

Taggart, P. 2000. *Populism*. Buckingham: Open University Press.

Thomassen, J. J. A. 2012. "The Blind Corner of Representation." In Special Issue titled "Inequality and Representation in Europe," edited by Z. Lefkofridi, N. Giger, and K. Kissau. *Representation. Journal of Representative Democracy* 48 (1): 13–27.

Van Beek, U. 2010. *Democracy under Scrutiny: Elites, Citizens and Cultures*. Toronto: Barbara Budrich Publishers.

Van der Eijk, C., and M. N. Franklin. 1991. "European Community Politics and Electoral Representation: Evidence from the 1989 European Elections Study." *European Journal of Political Research* 19 (1): 105–127. https://doi.org/10.1111/j.1475-6765.1991.tb01179.x.

Van Kessel, S. 2013. "A Matter of Supply and Demand: The Electoral Performance of Populist Parties in Three European Countries." *Government and Opposition* 48 (2): 175–199. http://doi.org/10.1017/gov.2012.14.

Volkens, A., J. L. Bara, I. Budge, M. D. McDonald, and H.-D. Klingemann, eds. 2013. *Mapping Policy Preferences from Texts. Statistical Solutions for Manifesto Analysts*. Oxford: Oxford University Press.

Zhirkov, K. 2014. "Nativist but not Alienated: A Comparative Perspective on the Radical Right Vote in Western Europe." *Party Politics* 20 (2): 286–296. https://doi.org/10.1177/1354068813511379.

CHAPTER 8

Internal Sanctions for Rule of Law Breaches under Article 7 TEU: Why Is the EU Dragging Its Feet?

Clara Portela and Ruth Ferrero-Turrión

Introduction

The imposition of sanctions by regional organizations has proliferated in recent years, with Africa and to some extent Latin America having adopted sanctions practices that remain absent from regional entities in Asia and the post-Soviet space (Hellquist and Palestini 2021; Hellquist 2015). Among regional organizations worldwide, the EU tops the ranking of the most prolific sender of sanctions (Borzyskowski and Portela 2018). EU sanctions, which are framed in the context of its Common Foreign and Security Policy (CFSP), have become common practice, and it has been increasing in both frequency and severity over the past decade (Helwig et al. 2020).

Yet, a fundamental difference sets the EU apart from other regional organizations: the EU is the only regional organization that does not impose sanctions internally, that is, on its own members. This contrasts with the standard practice among regional organizations elsewhere: their constitutive documents often foresee the suspension of members that breach the guiding principles of the organization or that otherwise depart from its membership obligations. This led to the suspension of members from several organizations, effected by the executive organs of the regional entities. Indeed, suspension of membership rights is a standard form of sanction in international organizations, in line with the provisions of the Vienna Convention on the Law of the Treaties. In the case of the African regional organizations—the African Union (AU) and the Economic Community of West African States (ECOWAS)—member states in breach of fundamental norms embraced by the organization sometimes face more severe measures such as visa bans and arms embargoes (Striebinger 2013). By contrast, the EU refrains from suspending its own members.

The introduction of a suspension mechanism for breaches of constitutive principles of the organization enshrined in Article 7 Treaty of the European Union (TEU) came late in the life of the EU—it was introduced in connection with the Eastern enlargement of the 2000s that had been in the making for an entire decade. This differs from the treaty arrangements for the imposition of foreign policy sanctions, which had been in place since the 1980s. Even more conspicuous than the timing chosen for the introduction of legal bases is the record of activation of "external" conditionality and sanctions mechanism versus "internal" sanctions: the vast practice of foreign policy sanctions is in contrast to the lack of activation of internal sanctions. This discrepancy had already been noticed in scholarship, which characterized it as the EU's "contradictory approach to sanctions at home and abroad" (Hellquist 2019).

The contrast between an abundant external sanctions record, with its particular emphasis on its neighborhood (Portela 2017), and the absence of internal sanctions has become all the more acute in recent years when breaches in rule of law standards accompany growing autocratic tendencies occurred in two member states that joined the EU in 2004, namely, Hungary and Poland. The question then arises as to why the EU is finding it difficult to activate Article 7 TEU, or any other mechanism, to respond to breaches in fundamental principles, despite the availability of a dedicated instrument in its toolbox. Why is it "dragging its feet"? The lack of activation is not without political consequences. It poses a credibility problem for the EU among several kinds of audiences: third countries traditionally suspicious of Western sanctions policies, civil society activists in Hungary and Poland, and an informed public opinion that generally condemns the selectivity in the imposition of sanctions (Crawford and Kacarska 2019; Portela and Orbie 2014).

The fact that the rule of law crises were unleashed under the rule of political parties represented at the European Parliament (EP) has no bearing on the activation of Article 7 TEU, a mechanism whose control remains, as detailed below, in the hands of the European Council. It further puts into question the credibility of the EP as the embodiment of democratic representation among EU institutions. First, the parties in power in the countries in question—Fidesz in Hungary and Law and Justice (Prawo i Sprawiedliwość; PiS) in Poland—were represented in its political groups, until the suspension of Fidesz in March 2021. Second, as the locus of democracy at the EU level, it emphasizes respect for the organization's fundamental principles in its member states as they are key to the democratic credentials of the organization. Thus, it is worthwhile examining how the EP has managed the current crisis, and to what extent it has mobilized support among its members to impose a sanctions-like condemnatory action on the transgressing parties.

Moreover, it is even more puzzling that the EU has not reacted more forcefully to democratic backsliding in light of the availability of alternative tools to Article 7. Indeed, conditionality mechanisms, which have been perfected by the EU over decades, have become a flagship tool. Also, the EU distinguishes itself among regional organizations worldwide for its conditionality policies in support of democratic standards, human rights, and the rule of law. In its external relations, the EU has developed a practice of linking its aid and trade to the fulfillment of human rights and democratic standards that has become a defining feature of its global actorness (Velluti 2016; Prickartz and Staudinger 2019). Political conditionality involves the suspension of a benefit in the event that certain commitments have been breached by the beneficiary party. It differs from sanctions in the sense that its activation results in a sanction. However, sanctions are often wielded in the absence of previously stipulated conditionality provisions. The EU's political conditionality reached its maximum level of sophistication in the context of its Eastern enlargement, following the definition of the so-called Copenhagen criteria at the European Council meeting of June 1993. Although less publicized, the practice of conditioning development cooperation for African, Caribbean, and Pacific (ACP) countries on respect for human rights, democracy, and the rule of law also has a long history (Del Biondo 2015; Saltnes 2018). The granting of trade preferences to developing countries, facilitating the access of their products to the EU market, is also conditioned on the respect for international norms regarding labor standards, human rights, the fight against corruption, and the preservation of biodiversity (Portela 2021; Vogt 2015). In addition to the fact that as a mechanism it can give rise to the imposition of sanctions if a breach occurs, conditionality is considered as a mechanism incentivizing compliance with norms in its own right. Thus, conditionality is seen as encouraging compliance prior to, or in the absence of, its activation.

Yet, despite its long experience with conditionality mechanisms in the foreign policy domain, the EU has not shown a proclivity to use them in response to democratic backsliding in its member states. The scholarly debate on how to effectively tackle democracy backsliding has given rise to several proposals for instruments that can mitigate the damage caused to the rule of law in some countries of the EU. However, the scholarly consensus is that the EU is unable to act against the perpetrators of infractions (Kelemen 2020; Pech 2020; Kochenov 2019; Closa 2021). Scholars nevertheless point out that the EU has various rule of law mechanisms at its disposal that help deal with different problematic situations. In this sense, these instruments can be divided into preventive tools, such as the Justice Scoreboard, Rule of Law Framework, Annual Rule of Law Dialogue, or the Cooperation and Verification Mechanism, and reactive tools, such as the Article 7 TEU, Infringement Actions by the TJEU, and Conditionality Funds mechanisms. However, the boundary between them is not clearly defined as some tools like Article 7 and the Rule of Law Mechanism marry both preventive and reactive approaches.

In order to explore this puzzle, we formulate three hypotheses, one of them pertaining to institutional design and two that focus on the (lack of) political will:

H1: According to our first hypothesis, the lack of activation of Article 7 is due to a flawed design. In this reading, the mechanism is unsuited to address the breach at hand.

H2: An alternative hypothesis postulates that domestic political factors interfere with the framing of a resolute reaction vis-à-vis democratic backsliding.

H3: Yet a third hypothesis locates the origins of the deadlock in EU institutions, whose studied balance hinders rather than facilitate the reaction to backsliding.

Simply put: is it the mechanism design, is it member states politics, or is it EU institutions that "get in the way," of preventing a more forceful reaction?

The first section of this chapter explores the design of Article 7 TEU and its alternatives, taking issue with its deficits. The second section explores the politics behind the nonactivation of Article 7. First, the role of member states in framing the EU response to the rule of law crises unleashed in Hungary under the Fidesz party and in Poland under the Law and Justice party is examined. Second, the EP's treatment of the parties that are responsible for the breaches in its own institutional context are analyzed. This is followed by a discussion of our findings, connecting the evidence revied to our original hypotheses and contextualizing them in the broader framework of regional organizations' internal sanctions. A final reflection concludes the chapter.

The institutional design of EU internal sanctions: Article 7 TEU and its alternatives

The EU enshrines the rule of law as part of its fundamental values. Article 2 TEU alludes to "the values of respect for human dignity, freedom, democracy, equality, rule of law and respect for human rights, including the rights of persons belonging to minorities."[1] Article 49 TEU explicitly demands compliance with Article 2, making adherence to the rule of law one of the essential requirements for membership in the organization.

With regard to the enlargement policy, this requirement finds reflection in the accession criteria established in the Copenhagen European Council in June 1993. In addition to the rule of law, the so-called Copenhagen criteria encompassed the existence of stable institutions that guarantee democracy, respect for human rights, and protection of minorities; a functioning market economy and the ability to cope with competitive pressure and market forces within the EU; and the ability to assume the obligations arising from membership (European Council 1993). These Copenhagen criteria were further specified and reinforced at the European Council meeting held in Madrid in 1995 (Kochenov 2004).

---

[1] Consolidated version as of March 1, 2020, published in DO, No. C 202, June 7, 2016. https://eur-lex.europa.eu/legal-content/ES/TXT/?uri=CELEX:02016M/TXT-20200301 (Accessed December 15, 2020).

Mechanism design

The EU has three instruments at its disposal to address the breaches of the rule of law in its member states (Mańko 2019).

1. The standard method is the judicial route. The European Commission, as "the guardian of the Treaties," can use its powers of control through Article 7, 17.1 TFEU, and 354 TFEU, and, in addition, has the power to initiate an infringement procedure (Article 258–260 TFEU) before the Court of Justice of the EU (CJEU) if it considers that any member state fails to comply with the obligations to which it is subject in accordance with the treaties. This judicial instrument was introduced in the Treaty of Amsterdam of 1997 (Merlingen et al. 2001).
2. A second method is Article 7 of the TEU. The nature of this article falls under the supranational logic of the EU in which three institutions are involved. The peculiar architecture of Article 7 being this way renders it less effective than in an intergovernmental procedure. As Closa (2021) argues, the institutional design of Article 7 constructs a non-jurisdictional sanctions mechanism ultimately dependent finally on national governments' willingness to enforce it and assume its costs (Closa 2021).
Article 7 has two parts, the preliminary "alert" mechanism (Article 7.1) and, in case of verification of the infraction, a sanction mechanism (Article 7.2) (Mangas Martín 2018). The "alert" mechanism was established with the Treaty of Nice, long after the judicial mechanism was in place. It is clearly a preventive mechanism against backsliding, while Article 7.2 is a reactive mechanism. Differences exist in their application. When the Council determines the existence of a risk of breaching EU values by any of its members, Article 7.1 allows for an "alert" before the infringement takes place, something unprecedented in the framework of international law. This pathway can be activated by the Commission, one-third of the member states, and/or the EP and must be approved by a four-fifths majority in the Council and receive the consent of two-thirds of the EP. By contrast, Article 7.2 requires unanimity in the Council after approval by a two-thirds majority in Parliament and an absolute majority of votes to determine the existence of a "bankruptcy" of European values (Oliver and Stefanelli 2016). After receiving observations from the affected state, the Council may suspend certain rights, including the right to vote, and this decision will be approved by a qualified majority.
Article 7.1 was first activated against Poland in 2017, on a proposal by the Commission, while the second time it was used against Hungary in 2018 on the request of the EP, with the abstention of members from the Spanish

Popular Party (Partido Popular), which did not follow the European Popular Party's voting instructions.

3. The third and most recent mechanism is the so-called conditionality of funds linked to the "Rule of Law Framework" (European Commission 2014). The objective of the Rule of Law Framework is to foster direct negotiations with the state in question to prevent the structural deterioration of the rule of law. The Commission maintains that, although the precise content of the principles and norms that derive from the rule of law may vary from state to state, they all emanate from the same constitutional tradition that shares six elements: the principle of legality, legal certainty, prohibition of the arbitrariness of the executive powers, independent and effective jurisdictional control, the right to a fair trial, the separation of powers, and equality before the law. Thus, as Kochenov and Pech (2015) suggest, it is possible to construct an essential definition of the rule of law within the EU framework. However, the Rule of Law Framework foresees a dialogue with national institutions as well as the issues recommendations for actions to prevent the threat from materializing (Mangas Martín 2018), and not to solve it when there is already a systemic infraction. This mechanism was reinforced in 2020 when it was transformed into a reactive mechanism to fight against breaches of the rule of law. This was accomplished with the adoption of a regulation titled "rule of law conditionality." Under this formula, which entered into force in January 2021, "EU budget payments can be withheld from countries in which established breaches of the rule of law compromise management of the EU funds" (European Parliament 2020a).

Compliance

However, none of the three mechanisms has worked adequately. This situation of inaction has been labeled "compliance dilemma," which results from the lack of coercion and from the reliance on member states' willingness to comply, which more often than not, ultimately depends on domestic politics (Closa 2021). Thus, the judicial route has proven slow and ineffective due to the absence of enforcement powers and the lack of cooperation of the affected state (Iñiguez 2020a). Sanctions are not working as disincentives as they come at a low cost for the offenders and a very high cost for the executors. Despite facing the annulment of the judicial reform in Poland; the illegalization of the transparency law on foreign NGOs in Hungary; or condemnation for not complying with the relocation agreements approved by the Council in 2015 in Poland, Hungary, and the Czech Republic, none of the affected states backed down from their positions. This caused Timmermans, promoter of the procedures during the Juncker Commission, to renounce his aspirations to preside over the Commission upon receiving the veto of these countries (Iñiguez 2020a).

For its part, the Rule of Law Framework has not turned out to be effective either, perhaps because, once again, the cooperation of the state in question was invariably missing. Various authors attribute the existence of this mechanism to the tepidity with which the issue of authoritarian drift was addressed already in 2013 (Pech and Scheppele 2017). However, the approval of this framework was carried out when gaps that were still far removed from constituting a flagrant violation of the rule of law were detected in Hungary. The triggering of Article 7 could have been more disruptive than constructive as it would inflame Eurosceptic tendencies, already very present in Hungarian society. On the contrary, Poland had not yet entered the democratic regression in which it currently finds itself. Lastly, the failure to activate Article 7 due to the difficulty of reaching unanimity within the framework of the Council, together with the game of alliances of the different political families, prevented the conclusion of ongoing procedures (Iñiguez 2020a; Scheppele 2016).

This situation of deadlock brought to the fore the need to launch new conditionality instruments capable of controlling the authoritarian drifts of some member states (Halmai 2018), similar to what happened during the negotiations for receiving European funds toward post-pandemic recovery (Iñiguez 2020b). After four months of negotiation, over which the risk of blocking the fund hovered, an agreement was reached that partially fulfilled the Polish and Hungarian objectives, which, once again, demonstrated their blocking capacity in the Council. The linkage between the approval of the budget and the recovery fund with the conditionality of the rule of law, promoted during the German presidency, put Ursula Von der Leyen, highly dependent on the support of the Visegrad group, on the ropes. As a result, Poland and Hungary avoided pressure that was not judicially substantiated (European Council 2020) owing to a slow and ineffective legal procedure.

Politics behind the lack of activation of Article 7: The crisis with Hungary under Fidesz party and Poland under Law and Justice party

In recent years, the political systems in Hungary and Poland have evolved into examples of electoral authoritarianism (Levitsky and Way 2010).

Despite their EU membership, their ruling regimes dismantle the rule of law and limit freedoms among their citizens with the aim of avoiding opposition movements contesting their worldviews, not only in political terms but also in the social, cultural, and economic spheres. And this has been the trend for about ten years, during which the conservative governments, both in Poland (PiS), and in Hungary (Fidesz), have performed what is known as "state capture" (Innes 2014), by taking control of the country's structures little by little and by breaking with the system of division of powers and the principle of checks and balances, which are essential to keep liberal democracies afloat.

The modification of national legislation toward increasingly illiberal positions has progressively restricted freedom of the press, of opinion, and of education (Ágh 2018). The framework on which these changes are made is always the same—the threat to the identity and integrity of the nation is above those freedoms. The authoritarian drifts in countries of the region are characterized by very similar patterns. The increase in governmental control of the judiciary, both in the case of Poland and Hungary, was the signal that alerted Brussels. In both cases, the retirement age of judges was lowered, something that violates the EU principle of judicial independence and nondiscrimination based on age. In Poland, moreover, disciplinary measures were introduced against judges by other judges elected by Parliament.

In April 2020, the EP published a statement denouncing that all these measures are incompatible with European values (European Parliament 2020b). During the same parliamentary session, two relevant constitutional claims were introduced with regard to the constitutional amendments in Hungary. The first concerned the definition of public funds undermining supervision and transparency, and the second was the reform of the electoral law that doubles the number of electoral districts in which political parties have to present a minimum number of candidates, which substantively limits the electoral competition capacity of the opposition.

In Poland, constraints on the freedom of the press are notable since 2015, the year of the rise of the Law and Justice party, dropping in the global ranking of press freedom from position 18 in that year to 65 in 2022 (Reporters without Borders 2022). During Law and Justice party's first term, public service media were de facto transformed into the so-called national state media under the so-called Media Law. This law allowed the government to hire and fire state media directors, making them de facto government propaganda outlets. This dovetails with the electoral program in which the PiS promised a "new media order."

Restrictions on sexual freedom are also a leitmotif in both cases, mostly targeting the LGBT community and women's rights. On December 11, the Council reached an agreement on linking the rule of law to the reconstruction funds. On the 15th of the same month, the Hungarian legislature, controlled by Orbán's national conservative party, approved a law prohibiting adoptions by same-sex couples (DW 2020). The creation of cities free of LGBT ideology in Poland has sparked several international criticisms of the Polish government. President Duda won the last presidential elections after describing LGBT rights as an ideology more dangerous than communism (BBC 2020). Prime Minister Morawiecki denied that LGBT people were deprived of rights in Poland and Vice President and MEP for Law and Justice Joachim Brudzinski proposed that the next complaint be in defense of murdered Christians, imprisoned Pro-Life activists, and those persecuted for citing the Bible. Also in Poland, the rights of Polish women have been restricted through a ruling by the Constitutional Court that thus eliminated any possibility of legally accessing abortion.

In 2017, Brussels reacted by triggering Article 7. The European Commission initiated a procedure under Article 7 in response to the risks of the rule of law in Poland. The EP supported this procedure in a resolution of March 2018 (European Parliament 2018a). Similarly, a few months later, on September 8, 2018, the Parliament launched a procedure against Hungary also under Article 7 (European Parliament 2018b). However, this procedure was delayed as a result of the difficulties in achieving unanimity within the Council, with member states avoiding a vote to determine whether or not there was a "clear risk" of a "serious breach" of EU values.

The Commission repeatedly expressed concerns about growing democratic deficits in Poland and Hungary. In the case of Poland, in addition to the issues that prompted the resolutions of the Commission and Parliament of 2017 and 2018 on the need to launch Article 7, a ruling by the Polish Constitutional Court in October 2021 questioned the primacy of the EU law when it collided with the Polish Constitution (Republic of Poland 2021). The ruling of the Polish court foregrounded the differences between Poland and the rest of the bloc on several principles of democracy, such as judicial independence, freedom of the media, as well as the rights of women, migrants, and the LGBT community. This prompted the Commission to temporarily block access to €36bn in grants and loans requested by Poland to help the country recover from COVID-19. However, the Rule of Law Mechanism, approved at the end of 2020 and in force since the beginning of 2021, was yet to be rolled out by the Commission as it was holding out for the ruling of the CJEU. Regarding Hungary, the Commission was extremely concerned about issues related to the award of public contracts involving conflicts of interest as well as the corrupt spending of EU funds. In both cases, the EP, which is in charge of approving multi-annual budgets, has been pressuring the Commission to cut access to funds for these countries immediately. In fact, the EP launched an inaction procedure against the Commission on October 29, 2021.

The approval of the Rule of Law Framework and its link with the budgets and recovery funds failed to convince the most assertive positions shown by Hungary and Poland. In 2021, both countries filed a case to the CJEU against the conditionality mechanism that aims to punish violations of the rule of law in the member states by withholding funds destined for them. The CJEU responded to the challenge that Hungary and Poland had filed against the "conditionality mechanism" with a ruling in February 2022 (Court of Justice of the EU 2022). The ruling determined that Brussels could cut funding to those countries that violate the rule of law. This ruling confirms the Commission's ability to withhold funds by virtue of the defense of common values on which the EU is based. Especially relevant is the recognition of the internal conditionality applied through the budget, since it is considered one of the main instruments that allow EU policies and activities to be enforced (Court of Justice of the EU 2022).

This situation prevailed within the EU until the Russian invasion of Ukraine on February 24. The fact that Europe is experiencing a war changed the Commission's approach fundamentally. The criteria on which the Commission had blocked the €36,000 million to Poland was made more flexible, as concerns about the Polish government's ability to ensure proper spending of community money due to a politicized judicial system seem alleviated. The Commission is unlikely to demand that Poland reinstate the judges expelled during the reform of the judiciary, which was, in the first instance, what put Brussels on alert in 2017. Freezing funding to a member state which is facing great pressure as a result of the war in a neighboring country as well as hosting millions of refugees is regarded as politically unsound. In June

2022, Commission President Von der Layen announced the provision of recovery funds to Poland, although it stated that it would continue insisting on reforms to guarantee the independence of the judiciary (Bayer 2022).

Regarding Hungary, the Commission waited until the Hungarian general elections on April 3, 2022, to adopt its decision. On April 27, the Budapest government was notified that Brussels had activated the cross-compliance regulation due to systemic deficiencies of the rule of law that threaten the financial interests of the EU. Those shortcomings include charges of systemic irregularities in public procurement, failure to prosecute corruption, and failure to cooperate with the European Anti-Fraud Office. In any case, based on the conditionality stipulations, the Commission can only propose possible sanctions since, ultimately, the decision-making power rests with the Council. Therefore, we will still have to wait to see if, indeed, the instruments that began to operate at the beginning of 2021 will be sufficient to address the deterioration of liberal democracies within the EU framework.

The institutional balance and Article 7: The isolation of Law and Justice and Fidesz parties at the EP

Given that the activation of Article 7 is in the hands of the Council, and that it rests on a quasi-unanimous decision, the role of member states is paramount. This begs the question as to whether a different institutional design that involved the stronger participation of other key institutions bears the promise of a lower threshold for activation. In this regard, the role of the EP deserves special attention. In addition to being the EU institution with the least-weakest role in Article 7 procedure, it is the locus of democratic accountability par excellence in Brussels' institutional setup.

Faced with a challenge of the rule of law, the EP can be expected to play a central role in promoting corrective action. First, such a role dovetails with its self-promoted image as the locus of democratic accountability in the EU's institutional machinery and its advocacy of human rights and rule of law principles. Second, the EP has played a historical role in scrutinizing compliance with EU norms along the accession process of candidate countries, providing it with a formal influence that it lacks in most areas of European foreign policy (Irrera and Stavridis 2015). Thus, the EP has a particular stake in monitoring compliance with rule of law standards among its members. This is without detriment to the role of guardian of the treaty that falls squarely on the Commission, thus making it responsible for monitoring adherence to norms. The Parliament is not subject to the incentive structure faced by the Commission, which compels it to act according to tactical calculations. While the Commission can be expected to launch an initiative only when it anticipates the support of a sizable portion of members of the Council and of Parliament (Closa 2021), the EP is free from such constraints.

The EP has indeed been the most active institution in engaging with rule of law breaches through debates and resolutions; however, it has been slow in promoting the activation of Article 7. It did not launch the preventive or "alert" stage against the Hungarian government until 2018, while in the case of Poland, it moved only after the Commission took the initiative, seconding its move (see above). The EP also supported the Commission's threats to block EU funds for members in breach of rule of law obligations.

Separately from its role in triggering Article 7 procedures, the EP also had another tool at its disposal to react to the deterioration of the rule of law in Hungary and Poland. The membership of members of the EP (MEPs) from Fidesz and Law and Justice who are elected from their political groups could be threatened with suspension—a decision in the hands of the groups themselves. This measure, although not routinely cataloged as a sanction, can be considered as such by analogy with the membership suspension at the parliamentary level. The suspension of voting rights of delegates from the Russian Federation in the Parliamentary Assembly of the Council of Europe (PACE) following the annexation of Crimea in 2014 is a case in point (Radio Free Europe 2014).

Yet, the isolation of the two political parties in question was far from automatic. The Law and Justice Party (PiS) belonged to the European Conservatives and Reformist Group, which also includes the German Populist Party "Alternative für Deutschland" (AfD). PiS is represented in the group by 24 MEPs. Since the European Conservatives and Reformist Group is only the sixth group in the post-Brexit hemicycle, representing a mere 8.8% of MEPs, and it is ideologically at odds with the EU, PiS's continued membership to the group was hardly questioned. By contrast, Fidesz is part of the European People's Party (EPP), the largest political group in the EP with a share of 26.6 % of MEPs in the post-Brexit era. The EPP's position as a dominant, mainstream party made it difficult to ignore the breaches perpetrated by one of its members. Yet, the suspension of the Fidesz party from the EPP was discussed for a decade before it was effected. In July 2013, the Green MEP Rui Tavares presented a report criticizing the Hungarian government which failed to attract the support of most EPP MEPs. Yet, as relations deteriorated between Fidesz and its European partners—particularly with Commission President Juncker—Green MEP Judith Sargentini presented a new critical report in 2018, which was adopted with a sizeable number of EPP votes. This deterioration peaked with a campaign by the Hungarian government openly attacking Jean-Claude Juncker in February 2019. After 13 members of the EPP (out of a total of 83) demanded Fidesz's expulsion from the group in March 2019, Fidesz was "suspended" with 190 votes against 3. Suspension effectively meant that the party was deprived of voting rights within the group, was not invited to party meetings, and was not allowed to propose candidates for party leadership positions (Macek 2021).

Discussion

The tardiness and slow pace at which Article 7 procedures were launched in response to the deterioration of the rule of law in Hungary and Poland evidence a marked reluctance to their use by all actors involved in its activation. The present chapter explores this lukewarm response in an attempt to shed some light on its rationales. Some observers have noted the presence of the so-called compliance dilemma, referring to the uncomfortable choice between risking alienating offending states with sanctions or seeking their compliance with engagement (Closa 2021). Conspicuously, while the same dilemma theoretically applies to foreign policy sanctions, Brussels does not shy away from imposing these measures externally. Others have highlighted the perverse equilibrium owing to which governments slide toward authoritarianism benefit, and this is perpetuated by funds provided by the very organization they seek to undermine (Kelemen 2020).

Our brief review concurs with the analysis that it is a combination of factors that accounts for the EU's remarkably slow and meek reaction to democratic backsliding. All three sources analyzed played a role in preventing a resolute and speedy response. The design of Article 7 presents weaknesses that could be easily exploited: it reserved a privileged role to member states, instituting a voting rule that makes it easy for leaders at fault to be protected by like-minded governments. Equally importantly, it left penalties unspecified, depriving the tool of a proper deterrent effect. However, shifting decision-making power to the other institutions, in particular to the EP, would do little to improve the situation. The lack of political will demonstrated by member states in the context of the Council stems from domestic dynamics that affect the behavior of EP political groups just as much as national governments. Admittedly, the three sources we set to examine are hardly independent of one another. If domestic political dynamics, notably the rise of populist parties all over the EU, speak against the activation of Article 7, these will permeate Council politics as much as EP internal dynamics. Not even the Commission as the "guardian of the treaty" and thus the guarantor of the rule of law within the Union is insulated from these influences, given the president's dependence on support from Visegrad countries, and its reliance on the other key EU institutions. All these factors combine to exploit the vulnerabilities of a suspension mechanism designed to discipline an isolated offender government, but not an entire continent under the rising specter of populism (García Rivero, this volume). Nevertheless, the current trend toward funding conditionality (Végh 2022) might be advantageous after all: it might be effective in depriving the leaders at fault of key funding they need to sustain their networks, thus weakening their political base, without triggering a political commotion of the intensity associated with Article 7.

Conclusion: Why nobody is willing to activate Article 7

In view of the lack of appetite for the activation of internal sanctions mechanisms, it is pertinent to wonder whether Article 7 was ever intended for activation. The design of the tool, as well as the EU's long experience with external relations conditionality, suggests otherwise. The suspension mechanism, with its various stages, might have been designed in order to discourage both democratic and rule of law backsliding, or to incentivize their correction, rather than to lead to a full suspension. This reading would explain not only the indecisiveness of Brussels institutions to bring Article 7 procedures to a conclusion but also the consecutive addition of two "antechamber" stages—the "alert" mechanism and the "Rule of Law Framework"—whose effect is that of deferring the materialization of a suspension under Article 7.2. It would also account for the very absence of concrete sanctions measures specified in the mechanism, as a consequence of which governments at fault are unaware of what penalty could be waiting for them at the end of Article 7. Interestingly, this approach would be in line with sanctions scholarship, which claims that sanctions threats are more effective in promoting compliance than sanctions imposition (Hovi et al. 2005; Morgan et al. 2021). If this reading was correct and if Article 7 had been put in place in order to never be activated, member states and EU institutions would have seen its worth in its sheer deterrent effect. Be it as it may, EU actors have demonstrated that, despite the boldness of treaty provisions, when it comes to dealing with each other's breaches, they still feel more comfortable employing traditional conditionality tools than with the "nuclear" option embodied in an Article 7 suspension.

At the outset of our chapter, we contrasted the EU's active sanctions practice in its external relations with its reticence to activate sanctions internally. At the same time, we highlighted the more puzzling contrast between the growing practice of membership suspension in regional organizations in Africa for breaches of constitutional principles with the EU's reluctance to make use of the same. In light of our analysis, we can conclude that the EU's commitment to discipline those members is considerably weaker than in extra-European organizations. Determining the factors that account for such divergence is an intriguing question that ought to be explored in the future research agenda.

Bibliography

Ágh, A. 2018. "The Decline of Democracy in East-Central Europe. Hungary as the Worst-Case Scenario." *Problems of Post-Communism* 63 (5–6): 277–287.

Bayer, L. 2022. "Amidst Commission Rebellion, von der Layen Defends Polish Recovery Cash Plan." *Politico*, June 2.

BBC. 2020. "Polish Election: Andrezj Dda Says LGTB "Ideology" Worse Than Communism." BBC, June 14. https://www.bbc.com/news/world-europe-53039864 (Accessed June 15, 2022).

Biondo, K. del. 2015. "Donor Interests or Developmental Performance? Explaining Sanctions in EU Democracy Promotion in sub-Saharan Africa." *World Development* 75:74–84.

Borzyskowski, I. V., and C. Portela. 2018. "Sanctions Cooperation and Regional Organisations." In *Inter-Organisational Relations in International Security: Cooperation and Competition*, edited by S. Aris, A. Snetkov, and A. Wenger, 240–261. Abingdon: Routledge.

Closa, C. 2021. "Institutional Logics and the EU's Limited Sanctioning Capacity under Article 7 TEU." *International Political Science Review* 42 (2): 501–515.

Court of Justice of the European Union. 2022. "Judgments in Cases C-156/21 Hungary v Parliament and Council and C-157/21 Poland v Parliament and Council." Press Release No.

28/22. Luxembourg, February 16. https://curia.europa.eu/jcms/upload/docs/application/pdf/2022-02/cp220028en.pdf (Accessed May 16, 2022).

Crawford, G., and S. Kacarska. 2019. "Aid Sanctions and Political Conditionality: Continuity and Change." *Journal of International Relations and Development* 22 (2): 184–214.

DW. 2020. "LGBT rights: Hungary Passes Law Banning Same-Sex Adoption." December 15. https://www.dw.com/en/lgbt-rights-hungary-passes-law-banning-same-sex-adoption/a-55947139 (Accessed May 16, 2022).

European Commission. 2014. "A New European Parliament and the Council. A New EU Framework to Strengthen the Rule of Law." COM (2014) 158, Final, March 11, 2014. Communication from the Commission to the European Parliament and the Council.

European Commission. 2017. "Proposal for a Council Decision on the Determination of a Clear Risk of a Serious Breach by the Republic of Poland of the Rule of Law." COM/2017/0835, Final, 2017/0360 (NLE).

European Council. 1993. Presidency Conclusions, Copenhagen, June 21–22.

European Council. 2020. European Council Conclusions, Brussels, December 10–11, 2020 EUCO 22/20. https://www.consilium.europa.eu/media/47296/1011-12-20-euco-conclusions-en.pdf (Accessed June 15, 2022).

European Parliament. 2018a. Resolution of March 1, 2018, on the Commission's Decision to Activate Article 7(1) TEU as Regards the Situation in Poland (2018/2541(RSP)).

European Parliament. 2018b. Resolution of 12 September 2018 on a Proposal Calling on the Council to Determine, Pursuant to Article 7(1) of the Treaty on European Union, the Existence of a Clear Risk of a Serious Breach by Hungary of the Values on Which the Union Is Founded (2017/2131(INL)).

European Parliament. 2020a. Motion for a Resolution on the Multiannual Finance Framework 2021–2027, the Interinstitutional Agreement, the EU Recovery Instrument and the Rule of Law Regulation, December 16. https://www.europarl.europa.eu/doceo/document/B-9-2020-0428_EN.html (Accessed June 15, 2022).

European Parliament. 2020b. Comisión Libertades Civiles (LIBE) El Parlamento Europeo muestra su preocupación por las medidas tomadas por Hungría para combatir el COVID19, March 24. https://www.europarl.europa.eu/spain/es/prensa/communicados_de_prensa/pr-2020/03-2020/el-parlamento-europeo-muestra-su-preocupacion-por-las-medidas-tomadas-por-hungria-para-combatir-el-covid-19.html (Accessed June 15, 2022).

Halmai, G. 2018. "Abuse of Constitutional Identity: The Hungarian Constitutional Court on Interpretation of Article E) (2) of the Fundamental law." *Review of Central and East European Law* 43 (1): 23–42.

Hellquist, E. 2015. "Interpreting Sanctions in Africa and Southeast Asia." *International Relations* 29 (3): 319–333.

Hellquist, E. 2019. "Ostracism and the EU's Contradictory Approach to Sanctions at Home and Abroad." *Contemporary Politics* 25 (4): 393–418.

Hellquist, E., and S. Palestini. 2021. "Regional Sanctions and the Struggle for Democracy." *International Political Science Review* 42 (2): 437–450.

Helwig, N., J. Jokela, and C. Portela. 2020. "EU-Sanktionspolitik in geopolitischen Zeiten." *Vierteljahresschrift für Integration* 4:278–294.

Hovi, J., R. Huseby, and D. Sprinz. 2005. When Do (Imposed) Economic Sanctions Work?, *World Politics* 57 (4): 479–499.

Iñiguez, G. 2020a. "El Estado de derecho y la condicionalidad del fondo de recuperación: ¿bloqueo institucional o falta de voluntad política?." *Araucaria. Revista Iberoamericana de Filosofía, Política, Humanidades y Relaciones Internacionales* 22 (45): 18–205. https://dx.doi.org/10.12795/araucaria.2020.i45.08.

Iñiguez, G. 2020b. "El regreso del Estado de Derecho. 11 noviembre 2020." *Política Exterior.* https://www.politicaexterior.com/el-regreso-del-estado-de-derecho/ (Accessed May 2, 2022).

Innes, A. 2014. "The Political Economy of State Capture in Central Europe." *Journal of Common Market Studies* 52 (1): 88–104.

Irrera, D., and S. Stavridis, eds. 2015. *The European Parliament and its International Relations.* Abingdon: Routledge.

Kelemen, D. 2020. "The European Union's Authoritarian Equilibrium." *Journal of European Public Policy* 27 (3): 481–499. https://doi.org/10.1080/13501763.2020.1712455.

Kochenov, D. 2004. "Behind the Copenhagen Façade. The Meaning and Structure of the Copenhagen Political Criterion of Democracy and the Rule of Law." *European Integration Online Papers* (EIoP) 8 (10): 1–24. http://eiop.or.at/eiop/texte/2004-010a.htm (Accessed May 2, 2022).

Kochenov, D. 2019. "Elephants in the Room: The European Commission's 2019 Communication on the Rule of Law." *Hague Journal on the Rule of Law* 11:423–438.

Kochenov, D., and L. Pech. 2015. "Upholding the Rule of Law in the EU: On the Commission's 'Pre-Article 7 Procedure' as a Timid Step in the Right Direction." *European Constitutional Law Review* 11 (April): 512–540 [A more extensive version can be found in "Monitoring and Enforcement of the Rule of Law in the EU: Rhetoric and Reality." Robert Schuman Centre for Advanced Studies Research Paper No. RSCAS 2015/24. http://dx.doi.org/10.2139/ssrn.2625602 (Accessed April 21, 2022).

Kurtz, M. J., and A. Barnes. 2002. "The Political Foundations of Post-Communist Regimes: Marketization, Agrarian Legacies, or International Influences." *Comparative Political Studies* 35 (5): 524–533.

Levitsky, S., and L. Way. 2010. *Competitive Authoritarianism.* Cambridge: Cambridge University Press.

Macek, L. 2021. *History of a Breakdown: Fidesz's Departure from the EPP group at the European Parliament.* Paris: Notre Europe.

Mangas Martín, A. 2018. "Polonia en el punto de mira: 'Sólo riesgo de violación grave del Estado de Derecho.'" *Revista General de Derecho Europeo* 44:1–12.

Mańko, R. 2019. "Protecting the Rule of law in the EU. Existing Mechanisms and Possible Improvements." European Parliamentary Research Service (EPRS), PE 642.280.

Merlingen, M., C. Mudde, and U. Sedelmeier. 2001. "The Right and the Righteous? European Norms, Domestic Politics and the Sanctions against Austria." *Journal of Common Market Studies* 39 (1): 59–77.

Morgan, C., N. Bapat, and Y. Kobayashi. 2021. "The Threat and Imposition of Economic Sanctions project: A Retrospective." in *Research Handbook on Economic Sanctions*, edited by P. Van Bergeijk, 44–61. Cheltenham: Edward Elgar.

Oliver, P., and J. Stefanelli. 2016. "Strengthening the Rule of Law in the EU: The Council's Inaction." *Journal of Common Market Studies* 54 (5): 1075–1084. https://doi.org/10.1111/jcms.12402.

Pech, L. 2020. "The Rule of Law in the EU: the Evolution of the Treaty Framework and Rule of Law Toolbox." Working Paper No. 7, Reconnect Project, March. https://reconnect-europe.eu/wp-content/uploads/2020/03/RECONNECT-WP7-2.pdf (Accessed April 21, 2022).

Pech, L., and K. L. Scheppele. 2017. "Illiberalism Within: Rule of Law Backsliding in the EU." *Cambridge Yearbook of European Legal Studies* 19:3–47.

Portela, C. 2017. "Sanctions and the European Neighbourhood Policy." In *The Routledge Handbook on the European Neighbourhood Policy*, edited by T. Demmelhuber et al., 270–278. London: Routledge.

Portela, C. 2021. "Trade Preference Suspensions as Economic Sanctions." In *Research Handbook on Economic Sanctions*, edited by P. Van Bergeijk, 263–271. Cheltenham: Edward Elgar.

Portela, C., and J. Orbie. 2014. "Sanctions under the EU's Generalised System of Preferences (GSP): Coherence by Accident?." *Contemporary Politics* 20 (1): 63–76.

Prickartz, A. C., and I. Staudinger. 2019. "Policy vs Practice: The Use, Implementation and Enforcement of Human Rights Clauses in the European Union's International Trade Agreements." *Europe and the World Law Review* 3 (1): 1–12.

Radio Free Europe. 2014. "PACE Deprives Russia of Voting Rights." April 10. https://www.rferl.org/a/russia-ukraine-pace-/25327665.html (Accessed June 15, 2022).

Reporters without Borders. 2022. World Press Freedom Index. https://rsf.org/en/ranking.

Republic of Poland. 2021. Case No K 3/21 Judgment in the Name of the Republic of Poland Assessment of the Conformity to the Polish Constitution of Selected Provisions of the Treaty on European Union, Warsaw, October 7. https://trybunal.gov.pl/en/hearings/judgments/art/11662-ocena-zgodnosci-z-konstytucja-rp-wybranych-przepisow-traktatu-o-unii-europejskiej (Accessed May 16, 2022).

Saltnes, J. D. 2018. "The European Union's Human Rights Policy: Is the EU's Use of the Human Rights Clause Inconsistent?." *Global Affairs* 4 (2–3): 277–289.

Scheppele, K. L. 2016. "EU Can Still Block Hungary's Veto on Polish Sanctions." *Politico*. https://www.politico.eu/article/eu-can-stillblock-hungarys-Orbán-veto-on-polish-pis-sanctions/ (Accessed June 15, 2022).

Striebinger, K. 2013. "When Pigs Fly: ECOWAS and the Protection of Constitutional Order in the Event of Coup d'état," in *Roads to Regionalism*, edited by T. Börzel et al., 179–198. Farnham: Ashgate.

Végh, Z. 2022. "Mind the Gaps: The Pending Suspension of Hungary's EU Funds." ECFR Commentary, European Council of Foreign Relations, October 5.

Velluti, S. 2016. "The Promotion and Integration of Human Rights in EU External Trade Relations." *Utrecht Journal of International and European Law* 32 (83): 41–68.

Vogt, J. 2015. "A Little Less Conversation. The EU and the (Non) Application of Labour Conditionality in the Generalised System of Preferences (GSP)." *International Journal of Comparative Labour Law and Industrial Relations* 31 (3): 285–304.

PART III

Populist Parties in Different European Regions

CHAPTER 9

Populism in Western versus Eastern Europe

José Rama and Andrés Santana

INTRODUCTION

The word "populism" was declared 2017 "Word of the Year" by the *Cambridge Dictionary*. Despite the time that has passed and far from losing momentum in academia, media, and especially in society, the truth is that populism remains a fashionable and notorious phenomenon. As we are writing this chapter (February 2022), a (former) populist left party is part of the coalition government in Spain; populist radical right parties (PRRPs) lead the government in Hungary and Poland or are the first political option in the National Council in Switzerland; and like-minded political forces are the second preferred options in Belgium, Finland, and France, and comprise the third option in Austria, Spain, and Sweden. Beyond Europe, populist leaders *lured* the people with their oversimplified messages, as the cases of Mexico, Brazil, Chile, Peru, and even India and the Philippines illustrate. Thus, while some political scientists foretold a swift end of the populist wave, and some others, like Larry M. Bartels (2017), even reckoned it to be just a myth, the examples above attest to the current political relevance of populism.

From an academic perspective, there are at least five main areas of interest regarding populism. First, how do we define and interpret the concept, with schools distinguishing between those who consider it an ideology, as, for instance, Cas Mudde (2004); a discourse, as Ernesto Laclau (2005); a political strategy, in the vein of Kurt Weyland (2001); or a performance, in the likes of Pierre Ostiguy et al. (2020). Second, with regard to its supply side, the question arises as to what do populist parties say and stand for. One example of bourgeoning research in this area is the comparative analysis of PRRPs' Euroscepticism by Andrea Pirro and Stijn van Kessel (2017). Third, how does one classify political parties into populist and non-populist—leading to the proposals from Maurits J. Meijers and Andrej Zaslove (2021), Pipa Norris (2020), as well as a group of experts from the PopuList, elaborated by Matthijs Rooduijn et al. (2020)—or rather how do we measure populist attitudes, as illustrated by a battery of questions and indexes advanced by Agnes Akkerman et al. (2014). Fourth, and this concerns the demand side of it, who exactly are the populist voters? A study exemplifying this line of research is the comparative analysis of the factors that unite the voter bases of Western populist parties by Rooduijn (2018). Finally, what is the relationship between populism and democracy, as illustrated by Stefan Rummens (2017) in *The Oxford Handbook of Populism*.

Our chapter tries to fill an empirical lacuna related to the interplay between the fourth and the last of the aforementioned areas: the relationship between democratic preferences and the vote for populist parties. Importantly, we do not know whether the relationship between individuals' support for democracy (SFD) and their tendency to vote for populist parties is different from the one between their satisfaction with democracy (SWD) and such voting tendency.

This chapter builds on Chapter 1 of this book, in which Enrique Clari and Carlos García-Rivero focus on the contextual and individual factors that help explain the different political cultures in a given country, distinguishing among critical, satisfied, cynical, and illiberal citizens. In this chapter, we focus on the individual level and explore how attitudes toward democracy (SFD and SWD) explain the vote for PRRPs in Western and Eastern Europe.

To do this, we employ data from the European Election Study 2019 (EES 2019), retrieved by Hermann Schmitt et al. (2022), and carry out logistic regressions where the dependent variable is the vote recall for PRRPs (codified as 1) *versus* other parties (coded as 0). We analyze data from 16 European countries, both from the Western and Eastern continent.

Our results show that SFD and SWD follow different dynamics, at least, in Eastern Europe. While SFD reduces the chances of voting for PRRP both in Western and Eastern Europe, SWD works in the opposite direction in the two regions: in Western Europe, it further reduces the propensity to vote for a PRRP, but in Eastern Europe, it tends to increase rather than curtail that propensity.

PRRPs and Democracy in Europe

It is well known that populism and democracy are contested concepts. Depending on how we understand populism (as an ideology, style, strategy, or rhetoric), which area of the world we are interested in (Europe, the Americas), which breed of populism we consider (radical right, radical left, others), and our conception of democracy (minimalistic versus maximalistic views), different interpretations of their relationship will arise. In general terms, scholars are divided into three schools or groups. First, those who hold a negative stance on populism and its effects on democracy, as exemplified by Pierre Rosanvallon (2008), Panizza (2005), and Norris and Ronald Inglehart (2019). Second, those who, like Laclau (2005), evaluate populism as a corrective for democracy. Third and last, those who contend that the impact of populism on democracy needs to be addressed empirically, in the spirit of Mudde and Cristóbal Rovira Kaltwasser (2017). Thus, it is fair to recognize that the relationship between populism and democracy (without adjectives on either side) is far from being settled, as the works of Rama and Fernando Casal Bértoa (2020), Rovira Kaltwasser and Steven M. van Hauwaert (2020), and Lisa Zanotti and José Rama (2021) attest.

Following the approach of Ángel Rivero in Chapter 2 of this volume, here we conceive of populism as a political ideology antagonist of liberal democracy. Working with this definition, populism is not against democracy without adjectives but, by advocating the supremacy of the will of the people without any constraints, it "fundamentally rejects the notion of pluralism and, therefore, minority rights as well as the institutional guarantees that should protect them" (Mudde and Rovira Kaltwasser 2017, 81), and is, therefore, clearly at odds with the principles of liberal democracy.

We are moreover concerned with the effects of populism on democracy in Europe, an area where, because of the predominance of PRRPs, it is difficult to differentiate the effect of the populist and the radical right (especially, the nativist) components on democratic regimes. According to Mudde (2007), there are two types of far-right parties: extreme and radical ones. While the former reject democracy as the best political regime and aim to change it, the latter do not aim at overthrowing democracy, at least as a whole. In view of the specialized literature revised above, neither the populist nor the radical right nature of PRRPs implies that these parties are against democracy as such,[1] so we advance our first expectation:

Expectation 1: We do not expect any systematic relationship between SFD and the vote for PRRPs.

With respect to the relationship between SWD and the populist radical right, the literature reviewed clearly implies that PRRPs are at odds with the way democracy works in Europe, and more precisely, with its liberal component, which they wish to dismantle. In this sense, and focusing on radical right parties, Marcel Lubbers et al. (2002, 353) found a negative relationship between SWD and the vote for these parties. Hence, our second expectation:

Expectation 2: The lower the SWD, the higher the tendency to vote for PRRPs.

Data and methods

For our empirical analyses, we use data from the European Election Study 2019 (hereafter EES 2019) (Schmitt et al. 2022). The EES 2019 is a post-election study, conducted by Gallup International in all 28 EU member states after the elections to the European Parliament were held between May 23 and May 26, 2019. The data collection spanned from June 14 to November 7, and it was mostly conducted online, by means of self-administered computer-assisted web-based questionnaires (CAPI), except for Malta and Cyprus, where reliable access panels were not available, and so computer-assisted telephone interviews (CAWI), combining landlines and mobile phones, were employed. The universe is the national population of the 28 European Union Member States, with the resident in each member

---

[1] Nonetheless, as Roberto Biorcio (2003, 7) reminds us, we cannot forget that some of these parties have their roots in authoritarian movements with radical right histories, as is the case of the National Front, now National Rally (NR), the Freedom Party of Austria (FPÖ), and the Sweden Democrats.

state aged 18 years and over (16 years old and over in Austria). Foreign EU nationals with a sufficient command of the national languages to answer the questionnaire are also covered. The respondents were selected randomly from access panel databases using stratification (quota) variables (gender, age, region, and level of urbanization), except for Malta and Cyprus, where a multistage Random Digit Dialing approach was used. In all countries, the samples were stratified by gender, age, region, and urbanization. The sample size is roughly 1,000 interviews in each member state (except Cyprus, Luxembourg, and Malta, where it is close to 500). The total sample size is 26,538.

The EES 2019 is especially well suited to the purposes of the current chapter because it includes a wealth of comparative electoral data (136 variables) for Western and Eastern European countries retrieved at approximately the same date. Most importantly, it contains information on our two key independent variables: SFD and SWD. Other comparative surveys covering a broad range of Western and Eastern European countries that are widely used in electoral research, like the European Social Survey, do not retrieve information on SFD.

The dependent variable is the vote recall for PRRPs (codified as 1) versus other parties (coded as 0). Abstentionists and those who do not recall whom they voted for are treated as missing. For robustness purposes, we also test models in which we add abstentionists to the reference category. Following what is becoming increasingly standard practice in the discipline, to code a party as a PRRP, we consider all the parties that, according to the PopuList (Rooduijn et al. 2020), are classified as both populist and radical right. We consider all the countries with significant PRRPs, namely ten from Western Europe (Austria, Belgium, Denmark, Germany, Finland, France, Italy, the Netherlands, Spain, and Sweden) and six from Eastern Europe (Croatia, Estonia, Hungary, Poland, Slovakia, and Slovenia). Table 9.1 displays the list of countries and parties considered.

Our first key independent variable is SFD. In the EES 2019, it is captured by the following question: "How important is it for you to live in a country that is governed democratically?" (11-point scale, 0–10, where 0=not at all important, and 10=absolutely important). To facilitate the interpretation of the results, in some of our figures, we have divided the original variable by 10 to rescale it from 0 (minimum) to 1 (maximum).

Table 9.1 Populist radical right parties in Western and Eastern Europe that contested in the 2019 elections to the European Parliament

Countries	Political Parties
Western Europe	
Austria	Freedom Party of Austria (FPÖ)
Belgium	Flemish Interest (VB)
	People's Party (Pp)
	National Front (FN)
Denmark	Danish People's Party (DF)
Finland	Finns Party (PS)
France	National Rally (RN)
	La liste Debout La France (DLF)
Germany	Alternative for Germany (AfD)
Italy	Lega
	Fratelli d'Italia (FDI)
Netherlands	Party for Freedom (PVV)
	Forum for Democracy (FvD)
Spain	Vox
Sweden	Sweden Democrats (SD)
Eastern Europe	
Croatia	Croatian Democratic Alliance of Slavonia and Baranja (HDSSB)
Estonia	Estonian Conservative People's Party (EKRE)
Hungary	Our Homeland Movement (MH)
	Fidesz—Hungarian Civil Alliance
	Jobbik—The Movement for a Better Hungary
Poland	Prawo i Sprawiedliwość (PiS)
	Kukiz'15 (K15)
Slovakia	Slovak National Party (SNS)
	We are Family (SR)
Slovenia	Slovenska nacionalna stranka (SNS)
	Slovenska demokratska stranka (SDS)

Notes: Cells sorted by region and country name. Parties or countries not considered in the EES or without significant populist radical right parties are not shown in the table.

Source: Own elaboration, based on Rooduijn et al. (2020).

Our second key independent variable is SWD. In the EES 2019, it is tapped with a question that reads as follows: "On the whole, how satisfied are you with the way democracy works in *country*?" (1=very satisfied; 2=fairly satisfied; 3=not very satisfied; and 4=not at all satisfied). To facilitate the interpretation of the results, we have inverted the scale.

Following standard practice, we include a series of controls in all our models. We introduce three sociodemographic variables, namely sex (a binary variable, 2=female, 1=male); age group (a five-fold ordinal variable, 1=18–24 years, 2=25–39, 3=40–54, 4=55–64, 5=65 years or older); and education level (an ordinal variable with three categories, 1=low education, 2=middle education, 3=high education). We also control for three attitudinal variables: left-right ideological position (11-point scale, 0–10, 0=left, 10=right); attitudes toward immigration (11-point scale, 0–10, 0=fully favor restrictive policies, 10=fully oppose restrictive policies); and the retrospective evaluation of the economic situation (an ordinal variable with five categories, 1=compared to 12 months ago, the economy is a lot better, 2=a little better, 3=stayed the same, 4=a little worse, 5=a lot worse).

Table 9.2 shows the descriptive statistics as well as the variance inflation factors (VIFs) of the variables. Given that all the VIFs lie well below the levels that would raise collinearity concerns, all the independent and control variables can be simultaneously incorporated into our models.

Given that the dependent variable is binary, we carry out binary logistic regressions with country clusters. As the number of countries is moderate (16), this strategy is probably preferable to multilevel regression models. In all our models, we include political weights that redress the effective voting distributions in the 2019 European elections (these weights are made available by the EES 2019 in variable WGT4).

To uncover the overall similarities and differences between West and East in the relationship between democratic attitudes (SFD and SWD) and PRRP vote, we pool the data for all the Western countries and parties in Table 9.1, as well as for all their Eastern counterparts. In our pooled analysis, we test four models: models M1 and M2 use our first specification of the dependent variable (vote for a PRRP versus other parties, treating abstainers as missing) for Western and Eastern European countries, respectively. Models M3 and M4 employ our second specification of the dependent vari-

Table 9.2 Descriptive statistics and variance inflation factors of the variables

	N	Mean	Std. dev.	Min	Max	VIF
Dependent variables						
Populism vs. other	10,730	0.21	0.41	0	1	
Populism vs. other+abstainers	15,008	0.15	0.36	0	1	
Independent variables						
Female	14,988	1.51	0.50	1	2	1.01
Age	15,008	3.05	1.31	1	5	1.08
Education	13,372	2.49	0.60	1	3	1.02
Ideology	13,303	5.12	2.64	0	10	1.10
Support for democracy (SFD)	14,421	8.55	2.10	0	10	1.09
Satisfaction with democracy (SWD)	14,600	2.28	0.88	1	4	1.30
Immigration	14,146	4.36	3.29	0	10	1.08
Economy	14,237	3.09	1.02	1	5	1.28

Source: Own elaboration, EES 2019 data. *Notes*: N=number of valid observations, Std. dev.=standard deviation, Min=minimum, Max=maximum, VIF=variance inflation factor.

able (vote for a PRRP versus other parties or abstention). Hence, M1 and M2 employ fewer cases than M3 and M4, respectively.

Our chapter aims to go beyond the overall patterns of similarities and differences between Western and Eastern countries with regard to the relationship between attitudes toward democracy and the vote for PRRPs. We also aim at clarifying the cross-party variability within each region. To clarify the specific relationships between democratic attitudes and the vote for each PRRP, we carry out specific country analyses for each party (for these analyses, we treat abstainers as missing). Following the approach of other studies in the field, we do so for all those parties in Table 9.1 with at least 50 successful observations, that is, 50 PRRP voters: the Austrian FPÖ (161 observations), the French RN (141), the German AfD (101), the Italian Lega (243), the Spanish Vox (56), and the Swedish SD (142) in Western Europe; and the Croatian HDSSB (61), the Estonian EKRE (98), the Hungarian Fidesz (224) and Jobbik (67), and the Polish PiS (240) and K15 (70) in

Eastern Europe. Hence, we perform individual party analyses for 12 parties, 6 in each region.

Results

The results of the pooled regressions, displayed in Table 9.3, show a partly different effect of our two key independent variables. On the one hand, M1 and M2 reveal that the stronger the preference for a democratic regime, the lower the propensity to vote for a PRRP as compared to other parties, both in Western Europe and, albeit less strongly so, in Eastern Europe. This runs counter to our first theoretical expectation of null effects of SFD on the vote for PRRPs. This means that, although they may not share extreme parties' negative stance on democracy as such, PRRPs' uneasiness with the liberal component of democracies suffices for them to harbor a significantly less prodemocratic electoral basis. This relationship, which is statistically significant in M1 and M2, is masked when abstentionists are lumped into the reference category, as models M3 and M4 show, where preferences over regimes cease to be statistically significant. This makes sense, as preferences for a democratic regime are likely to enhance the levels of factors such as the belief that voting is a duty (from here on, "Duty") or that voting has an inherent or intrinsic value because it contributes to sustaining democracy ("Demo"), and both have been shown to increase the propensity to vote, as the books of André Blais (2000) and Andrés Santana (2014) document, and as Anthony Downs (1957) had hypothesized long ago.

On the other hand, all our models suggest that the effect of SWD is conditional on contextual factors: it runs in different directions in Western and Eastern Europe. In the West, the greater the SWD, the lower the propensity to vote for a PRRP. This is consistent with our second expectation as well as with common assumptions and (possibly because the literature has a certain Western bias) the bulk of the scholarly literature on the topic, as illustrated by the research of Donovan (2019), Lubbers et al. (2002), and Teun Pauwels (2017). However, in the East, the effect works in the opposite direction: the greater the SWD, the *larger* the propensity to vote for a PRRP. This differential eastern effect is consistent with the results shown by Santana et al. (2020) for political mistrust and by Zagórski and Santana (2021) for trust in the national elites and SWD. Probably, this positive effect in Eastern Europe is because some of the most salient populist parties in this region are currently in government (more on this later). Interestingly, while the effects are consistently weaker in the models that include abstainers in the reference category (M3 and M4), such inclusion does not mask the effects of SWD to the point of rendering its effect nonsignificant. This has an implication for scholars studying turnout and the decision to vote, since it suggests that "Duty" and "Demo" (and thence, turnout) are much more conditioned by democratic preferences than by SWD.

As for the controls, unsurprisingly, both in the West and in the East, the more right-wing and the more anti-immigration the individuals are, the more likely they are to vote for a PRRP. The economic situation matters only in Eastern Europe, where its worsening reduces the odds of PRRP voting (possibly because the largest PRRPs in this region are in government). Sex, which has been shown to be a good predictor of PRRP vote, as illustrated by the recent comparative analysis of Eelco Harteveld et al. (2015) and the meta-analysis of Daniel Stockemer et al. (2018), matters only in the West, where women are less likely to vote for PRRPs. This context-dependency of the effect of sex on PRRP voting is consistent with the findings of Tim Immerzeel et al. (2015). Something similar happens with education: high education (i.e., university education) only reduces the prospects of the PRRP vote in Western Europe. Finally, age fails to have significant effects in either region, possibly because the effects of this factor on PRRP vote are mixed and depend on the specific parties under consideration. Naturally, in models M3 and M4, which include abstainers in the reference category, the effect of age becomes positive. This is so because as age increases, abstention falls, as previous research has consistently proved: see, for instance, the chapter by Ruth Dassonneville (2017) in the *Sage Handbook of Electoral Behavior*.

Table 9.3 provides information on the sign and significance of the coefficients but, being the dependent variable binary, the information it conveys on the magnitude of the effects is limited. Figure 9.1 addresses this issue by illustrating the predictive margins of SFD on the propensity to vote for PRRPs instead of other parties (hence, it focuses on models M1 and M2). It shows that holding all the other variables at their means, passing from the minimum to the maximum of SFD reduces the likelihood of voting for a

Table 9.3 Effects of democratic support and satisfaction on the propensity to vote for populist radical right parties in Western and Eastern Europe, 2019 European elections

	Populist vs. Others		Populist vs. All	
	M1: Western	M2: Eastern	M3: Western	M4: Eastern
Support for democracy (0–10)	**-0.83****	**-0.46*****	-0.07	0.22
	(0.34)	**(0.17)**	(0.38)	(0.25)
Satisfaction with democracy (baseline: not at all satisfied)				
Not very satisfied	**-0.63*****	0.24	**-0.50*****	0.28
	(0.14)	(0.41)	**(0.15)**	(0.37)
Fairly satisfied	**-1.35*****	**1.43*****	**-1.03*****	**1.40*****
	(0.29)	**(0.52)**	**(0.30)**	**(0.34)**
Very satisfied	**-1.53*****	**2.69*****	**-1.10****	**2.42*****
	(0.42)	**(0.41)**	**(0.44)**	**(0.22)**
Gender (Female)	**-0.34*****	-0.07	**-0.33*****	-0.12
	(0.12)	(0.16)	**(0.10)**	(0.14)
Age (baseline 18–24)				
25 to 39 years	0.19	0.09	0.25	**0.30****
	(0.24)	(0.13)	(0.16)	**(0.12)**
40 to 54 years	**0.39****	-0.35	**0.42*****	0.24
	(0.20)	(0.25)	**(0.11)**	(0.20)
55 to 64 years	0.33	-0.24	**0.45*****	**0.48*****
	(0.23)	(0.19)	**(0.13)**	**(0.13)**
65 years or more	0.10	-0.18	**0.32****	**0.73****
	(0.26)	(0.24)	**(0.14)**	**(0.29)**
Education (baseline: low)				
Medium	-0.29	-0.19	-0.11	-0.42
	(0.20)	(0.27)	(0.18)	(0.29)
High	**-0.91*****	-0.12	**-0.53****	-0.24
	(0.22)	(0.23)	**(0.21)**	(0.26)
Left-right ideology (0–10)	**4.18*****	**3.85*****	**3.88*****	**3.60*****
	(0.61)	**(0.39)**	**(0.48)**	**(0.22)**

(Continued)

Open immigration policies (0–10)	-0.98***	-0.75**	-0.85***	-0.62*
	(0.32)	(0.37)	(0.26)	(0.35)
The economy worsened (1–5)	0.09	-0.34***	0.07	-0.35***
	(0.06)	**(0.11)**	(0.06)	**(0.09)**
Constant	-2.03***	-1.72***	-3.52***	-3.57***
	(0.52)	(0.61)	(0.52)	(0.51)
Observations	6,053	2,550	7,456	3,650

Source: Own elaboration, EES 2019 data.

Note: Binary logistic regressions with country clusters. Robust standard errors in parentheses. *** $p<0.01$, ** $p<0.05$, * $p<0.1$.

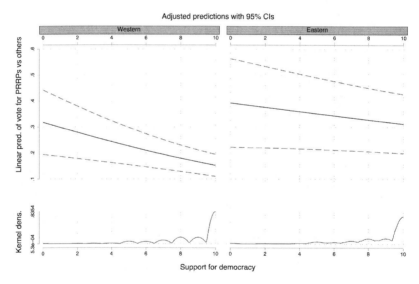

Figure 9.1 Effect of democratic preferences on the probability of voting for a populist radical right in Western and Eastern Europe

Source: Own elaboration, EES 2019 data.

Note: Predictive margins (adjusted predictions) of the probability of voting for a populist radical right party (instead of other parties) as a function of the level of support for democracy, holding all the other variables at their means. Computations are based on models M1 (Western Europe) and M2 (Eastern Europe). The dashed lines are the 95% confidence intervals of the adjusted predictions.

PRRP by 16 percentage points in the West (from 31 to 15%) and by 8 percentage points in the East (from 39 to 31%).

Let us now turn to the effects of SWD. Figure 9.2 shows the predictive margins of SWD on the propensity to vote for PRRPs instead of other parties. It shows that holding all the other variables at their means, passing from the minimum to the maximum level of SWD reduces the likelihood of voting for a PRRP by 21 percentage points in the West (from 30 to 9%) but *increases* it by no less than 55 percentage points in the East (from 19 to 74%). As mentioned before, this large positive effect in the East is most likely driven by the government responsibilities of the two largest PRRPs in the region: the Hungarian Fidesz, and the Polish PiS (we will address this issue later).

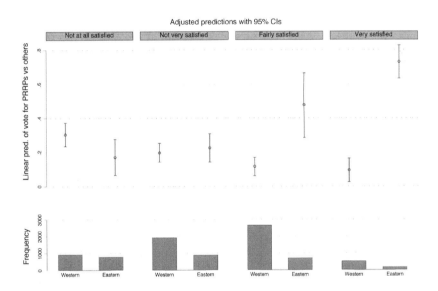

Figure 9.2 Effect of democratic satisfaction on the probability of voting for a populist radical right party in Western and Eastern Europe

Source: Own elaboration, EES 2019 data.

Note: Predictive margins (adjusted predictions) of the probability of voting for a populist radical right party (instead of other parties) as a function of the level of satisfaction with democracy, holding all the other variables at their means. Computations are based on models M1 (Western Europe) and M2 (Eastern Europe). The vertical lines around the point-estimations are the 95% confidence intervals of the adjusted predictions.

In order to focus on the similarities and differences between Western and Eastern countries with regard to the relationship between attitudes toward democracy (SFD and SWD) and the vote for PRRPs, the former analyses have pooled the data for all Western or all Eastern European countries. However, the possibility should not be ruled out that the relationship under study experiences variability within the countries or parties of each region. To address this point, we will test the models for each party separately.

Before doing so, it will be useful to provide information on the democratic profile of the voters of each party. We illustrate this with the aid of Figure 9.3, a two-way scatterplot that represents SWD in the vertical axis and SFD in the horizontal axis. Each party is represented by a point indicating the average position of its voters in each dimension: Western parties are represented by black circles and Eastern ones, by grey triangles. The dashed lines divide the space into four quadrants: the upper left one corresponds

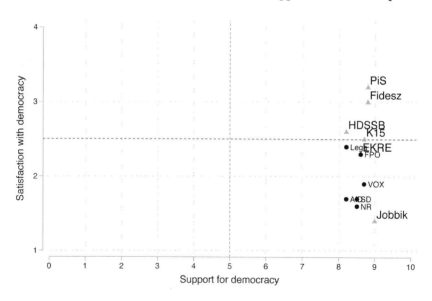

Figure 9.3 Democratic profile of the voters of each populist radical right party.

Source: Own elaboration, EES 2019 data.

Note: Vertical axis: satisfaction with democracy. Horizontal axis: Support for democratic regimes. Black circles: Parties in Western countries. Grey triangles: Parties in Eastern countries.

to nondemocratic satisfied voters; the upper right, to democratic and satisfied voters; the lower left, to nondemocratic unsatisfied voters; and the lower right, to democratic but unsatisfied voters.

Given the high prevalence of democratic support throughout Europe, the two left quadrants in Figure 9.3 are void. Substantively, this means that voters of all these 12 PRRPs are on average supportive of democracy as such, which is consistent with our common understanding of radical as opposed to extreme parties. Naturally, this does not prevent them from being less enthusiastic of the *liberal* component of democracy, but the EES does not have data on this. In any event, it is important to note that their overall prodemocratic outlook does not preclude SFD from influencing the propensity to vote for PRRPs, since the levels of SFD of the other parties could be even higher (in fact, our pooled analyses above suggest that this is precisely the case). Figure 9.3 also reveals that the differences regarding SWD among the voters of the 12 PRRPs are large. Thus, considering the two dimensions jointly, we can distinguish among three broad cases:

- *Democratic and satisfied voters*: this configuration can be found only in Eastern Europe and is characteristic of the voters of Fidesz and PiS, the parties governing in Hungary and Poland, respectively, at the time the 2019 European elections took place.
- *Democratic and neither satisfied nor unsatisfied voters*: this configuration can be found both in Western and Eastern Europe and is characteristic of the voters of PRRPs participating in their countries' governments as junior partners or giving external backing to the governing coalition. In the West, it is found among the voters of the FPÖ in Austria (junior partner of the government coalition at that time) and the Lega in Italy (again, junior partner of the government coalition at that time). In the East, it fits the positions of the voters of EKRE in Estonia (junior partner of the government coalition), HDSSB in Croatia (who had given external backing to the governing coalition), and K15 in Poland (the only PRRP in the opposition within this group).
- *Democratic but unsatisfied voters*: this configuration is typical of the voters of PRRPs in the opposition, whether in the West or in the East. It is prevalent in Western Europe and is found among the voters of four out of the six parties considered for the individual analyses in this region: AfD in Germany (in the opposition, and facing a *cordon sanitaire*), NR in France (same case as AfD), Vox in Spain (in the opposition), and SD in Sweden (also facing a *cordon sanitaire* at the time). It can also be found in Eastern Europe, most pre-

cisely, among the voters of Jobbik (Hungary's largest opposition party at the time the 2019 European elections took place).

To conclude with the empirical analysis, we will discuss the effects of SFD and SWD on the vote for each of the PRRPs in Western and Eastern Europe shown in Figure 9.4 (West) and Figure 9.5 (East). Each figure has six panels, one for each PRRP. The two points in each panel represent the best estimation of the effects of our two key independent variables on the probability of voting for the PRRP (instead of other parties). The horizontal lines around them stand for their 95% confidence intervals. If a confidence interval crosses the vertical lines drawn at the origin (zero) of the horizontal axis of each panel, the effect of the variable is not statistically significant. If they do not cross it and are located to its right, the effect is significantly positive, whereas if they are located to its left, the effect is significantly negative.

As to SFD, only for one party, the Italian Lega, are we able to find a statistically significant effect, which, in line with the previous analyses, is negative. This result is likewise consistent with the analyses of Lega's discourse by Paris Aslanidis (2016) and Gianluca Passarelli (2015), as well as with the empirical findings of Vincenzo Emanuele et al. (2021). Even if the sign of the effect is also negative for most of the remaining parties, with the sole exceptions of Jobbik (slightly positive and nonsignificant) as well as NR and K15 (positive, but close to zero), it fails to attain statistical significance. Our inability to detect statistically significant effects at the individual party level is most likely motivated by the moderate country-level subsamples of citizens who voted for each PRRP in the EES 2019 data. For instance, using this data, a negative effect of SFD does emerge for the Spanish Vox, but it fails to reach statistical significance. In contrast to this, research by Rama et al. (2021, 130–132), employing national survey data with substantially larger samples, proves that the effect is not only negative, but also statistically significant. This, coupled with the fact that most of the effects reported here run in the same direction, leads us to interpret that the effect found in the pooled analyses (SFD hinders PRRP voting) reflects an actually generalizable pattern of most of the parties analyzed in this chapter.

The results concerning SWD are extremely interesting. When we pooled data for all PRRPs in Western Europe, we found that SWD hindered the vote prospects for these parties in the West. Figure 9.4 shows that this was not driven by any specific PRRP in the region: SWD significantly reduces

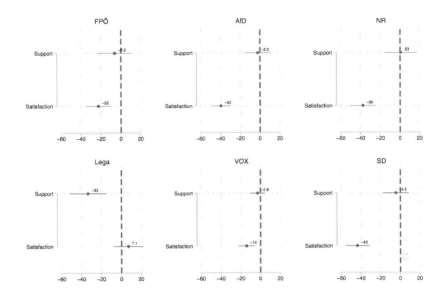

Figure 9.4 Effect of democratic support and satisfaction on the probability of voting for each populist radical right party in Western Europe

Source: Own elaboration, EES 2019 data.

Note: Predictive margins (adjusted predictions) of the probability of voting for each populist radical right party instead of other parties in the country (abstainers treated as missing) as a function of the level of democratic support or democratic satisfaction, holding all the other variables at their means. Computations are based on binary logistic models. The horizontal lines around the point-estimations are the 95% confidence intervals of the adjusted predictions. Effects are statistically significant if they do not cross the vertical dashed lines.

the probability of voting for the Austrian FPÖ, German AfD, French NR, Spanish Vox, and Swedish SD, and it has a positive but statistically nonsignificant effect for the Italian Lega (junior albeit powerful partner of the government coalition at the time).

When we pooled data for all PRRPs in Eastern Europe, we found that SWD significantly and substantially *enhanced* the vote prospects for these parties in the East. We suggested that this was probably related to the government responsibilities of the largest PRRPs in Eastern Europe—the Hungarian Fidesz and the Polish PiS. Figure 9.5 shows that it is precisely for

Fidesz and PiS that SWD significantly and very substantially increases vote prospects. The effect on the Croatian HDSSB (who had given external support to the governing coalition) is also statistically significant and positive, but considerably smaller than the one enjoyed by Fidesz and PiS, who were directly in charge of their governments. SWD has no statistically significant effects on the probability of voting for the Estonian EKRE (junior partner of the government coalition) or the Polish K15 (in the opposition). Finally, the effect was statistically significant and negative for Jobbik, something that

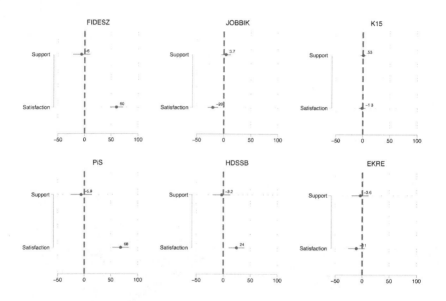

Figure 9.5 Effect of democratic support and satisfaction on the probability of voting for each populist radical right party in Eastern Europe

Source: Own elaboration, EES 2019 data.

Note: Predictive margins (adjusted predictions) of the probability of voting for each populist radical right party instead of other parties in the country (abstainers treated as missing) as a function of the level of democratic support or democratic satisfaction, holding all the other variables at their means. Computations are based on binary logistic models. The horizontal lines around the point-estimations are the 95% confidence intervals of the adjusted predictions. Effects are statistically significant if they do not cross the vertical dashed lines.

should come as no surprise considering that it was Hungary's largest opposition party when the 2019 European elections took place.

The pattern of relationships between SWD and vote for PRRPs found here helps to shed further light on the evidence of increasing satisfaction with decaying democracy uncovered in Chapter 1 by Clari and García-Rivero (those whom the authors dub as "illiberal citizens"). Our results do not mean that many Poles and Hungarians would necessarily feel better in any environment that is less democratic. They may feel better, however, in those scenarios where the democratic backlash is the result of measures undertaken by the party they voted for. Consider PiS voters in Poland and Fidesz voters in Hungary. It would make little sense to expect them to feel better if democratic quality had fallen due to measures undertaken by, say, a communist party. However, they may very well be satisfied in an environment in which cuts to democratic quality are led by "their" parties, for example, by PiS or Fidesz. There are two reasons for this. The first one is causal: they may like the specific type of democratic cuts undertaken by PiS and Fidesz. The second one is correlational: even if they did not value positively the democratic cuts undertaken by PiS or Fidesz, these cuts coincide with other measures these parties enact while being in government, which PiS and Fidesz voters are bound to like, thereby enhancing their SWD. Now, when they hold office, PiS and Fidesz also tend to undermine the liberal component of democracy, curtailing the quality of democracy. Hence, in Poland, many citizens (mostly PiS voters) will have a high SWD precisely when the quality of democracy has declined. Something similar applies to Fidesz voters in Hungary.

Conclusion

This chapter explores the relationship between attitudes toward democracy and the vote for PRRPs in Western and Eastern Europe, paying special attention to the differences and similarities in the two regions. We consider two key dimensions of democratic attitudes: support for democracy (SFD) and satisfaction with the way it works (SWD). The key question we address is thus the following: do SFD and SWD play different roles in the East and the West? To answer this question, we use data from the European Election Study 2019, which include appropriate measures of all our key variables for 16 countries. Our results uncover both similarities and differences in the relationship between democratic attitudes and the vote for PRRPs in the two regions. On the one hand, SFD hinders the vote for PRRPs both in Western and Eastern Europe. On the other, SWD works in different, opposite directions in the West and the East: while it further impairs the vote for these parties in Western Europe, it increases rather than curtails their electoral prospects in Eastern Europe.

Bibliography

Akkerman, A., C. Mudde, and A. Zaslove. 2014. "How Populist Are the People? Measuring Populist Attitudes in Voters." *Comparative Political Studies* 47 (9): 1324–1353. https://doi.org/10.1177/0010414013512600.

Aslanidis, P. 2016. "Is Populism an Ideology? A Refutation and a New Perspective." *Political Studies* 64 (S1): 88–104. https://doi.org/10.1111/1467-9248.12224.

Bartels, L. M. 2017. "The 'Wave' of Right-Wing Populist Sentiment Is a Myth." *Washington Post (Monkey Cage)*, June 21. https://www.washingtonpost.com/news/monkey-cage/wp/2017/06/21/the-wave-of-right-wing-populist-sentiment-is-a-myth/.

Biorcio, R. 2003. "Italian Populism: From Protest to Governing Party." Paper presented at the Conference of the European Consortium for Political Research, Marburg, September.

Blais, A. 2000. *To Vote or Not to Vote: The Merits and Limits of Rational Choice Theory*. Pennsylvania: University of Pittsburgh Press. https://doi.org/10.2307/j.ctt5hjrrf.

Dassonneville, R. 2017. "Age and Voting." In *The SAGE Handbook of Electoral Behaviour*, edited by K. Arzheimer, J. Evans, and M. S. Lewis-Beck, 137–158. London: Sage.

Donovan, T. 2019. "Authoritarian Attitudes and Support for Radical Right Populists." *Journal of Elections, Public Opinion and Parties* 29 (4): 448–464. https://doi.org/10.1080/17457289.2019.1666270.

Downs, A. 1957. *An Economic Theory of Democracy*. New York: Harper.

Emanuele, V., A. Santana, and J. Rama. 2021. "Anatomy of the Italian Populist Breakthrough: A 'Demarcationist' Fuel Driving Lega and Five-Star Movement Electoral Success?." *Contemporary Italian Politics* 14 (1): 49–67. https://doi.org/10.1080/23248823.2021.2000346.

Harteveld, E., W. Van Der Brug, S. Dahlberg, and A. Kokkonen. 2015. "The Gender Gap in Populist Radical-Right Voting: Examining the Demand Side in Western and Eastern Europe." *Patterns of Prejudice* 49 (1–2): 103–134. https://doi.org/10.1080/0031322X.2015.1024399.

Immerzeel, T., H. Coffé, and T. Van der Lippe. 2015. "Explaining the Gender Gap in Radical Right Voting: A Cross-National Investigation in 12 Western European Countries." *Comparative European Politics* 13:263–286. https://doi.org/10.1057/cep.2013.20.

Laclau, E. 2005. *On Populist Reason*. London: Verso.

Lubbers, M., M. Gijsberts, and P. Scheepers. 2002. "Extreme Right-Wing Voting in Western Europe." *European Journal of Political Research* 41 (3): 345–378. https://doi.org/10.1111/1475-6765.00015.

Meijers, M. J., and A. Zaslove. 2021. "Measuring Populism in Political Parties: Appraisal of a New Approach." *Comparative Political Studies* 54 (2): 372–407. https://doi.org/10.1177/0010414020938081.

Mudde, C. 2004. "The Populist Zeitgeist." *Government and Opposition* 39 (4): 541–563. https://doi.org/10.1111/j.1477-7053.2004.00135.x.

Mudde, C. 2007. *Populist Radical Right Parties in Europe*. Cambridge: Cambridge University Press.

Mudde, C., and C. Rovira Kaltwasser. 2017. *Populism: A Very Short Introduction*. Oxford: Oxford University Press.

Norris, P. 2020. "Measuring Populism Worldwide." *Party Politics* 26 (6): 697–717. https://doi.org/10.1177/1354068820927686.

Norris, P., and R. Inglehart. 2019. *Cultural Backlash: Trump, Brexit, and Authoritarian Populism*. Cambridge: Cambridge University Press.

Ostiguy, P., F. Panizza, and B. Moffitt, eds. 2020. *Populism in Global Perspective: A Performative and Discursive Approach*. London: Routledge.

Panizza, F., ed.. 2005. *Populism and the Mirror of Democracy*. London: Verso.

Passarelli, G. 2015. "Populism and the Lega Nord." In *The Oxford Handbook of Italian Politics*, edited by E. Jones and G. Pasquino, 224–239. Oxford: Oxford University Press. https://doi.org/10.1093/oxfordhb/9780199669745.001.0001.

Pauwels, T. 2017. *Populism in Western Europe: Comparing Belgium, Germany and the Netherlands*. London: Routledge.

Pirro, A., and S. Van Kessel. 2017. "United in Opposition? The Populist Radical Right's EU-Pessimism in Times of Crisis." *Journal of European Integration* 39 (4): 405–420. https://doi.org/10.1080/07036337.2017.1281261.

Rama, J., and F. Casal Bértoa. 2020. "Are Anti-Political-Establishment Parties a Peril for European Democracy? A Longitudinal Study from 1950 till 2017." *Representation* 56 (3): 387–410. https://doi.org/10.1080/00344893.2019.1643770.

Rama, J., L. Zanotti, S. J. Turnbull-Dugarte, and A. Santana. 2021. *VOX: The Rise of the Spanish Populist Radical Right*. London: Routledge.

Rooduijn, M. 2018. "What Unites the Voter Bases of Populist Parties? Comparing the Electorates of 15 Populist Parties." *European Political Science Review* 10 (3): 351–368. https://doi.org/10.1017/S1755773917000145.

Rooduijn, M., S. Van Kessel, C. Froio, A. Pirro, S. L. De Lange, D. Halikiopoulou, P. Lewis, C. Mudde, and P. Taggart. 2020. "The PopuList 2.0: An Overview of Populist, Far Right, Far Left and Eurosceptic Parties in Europe". The PopuList, March 3. https://popu-list.org/.

Rosanvallon, P. 2008. *Counter-Democracy: Politics in an Age of Distrust,* translated by A. Goldhammer. Cambridge: Cambridge University Press.

Rovira Kaltwasser, C., and S. M. Van Hauwaert. 2020. "The Populist citizen: Empirical Evidence from Europe and Latin America." *European Political Science Review* 12 (1): 1–18. https://doi.org/10.1017/S1755773919000262.

Rummens, S. 2017. "Populism as a Threat to Liberal Democracy." In *The Oxford Handbook of Populism*, edited by C. Rovira Kaltwasser, P. Taggart, P. Ochoa Espejo, and P. Ostiguy, 554–569. Oxford: Oxford University Press. https://doi.org/10.1093/oxfordhb/9780198803560.001.0001.

Santana, A. 2014. *La decisión de votar. "Homo economicus" versus "homo sociologicus."* Centro de Investigaciones Sociológicas.

Santana, A., P. Zagórski, and J. Rama. 2020. "At Odds with Europe: Explaining Populist Radical Right Voting in Central and Eastern Europe." *East European Politics* 36 (2): 288–309. https://doi.org/10.1080/21599165.2020.1737523.

Schmitt, H., S. B. Hobolt, W. Van Der Brug, and S. A. Popa. 2022. *European Parliament Election Study 2019, Voter Study, ZA7581 Data file Version 2.0.1*. GESIS Data Archive, Cologne. https://doi.org/10.4232/1.13846.

Stockemer, D., T. Lentz, and D. Mayer. 2018. "Individual Predictors of the Radical Right-Wing Vote in Europe: A Meta-Analysis of Articles in Peer-Reviewed Journals (1995–2016)." *Government and Opposition* 53 (3): 569–593. https://doi.org/10.1017/gov.2018.2.

Weyland, K. 2001. "Clarifying a Contested Concept: Populism in the Study of Latin American Politics." *Comparative Politics* 34 (1): 1–22. https://doi.org/10.2307/422412.

Zagórski, P., and A. Santana. 2021. "Exit or Voice: Abstention and Support for Populist Radical Right Parties in Central and Eastern Europe." *Problems of Post-Communism* 68 (4): 264–278. https://doi.org/10.1080/10758216.2021.1903330.

Zanotti, L., and J. Rama. 2021. "Support for Liberal Democracy and Populist Attitudes: A Pilot Survey for Young Educated Citizens." *Political Studies Review* 19 (3): 511–519. https://doi.org/10.1177/1478929920945856.

Chapter 10

Populism in Southern Europe

Belén Fernández-García and Ángel Valencia-Sáiz

Introduction

It has been argued that populism, whether from the left or the right, shares a popular conception of democracy that emphasizes majority rule and popular will (see Chapter 2). In this chapter, we ask whether populist parties in Southern Europe hold a common democratic agenda or, on the contrary, left-right ideological differences tend to prevail.

This chapter is structured as follows. First, we analyze the evolution of the ideological orientation of populism in the region, discussing the main national and regional factors that explain the rise of these actors. We argue that the rise of populism in Southern Europe largely responds to a crisis of representation and dissatisfaction with the functioning of democracy, especially in the context of the Great Recession (Fernández-García and Luengo 2019; Valencia 2021). In this regard, populist parties that emerged during the double economic and political crisis of 2012–2015 in the region did so with ambitious programs of democratic regeneration. However, the European context following the Great Recession, as well as other domestic factors, has favored the rise of the populist radical right in the region, which is more concerned with sociocultural issues such as national identity, security, and immigration.

Second, we compare the proposals and statements of the main populist parties in Southern Europe on democratic matters. The analysis shows that, while there are certain similarities, such as a common agenda of restoring trust in political representatives, the democratic proposals of Southern European populist parties are largely determined by the host ideologies of these actors as well as by contextual factors.

The Rise and Evolution of Populism in Southern Europe

Between 2012 and 2015, Southern European countries simultaneously faced a double economic and political crisis that had both domestic and European components (Della Porta et al. 2017; Hutter et al. 2018). This resulted in the political space revolving around two main conflicts, an economic one, which put austerity policies at the center of the debate, and a political one, centered on political renewal and democratic regeneration (Hutter et al. 2018). In the main countries of the region (namely, Italy, Spain, Greece, and Portugal), austerity policies were agreed and implemented by both center-right and center-left mainstream parties, largely contradicting the latter's electoral programs (e.g., on public social spending). This was interpreted as a betrayal of left-wing voters that, coupled with the lack of a real political and economic alternative and widespread corruption in the region, contributed to a crisis of representation (Della Porta et al. 2017). Moreover, the fact that the response to the economic crisis was led by supranational bodies, considered undemocratic and far removed from the interests of ordinary citizens, as well as by the German government was perceived as a violation of the sovereignty of southern countries. It is not surprising, then, that the driving forces of political change in the region were political parties that combined opposition to austerity policies with political programs of democratic regeneration and against the privileges of the political class.

In Greece, "the populist rupture" was led by SYRIZA (Synaspismos Rizospastikis Aristeras), a coalition of left-wing parties and groups that was founded in 2004 and that managed to establish close links with the citizens' protests against austerity policies (Stavrakakis and Katsambekis 2019). One of the main features of SYRIZA's populist discourse was the identification of the national political elites with the country's international lenders (i.e., IMF, European Commission, and European Central Bank). In the 2015 elections, SYRIZA was the first political force in votes and seats, which allowed it to form a government together with the national-populist ANEL (Anexartitoi Ellinesnosi). This populist alliance—at the time, unique in Europe–was made possible by the restructuring of the Greek political space around support for or opposition to the supranational bodies that had taken control of the economic crisis and their austerity policies.

In Italy, the discontent generated by the economic crisis and political corruption was channeled through the Five Star Movement (Movimento 5 Stelle; M5S). The party emerged with a strong populist discourse, trying to overcome the classic left/right divisions. It also had a marked Eurosceptic and anti-austerity agenda, proposing a left-oriented and protectionist economic program. It also sought to amend the dominant way of doing politics in the country by promoting the direct participation of citizens in the decisions of the "party movement." In the 2013 elections, the M5S burst onto the scene with 25.6% of the vote, becoming the leading electoral force in the country.

In Spain, Podemos emerged from the social movements and citizens' protests that took place in those years and that demanded an end not only to austerity policies but also to the excesses and privileges of the political class. Podemos focused its attacks on national rather than European elites, developing a less Eurosceptic discourse than its Greek and Italian counterparts. The party, following a populist logic, claimed to represent the social majority against the political caste, represented by the country's two major parties, severely affected by corruption scandals (Vallespín and Bascuñán 2018). In the 2015 elections, Podemos became the third party in terms of votes and seats in the country, with 20.7% of the votes.

During this period, although there was no populist rupture equivalent to that of the other countries, Portugal would witness the rise of two political formations that are very opposed to austerity policies, with intense anti-establishment and anti-corruption rhetoric and a strong Eurosceptic discourse: the Left Bloc (Bloco de Esquerda; BE) and the Unitary Democratic Coalition (Coligação Democrática Unitária; CDU).

We can, therefore, say that the political space in Southern Europe was restructured in this electoral stage due to the rise of populist anti-austerity parties and the decline of the center-left mainstream parties, especially in Greece, Italy, and Spain. In this regard, the orientation toward the economic left and progressivism on sociocultural issues, combined with an intense agenda of democratic regeneration and an anti-corruption rhetoric, will be specific features of populism in this region in the context of the Great Recession; this is in contrast to the exclusionary populism dominant in Europe.

This peculiarity of Southern European populism faded in the elections held between 2018 and 2022. This electoral stage is characterized by two fundamental aspects: first, the institutionalization and electoral decline of the populist left and, second, the rise of the populist radical right, except for in Greece. To understand the main changes occurring in this period, it is necessary to consider, in addition to certain national factors, the European context that has taken shape since 2015. In this regard, although it is true that economic recovery was slow in coming in the region, the drastic increase in migratory flows since 2015, especially through the Mediterranean, meant that migration and border security issues were overshadowing economic issues—until the pandemic and the war in Ukraine. Furthermore, between 2015 and 2017, Europe experienced a wave of attacks linked to jihadist terrorism, which favored the radical right-wing discourse linking multiculturalism and immigration with national insecurity.

On the one hand, the rise of the radical right in Italy has been the strongest in the region: first with the electoral resurgence of the transformed Lega in 2018 and, later, with the rise of the Brothers of Italy (Fratelli d'Italia; FDI) in 2022. Under the new leadership of Matteo Salvini, the central defining theme of the Lega will no longer be the autonomy of Northern Italy, but a nativist and protectionist agenda aimed at the entire Italian nation (Albertazzi et al. 2018), thus connecting with the new crisis scenario in Europe. With Salvini's transformation, the Lega increased its support significantly in 2018 (from 4.1% of the vote to 17.4%). The results of the 2018 elections, in which the two populist parties, the Lega and the M5S, reached 50% of the vote, led to the formation of a short-lived populist coalition government. After the fall of the populist government, Conte formed a coalition government with the Democratic Party (Partito Democratico; PD) which fell a year and a half later for lack of parliamentary support. In the midst of the health crisis, a government of national unity led by Mario Draghi was formed, bringing together the country's major parties, with the exception of the Brothers of Italy. The latter political party, representative of Italian post-fascism (Chiaramonte et al. 2018), clearly benefited from being the only party in opposition. The success of the right-wing alliance of the FDI, Lega, and Forza Italia in the 2022 elections as well as the decline of M5S suggest that the populist/anti-populist divide has succumbed to the left-right divide in the country.

The other country where the populist radical right will emerge strongly is Spain. The weakening of the Popular Party (Partido Popular; PP) after Mariano Rajoy's government, with the management of the territorial crisis following the Catalan referendum and the declaration of independence as well as the judicial conviction of the party for illegal financing in 2018 will open the political space on the right to new competitors. In this context, Vox, a party founded by former members of the PP that holds a strong centralizing nationalist agenda, authoritarian and anti-immigration stances, and a very belligerent attitude toward the feminist and LGTBI movements, has burst onto the Spanish political scene. Vox broke through in the 2018 Andalusian elections, and it became the third largest political force (15.1%) in the 2019 general elections, ousting Podemos, which fell to 12.8% of the votes (see Chapter 5). In this regard, although Podemos gains institutional power with its participation in the coalition government with the Spanish Socialist Workers' Party (Partido Socialista Obrero Español; PSOE) from 2019 onwards, it has suffered an intense electoral decline since then, aggravated by the split promoted by one of the founders of Podemos, Íñigo Errejón, in Más País.

Portugal has also witnessed the emergence of a populist radical right party, Chega (CH), a split from the Social Democratic Party (Partido Social Democrata; PSD). In the 2021 presidential and 2022 parliamentary elections, Chega has become the third largest national political force with 11.9% and 7.2% of the vote respectively. The emergence of this political party is related to the electoral decline of the center-right and right-wing parties since 2015, worn out by the management of the economic crisis and the economic moderation of the PSD (Carvalho 2022). Furthermore, although Portugal is a country where immigration is not a relevant issue, in recent years there has been a greater politicization of the country's racial diversity, reflected in the citizen demonstrations against the latent racism in Portuguese society. In response, Chega is mobilizing those who consider that "Portugal is not racist," thus polarizing the racial debate. Ideologically, Chega is an ultra-conservative, nationalist, economically neoliberal party with a strong anti-statist and anti-left discourse—a profile that brings it very close to that of Vox. The party also maintains a populist discourse directed against the national political class and the "globalist elites." As far as the Portuguese radical left is concerned, both the BE and the CDU have suffered a sharp decline (4.4% and

4.3% respectively) because of the recovery of António Costa's Socialist Party (Partido Socialista; PS).

In Greece, the worsening living conditions of the Greek working classes and high youth unemployment, among other factors, undermined SYRIZA's popularity in government, leading to a change in government in favor of New Democracy (Nea Dimokratia; ND). As for the radical right, Greece will follow a different trend from that shown in the other three countries. Golden Dawn (Laikos Syndesmos-Chrysi Avyi; XA) was left out of Parliament after failing to pass the 3% threshold in the 2019 elections. The party is currently considered a criminal organization and is out of the electoral competition after its leadership, including the national leader, was sentenced to prison for possession of weapons and for planning and ordering violent assaults. At present, the only more or less relevant party in this ideological space is the Greek Solution (Elliniki Lisi; EL), which obtained 3.7% of the vote in the last elections and is around 5% in the poll (as of October 2022). This party holds a nationalist, Eurosceptic, conservative, and nativist agenda, and like Golden Dawn, it has a left-wing economic orientation.

Summing up, in this second electoral stage we observe how the populist left parties are losing electoral strength. This may be explained by the participation of these actors in the executive institutions, as well as by the displacement of economic issues from the center of public debate in favor of others more linked to cultural identity, security, and national unity, which are enabling the rise of populist radical right parties in the region, except for Greece. Likewise, the populist/anti-populist—old/new political divide—that formed during the Great Recession appears to be fading in favor of greater left/right ideological polarization.

The democratic agenda of Southern European populist parties

As Canovan argues (2002, 25), populism is characterized by a political appeal to the people as opposed to the elite "and a claim to legitimacy that rests on the democratic ideology of popular sovereignty and majority rule." Thus, it is argued that, at least from the theoretical point of view, populism is essentially democratic, in the sense that it seeks to radicalize the government of the popular majority, although it is ambivalent toward the liberal character of contemporary democracies (e.g., Bonikowski et al. 2019; Canovan 2002; Mudde 2007). This tension toward liberal democracy, explained in detail in Chapter 2 of this book, has to do with the monist ideology of populism by which it appeals to a homogeneous people and an unequivocal popular will against the pluralistic conceptions of liberal democracy that admits and protects the diversity of interests and identities in society.

According to Mudde (2007), populist democracy is based on plebiscitary politics, the personalization of power, and the primacy of the political. That is, direct expression of the popular will through instruments of direct democracy, simplification of the structures of representation around a strong executive elected directly by the people, and the supremacy of the popular will over other institutional centers of power other than the people, including the judiciary. According to this idea of democracy, the general will of the people cannot be limited by anything, not even by constitutional mechanisms that seek to protect minority rights. Populism is thus considered incompatible with the "liberal pillar" of contemporary democracies because it is hostile to those mechanisms that seek to prevent the "tyranny of the majority" (Bonikowski et al. 2019). The latter idea connects with the most common position on the impact of populism in democratic politics: the one that considers that populism leads to authoritarianism (e.g., Halikiopoulou, in Bonikowski et al. 2019) as discussed in Chapter 2.

However, it is also argued that populist actors are not only characterized by their populist agenda but are also, and primarily, defined by their host ideology. In this regard, the left and right ideological orientation of populist parties is expected to determine certain positions toward liberal democracy, such as the protection of minority rights. As Bonikowski (2019) points out, the hostility toward liberal democracy is particularly marked in the politics of the radical right that combine populism, nationalism, and authoritarianism. In this line, the study of Huber and Schimpf (2017) shows that the populist radical right is associated with lower levels of quality of liberal democracy than the populist center and the populist left, especially when it comes to minority rights.

Populist parties in Southern Europe are no different in this respect: left-oriented parties (e.g., Podemos and the BE; the M5S is more ambiguous) have a more inclusive conception of the people, while right-wing parties hold a more exclusionary view of it. In this regard, in addition to defending the usual fundamental rights and freedoms (e.g., freedom of the press, freedom of expression, etc.), both Podemos and the BE seek to protect the rights of migrants, ethnic and racial minorities, women, and LGTBI groups, among others. Together with the M5S, they also hold a broader conception of rights, which is not limited to civil and political ones but also extends to various social, economic, and cultural aspects (e.g., housing, access to drinking water, information, digital rights, etc.). Therefore, when examining the relationship between populism and democracy, populism should not be considered as a phenomenon that is isolated from the ideology that accompanies it.

While these differences between the populist right and the populist left are well known (e.g., Ivaldi et al. 2017), in this section we will focus on the more procedural and institutional aspects of democracy. Figure 10.1 shows the salience of democracy and direct democracy in the 2018–2019 electoral programs of the main populist right and populist left parties in Southern

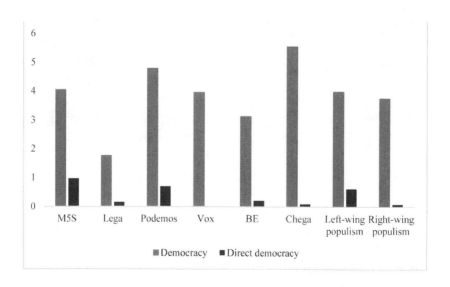

Figure 10.1 Favorable mentions of democracy and direct democracy in the election manifestos of 2018–2019

Source: Data from the Manifesto Project.

Europe.[1] As can be seen, except for the Portuguese parties, left-wing parties (including M5S) pay more attention to democratic issues than the right-wing ones, especially in relation to direct democracy (Brothers of Italy does not include any mention of democracy in their 2018 manifesto). The main measures proposed by the parties in democratic matters are detailed below.

THE DEMOCRATIC AGENDA OF POPULISM IN ITALY

Five Star Movement

The institutional reform proposed by the M5S (2018 election program) aims to "defend the values of the Constitution against the antidemocratic attacks that seek to overthrow it" (2018: 2), such as the processes of globalization in its most neoliberal vision and the antidemocratic practices of the political class. To this end, it advocates direct and participatory democracy; the improvement of the relationship between citizens and institutions; as well as transparency, meritocracy, and the fight against waste, conflicts of interest, and privileges that distance the state from solving society's needs.

Regarding the relationship between representatives and citizens, it proposes that this should be more direct and closer, undertaking various reforms to reestablish citizens' trust in their political representatives. It proposes, for example, limiting parliamentary salaries and reimbursements, as well as returning to the pension system that applies to ordinary citizens; restricting parliamentarians' mandates to two terms to avoid the professionalization of politics; and amending parliamentary rules so that parliamentary groups can be formed only by those political forces that have actually stood for election, thus putting an end to "shirt-switching" in Parliament and "betrayals" of the will of the voters. Furthermore, to improve the representativeness of Parliament, the M5S proposes lowering the voting age to 16, as well as the age for running for the Senate (in this case, it does not specify at what age).

In relation to the electoral system, the M5S denounces the complicity of the other political forces in the approval of "illegitimate electoral sys-

---

[1] Greece is not included because we seek to compare the positions of populist left and populist right in each country. In this regard, the Greek Solution is not included in the Manifesto Project yet. In the case of Portugal, we have selected the Left Bloc, a political force more assimilable to contemporary populist left than the Unitary Democratic Coalition, more linked to the traditional left.

tems" that have undermined the representativeness and political legitimacy of the Parliament. It proposes an electoral reform, the "Democratellum", to improve the representativeness of the system and to ensure the governability of the country by discouraging the fragmentation of political forces and the creation of fictitious coalitions that are formed for purely electoral purposes. The reform would set up a proportional system with medium-sized constituencies and a variable electoral threshold of around 5%. It also promises to reduce the size of the Parliament. This measure was promoted by the Conte government and finally approved in a popular referendum in 2020 with almost 70% of the votes. A drastic reduction in the size of both chambers was undertaken, from 630 to 400 seats in the Chamber of Deputies and from 315 to 200 elected seats in the Senate.

As far as the direct expression of popular will is concerned, the M5S is undoubtedly the party in the region that most clearly defends direct democracy and plebiscitary politics ("We believe in direct democracy!") (2018, 3). On the one hand, the party seeks to strengthen the "abrogative referendum" already provided for in Article 75 of the Constitution by eliminating the quorum currently required, which has been abused by political parties to ensure "most of the referendums of the last twenty years fail" (2018, 6). On the other hand, the party proposes the introduction of a "revolutionary" direct democracy tool, the "proactive referendum," whereby popular legislative initiatives supported by at least 500,000 voters would be submitted to a popular referendum if, within 18 months, the Parliament has not approved them or has done so with purely formal changes. This proposal, in the form of a constitutional bill, was passed by the lower house in February 2019 but was stopped when it reached the Senate. These measures seek to put an end to "the arrogance of the political class" that governs behind the backs of the people. The M5S illustrates this idea with the European integration, whereby quotas of sovereignty have been gradually ceded to the European institutions without considering the opinion of Italian citizens (according to the party). It, therefore, calls for any amendments to the treaties governing Italian participation in the EU to be submitted to a mandatory popular referendum. Finally, information and communication technologies also play a fundamental role in its model of direct democracy. In this regard, the party sets itself as an example of how to apply online direct democracy to elaborate its political program through the Rousseau platform.

In addition to reinforcing the plebiscitary elements of Italian democracy, the M5S also seeks to revolutionize the way politics is exercised, bringing decision-making closer to the citizenry. In this sense, it calls for the establishment of mechanisms for citizen control in the implementation of public policies; systems that encourage dialogue with citizens and the exchange of options to reach the best decisions; as well as decentralization in favor of the regions and local authorities as a way of bringing the adoption and implementation of public policies closer to the citizens.

In relation to the liberal or constitutional pillar, the M5S denounces the unequal access to justice in Italy. It criticizes that the Italian parties have never done anything because it benefits them that justice should be "weak with the strong and strong with the weak" (2018, 338). To reverse this situation, the party proposes strengthening economic and human resources to speed up judicial processes as well as lowering costs to make justice more accessible. Furthermore, to make equality before the law effective, it calls for the intervention of those parliamentary prerogatives that prevent political representatives from being subject to the same rules and processes as ordinary citizens. The party also called for no contamination of any kind between justice and politics, demanding the incompatibility of holding political office and returning to the judiciary.

The party also proposes the establishment of parliamentary oversight mechanisms for the government's implementation of public policies through the creation of a Parliamentary Oversight Committee. It also supports the work of independent administrative authorities such as the Antitrust Agency, the Energy Authority, the Anti-Corruption Authority, and the like in the appointment of which citizens or civic associations should be involved. However, the most important aspect of the M5S program in this regard is that of transparency as a way of controlling executive power. In this sense, one of the main objectives of the M5S program is the achievement of a transparent public sector at the service of the citizen, where meritocracy and citizen participation and scrutiny prevail, avoiding the interference of partisan interests, conflicts of interest, corruption, and arbitrariness of the public authorities.

Lega

The Lega's 2018 program for institutional reform begins by noting that "Democracy means government by the people. Its essence consists in the participation of the people in the government of the community" (2018, 20). The Italian party's reform, therefore, originates from a popular conception of democracy, the essence of which is clearly sculpted by Article 1 of the Italian Constitution according to Lega, which states, "Sovereignty belongs to the people, who exercise it in the forms and within the limits of the Constitution."

According to the party, the sovereignty of the people is threatened by the technocratic model of Europe that often imposes its decisions on the member states; by international institutions such as the UN and the WTO; by "the gigantic sovereign wealth funds that manipulate and affect national economies"; and by "the tendency of judges to take the place of the legislator" (2018, 20). To combat these threats, the party proposes a new balance of power and a strengthening of direct democracy, conceived as a corrective to possible distortions of representative democracy. Among these distortions, the constant parliamentary transformations that the M5S also denounces stand out. In this sense, the party proposes a constitutional reform that would introduce a "mandate obligation" to avoid such "betrayals" of the electorate.

It also seeks to strengthen the more plebiscitary character of Italian democracy by facilitating the holding of popular referendums (e.g., by eliminating the quorum requirement for referendums) and by forcing the Parliament to pronounce on popular initiative bills. The power of the people would also be strengthened by the direct election of the new head of the executive. In this sense, the Lega calls for the existence of "a strong chief executive" (2018, 21) that is directly elected by the people, "without having to pass through the confidence of the parliamentary chambers." The President of the Republic would combine the current powers of the Prime Minister and the President of the Republic, except for the presidency of the Superior Council of the Judiciary.

In relation to the powers of Parliament, the Lega maintains a somewhat negative position. In addition to reducing its size (it proposes the same reduction as the M5S), it also limits the Parliament's powers to legislative production, for example, when it says that "Parliament should make laws, if possible few, simple and clear" (2018, 21), questioning its function of control over the government (right after that, it points out that the head of the executive must not depend on the confidence of Parliament). It is also highly critical of the activity of the judiciary, identified, as mentioned above, as one of the threats to Italian democracy. In particular, the Lega criticizes judges for overstepping their functions, who "must apply the law, not create it" (2018, 21). In this sense, it proposes sanctioning judges who interpret laws in a manner contrary to that of the legislator.

Finally, as part of this new balance of powers, the Lega proposes to boost decentralization in favor of regions and municipalities. In this respect, it denounces how the space of the institutions closest to the territories has been restricted—for example, by limiting their funding and weakening the role of the regions. This is a negation of the principle of subsidiarity, which for the Lega is a necessary complement to popular sovereignty.

The Lega's program is more concise when it comes to the liberal or constitutional pillar of democracy. It defends, for example, the principle of equality before the law; however, it does so keeping in mind the party's need to protect its nativist agenda. In particular, the party points out that religious freedom is conditional on respect for the law, which must be equal for all citizens, with special mention of the Muslim population (it calls for "strict observance and application of the law to Muslims") (2018, 8). It also demands the independence and impartiality of the judiciary with respect to political interests, for example, when it proposes the incompatibility between remaining in the judiciary and holding political office. It proposes to change the way in which the Superior Council of the Judiciary is elected (but it is not specified in what sense) as well as to fix its tasks "in an imperative way" to prevent this body from exceeding its functions in addition to the creation of an external disciplinary commission to control the activity of judges. This hostility toward the judiciary has been reaffirmed with the Lega's participation in the Italian government. Salvini has, on numerous occasions, attacked the impartiality of judges who have overturned some of his policies on migration and security (e.g., red zones in cities).

The democratic agenda of populism in Spain

Podemos

Podemos' democratic program (2019 election program) begins by denouncing the collusion of the major economic powers with the main democratic institutions as well as with the media and political parties. It points out that the change people want to see is viable only if "we get rid of the corrupt and their control over public institutions" who capture the institutions "so that they can decide in favor of a few and against the majority" (2019, 47). Based on this populist diagnosis, the party proposes several measures aimed at empowering the people such as by making democratic institutions more representative and the management of public affairs more transparent and democratic.

On the one hand, the party proposes to improve the representativeness of the political system by lowering the voting age to 16; increasing the proportionality of the electoral system by changing the method of allocating seats; and reforming electoral regulations to facilitate voting abroad and to create a constituency for Spanish emigrants. It also proposes to end the "revolving doors" of political office, which leads politicians "to act against the people and in favour of the few" (2019, 50); to eliminate "the privileges of elected officials" (e.g., reduction of salaries and pensions) (2019, 52); to democratize electoral campaigns, establishing a minimum number of electoral debates per elections; and to democratize political parties, making primary elections mandatory for party executive positions as well as gender parity on electoral lists. To prevent the influence of financial interests on political representatives, it also wants to prohibit banks from financing the election campaigns of political parties.

On the other hand, the party advocates strengthening the plebiscitary elements of Spanish democracy, facilitating the presentation of popular initiatives; normalizing popular consultations on issues of national importance (e.g., military operations); subjecting the adoption of international treaties to parliamentary control and binding referendum; and eliminating the need for government authorization for local referendums. Podemos is the only party among those analyzed that proposes to introduce the power of citizens' revocation in the political system. Specifically, it proposes that citizens can initiate a recall process when 15% of the electoral roll considers that "the government has turned its back on it" (2019, 54), culminating in the holding of a referendum in which a binding decision is taken on whether the president of the government should remain in office and whether new elections need to be called. It is noteworthy, however, that these measures are absent from its agenda as a governing party.

Podemos also proposes opening new participatory spaces for citizen deliberation—for example, in the elaboration, management, and control of public policies—as well as promoting participatory budgets and favoring participation in legislative processes in the Parliament. Finally, Podemos' program seeks to democratize different processes and institutions such as international governance, with the creation of a democratically elected UN Parliamentary Assembly, the international financial system, public service broadcasting, and university governance.

The rest of the democratic measures are aimed at strengthening the liberal and constitutional pillar of Spanish democracy. A large part of the program in this area seeks to reduce political corruption (e.g., the creation of a National Anti-Corruption Plan), prevent the interference of economic powers in democratic institutions, and guarantee the independence of certain institutions and actors as mechanisms to strengthen democracy. For example, it proposes various transparency measures, such as regulating the activity of lobbies by making public the meetings they hold with political representatives or public administration officials. The party also proposes to guarantee the independence of the media from economic powers by prohibiting banks and other funds from owning media outlets.

The party also promises to reinforce the principle of equality before the law, abolishing "privileged jurisdiction" [*aforamientos*] of elected officials, the proliferation of which did not so much seek to protect public representatives from reprisals and threats from the most powerful but rather to offer judicial privileges to the political class, according to the party. It also calls for the abolition of the absence of accountability of the King, as well as to "the archaic formula" of administering justice "in the name of the King," when "justice in fact emanates from the people" (2019, 52). The party also promises to improve the quality and access to justice by reforming, for example, the law on court fees.

Podemos also proposes to strengthen the independence of the judiciary by reforming the system of election of its governing body, namely, the

General Council of the Judiciary. To this end, it proposes a system of direct election by citizens, but until this measure is adopted, which requires constitutional reform, the party proposes to improve the system of parliamentary elections by increasing the plurality and transparency of the election of this body, including the possibility of proposals endorsed by citizens. The promise to strengthen plurality clashes with the proposal made by the government of which Podemos forms part. Faced with the blockade in the renewal of the judicial body, the government proposed lowering the majorities required for the appointment of the council members, which was criticized by the European Commission and judges' organizations. The proposal was finally withdrawn by the Ministry of Justice (led by the PSOE), a decision that was criticized by Podemos. In relation to the Constitutional Court, Podemos calls for depoliticizing this institution by "establishing a system of appointments in which consensus and not party quotas prevail" but does not specify based on what mechanisms.

Finally, Podemos proposes working on the country's democratic memory in accordance with the principles of human rights, making reparations to the victims of Francoism, judging the crimes against humanity of fascism, and withdrawing decorations from the torturers of Francoism. It also seeks to place Spain at the forefront of human rights protection in the world.

Vox

The Vox electoral program for the 2019 elections is headed by the section "Spain, unity and sovereignty," which establishes national unity as the supreme value and the main purpose of the political organization. The party criticizes the design of the Spanish political system for allowing the government to depend on political forces whose "explicit purpose is to liquidate national unity" (2019, 2). In this sense, among the first proposals is the outlawing of parties, associations, or NGOs "that pursue the destruction of the territorial unity of the nation and its sovereignty" (2019, 2). This measure shows that for Vox, the principle of political pluralism is subordinate to the preservation of national unity and that its model of democracy revolves around this principle.

Vox's democratic agenda is rather short and focused on the lack of representativeness of the Spanish political system. In this sense, the party proposes to establish a direct link between the representatives and the represented, based on "a truly representative unicameral Parliament" (2019, 5) (it proposes to eliminate the Senate, the country's chamber of territorial representation). To this end, it wants to reform the electoral system, which it blames "for the huge disconnection between citizens and parliament" (2019, 5). It proposes that part of the deputies should be elected in a single national district so that the vote of all Spaniards is worth the same. This measure can be interpreted in the case of Vox as an attempt to reduce the weight of peripheral nationalist parties in the Congress of Deputies by reducing provincial representation in that institution. As the party points out, this reform would also serve to make MPs "answer to the voters and not so much to the political parties." An anti-party rhetoric is thus identified, denouncing in this sense how "the constitutional state has degenerated into a state of parties that defend their own interests more than those of all Spaniards" (2019, 26). This kind of rhetoric expresses the antiestablishment character of the organization, but the title that heads this section, "Spain above the parties," also warns of the party's anti-pluralism, positioning the Spanish nation above the diversity of interests and political identities in the country. In this regard, the party proposes to end public subsidies to political parties and their foundations, trade unions, employers' organizations, and other "ideological proselytizing" organizations. To improve the representativeness of the system, it also proposes to strengthen the rules on incompatibilities of politicians after leaving political office and the control over politicians during their mandates.

It is also noteworthy that at no point does Vox's program appeal to popular sovereignty or people's power (it only refers to national sovereignty). Nor does it propose to improve the more participatory or plebiscitary aspect of Spanish democracy. The remaining measures refer to the liberal or constitutional pillar of democracy. In particular, the independence of the judiciary, for which it calls for the introduction of the necessary human and material resources as well as effective procedures. A reform of the method of appointing the members of the Supreme Court and the General Council of the Judiciary is also proposed so that they would be elected by and from among judges. Regarding the Constitutional Court, the party proposes to abolish it, with the Supreme Court taking over its functions. It also links the territorial model of the state with the inequality of rights and freedoms of Spaniards, proposing to transform it "into a unitary state based on the rule of law that promotes equality and solidarity instead of privileges and division" (2019, 3).

Finally, in contrast to Podemos, Vox proposes the immediate repeal of the Law of Historical Memory. First, it denies the legitimacy of Parliament "to define our past" and, second, it proposes paying joint tribute "to all those who, from different historical perspectives, fought for Spain" (2019, 4). That is, it also proposes to pay homage to those who fought on the side that later installed a dictatorial regime—a measure that has been codified as antidemocratic by the Manifesto Project.

The democratic agenda of populism in Portugal

Left Bloc

The Left Bloc's program (2019 election program) on democratic reform begins by commemorating the popular struggles that overthrew the fascist dictatorship of the Estado Novo and paved the way for the construction of a democratic country. The party points out that the current role of the left is the democratization of the Portuguese political system and the qualification of the tools for citizen participation. Toward this, it proposes to improve the representativeness of the system by making it easier for Portuguese citizens abroad to exercise their right to vote and by reducing the voting age to 16; in addition, it opposes any possible reforms aimed at reducing the representativeness and proportionality of the electoral system. It also wants to improve citizens' representation by establishing a regime of exclusivity for elected officials and banning "revolving doors." The party also proposes several measures to increase political participation and deepen the more plebiscitary aspects of Portuguese democracy, such as reducing the number of signatures required to present popular legislative initiatives and citizens' initiatives for referendums. The Bloc also calls for participatory processes to involve citizens in the formulation and control of public policies as well as to democratize the regional level. This party considers democracy as a cross-cutting value that should guide the management of different public affairs, such as public education as well as access to scientific knowledge, the media, and new information and communication technologies. It also proposes democratizing the economy and access to energy. In this regard, the socialist orientation of the Bloc is highly evident in its concept of "sovereign democracy," defended against the big economic interests and the neoliberal dynamics of the European Union that limit Portugal's economic sovereignty.

In relation to the liberal or constitutional pillar of democracy, the party criticizes that the current system makes "justice a good of access reserved for those who have the means to pay" (2019, 111), thus undermining the principle of equality before the law. To correct this situation, it proposes the creation of a national justice service whose main principles will be free access and territorial proximity. The party also promises to democratize the administration of justice by expanding citizen participation through popular juries and calling for democratic scrutiny of the application of justice—although it does not specify what this would consist of. The party also wants to strengthen the rule of law in the country, proposing various measures to fight corruption as well as to establish a policy of absolute transparency whereby all assets and income of political representatives and high-ranking state officials are monitored. It also links the formation of absolute majorities in Parliament with corruption, opacity, abuse of power, and other practices that "atrophy democracy" (2019, 125).

Finally, the Left Bloc is the party with the strongest emphasis on media independence. The party dissociates itself from populism by pointing out that populists "organize themselves in the shadow of disinformation campaigns" (2019, 114). In the face of this threat, the Bloc points out that the existence of "serious and rigorous journalism is fundamental to safeguarding democracy itself," advocating state intervention to ensure the sustainability and the independence of the media from political and economic powers.

Chega

In contrast to the Bloc's view of the Portuguese democratic transition, Chega denounces (2019 election program) that the country lives in a limited democracy "as it is not based on a freely voted constitution" (2019, 7). In this regard, the party identifies a vice of origin in Portugal's democracy whereby the "left establishment" controlled the constituent process. Therefore, one of the Chega's main measures is the adoption of an "ideologically neutral constitution" that allows any government to exercise the power granted to it in free and democratic elections. Chega's democratic reform measures are also aimed at reducing the size of institutions and limiting the scope for state intervention in line with his neoliberal orientation. The party's guiding principles in this area are "representative democracy, the primacy of the rule of law, the limitation of state intervention and the separation of powers" (2019, 4).

In relation to the popular pillar of democracy, the party proposes several measures to improve the representativeness of the system, such as limiting the terms of office of representatives to two consecutive terms and abolishing any privileges of the political class. The party also proposes reforming the electoral system to mitigate the effect of the "useful vote" thereby allowing for the parliamentary representation of minor parties and reducing the "wasted votes" produced by the D'Hondt method. The party wants to reduce the number of constituencies from 22 to 14, as well as the number of MPs to a total of 100. It also proposes the extension of the legislature and municipal mandates to five years, as well as the presidentialization of the regime, with the powers currently attributed to the prime minister being accumulated in the figure of the "President of the Republic" (this measure disappears, however, in the 2022 electoral program).

As for popular sovereignty, Chega makes a single reference to the expression of popular will in the context of the constitutional reform it wants to carry out. The party considers that the current constitution was the result of the imposition of left-wing parties in collusion with the military and "not a genuine product of the sovereign will of the people," and therefore calls for a new constitutional text to be approved by popular referendum. We are therefore dealing with an organization that expressly defends representative democracy and in which the ideas of participatory and plebiscitary democracy are absent. In this sense, the concept of sovereignty is conceived in Chega's program in its national, not popular, conception, claiming it above all in the face of various external threats (e.g., globalization).

Finally, Chega develops numerous measures and appeals for the rule of law against arbitrariness and abuse of power. For this party, the role of the state is to guarantee the equal rights and duties of citizens and not to defend the interests and privileges of corporations. In this sense, it shows strong hostility toward civil society organizations, opposing state subsidies to foundations, associations, trade unions, and "ideological proselytizing" organizations. It also points out that the state should be subject to the same laws and judicial procedures as citizens and promises to make justice more accessible to citizens, lowering judicial costs, decentralizing the judicial map, and improving the functioning of the system. In relation to the judiciary, the party proposes a reform of the judicial system to guarantee the true independence of judges from political power (e.g., that members of the Supreme Court be elected on merit by and from among those who are part of the judicial community).

Conclusion

This chapter seeks to answer whether populist parties in Southern Europe maintain a common democratic reform agenda or not. The analysis shows that, while there are certain commonalities, the democratic agendas of Southern European populist parties are largely determined by the host ideologies of these actors as well as by national contextual factors.

There is, in general, a common agenda that seeks to reestablish trust in political representatives, highlighting the antiestablishment character shared by these actors. All parties denounce the lack of representativeness of the political systems in their countries due to the institutional design (e.g., electoral system) but, above all, to the abuses of the political class (professionalization of politics, privileges, corruption, etc.). They propose abolishing the procedural and economic privileges of the political class, reforming electoral systems to make them more proportional and representative, and, in some cases, reducing the size of legislative institutions (Lega, M5S, and Chega). However, there are also national particularities, such as the "mandate obligation" proposed by the Lega and M5S in the face of the continuous transformations of Italian parliamentary groups.

It is also common for populist actors to denounce the lack of independence of the judiciary and obstacles to access to justice. Except for the Bloc and the M5S, populist parties in Southern Europe propose to modify the appointment systems of the main judicial bodies, although they differ in the methods: while Podemos proposes that they be elected by popular vote, the right-wing parties propose that they be elected by and among judges (except Lega, which does not specify it). Even though all populist actors advocate judicial independence, we have seen how some who have come to power have questioned the legitimacy of judges (e.g., the Lega) or proposed methods that are not very pluralistic for the election of judicial bodies (e.g., Podemos). In this regard, questioning the independence of the judiciary can be the preliminary step to undermine its legitimacy once in government.

In relation to direct democracy, Italian parties are the only ones that speak openly in favor of this model of democracy, conceived as a corrective to the distortions produced by representative democracy, with the M5S being the party that most clearly defends it. Podemos and the BE also propose to extend the use of different tools of direct democracy (e.g., reducing the number of signatures needed to present popular initiatives or making popular consultations or referendums compulsory for certain topics). The Lega is the exception among the radical right parties analyzed, coming closer to the proposals of left-wing parties. In this sense, neither Vox nor Chega propose to intensify the plebiscitary character of democracy.

The left-wing parties and the M5S, for their part, go beyond this plebiscitary vision of democracy, proposing various mechanisms to ensure citizens' participation in decision-making and in the control of public policies, as well as the democratization of the management of different public affairs. This greater emphasis on participatory democracy is not only due to the ideological orientation of these organizations to the new left, which emphasizes grassroots democracy and new channels of direct participation and deliberation, but also because of the context in which these parties emerged of widespread discontent toward the functioning of democracy, expressed in various forms of protests and social mobilization. Finally, only Lega and Chega (although in the latter it disappears from the 2022 election program) propose the presidentialization of the political systems of their countries, so that the President of the Republic, who assumes the functions of the Prime Minister, is directly elected by the citizens.

By country, Italian populist parties are undoubtedly the ones that most converge on democratic issues, which explains the government agreement they reached after the 2018 elections. Both parties seek to reinforce the plebiscitary character of Italian democracy and defend a popular conception of democracy. They share many appeals against the political class and propose, in both cases, a drastic reduction in the size of the Italian Parliament. They also advocate decentralization as a way of bringing institutions closer to citizens and encouraging participation. The main differences are the M5S's defense of a truly participatory democracy, with a strong electronic component and an emphasis on transparency as a guiding principle in politics and administrative actions. In the case of the Lega, it proposes a rebalancing of the three branches of government, with the power of the executive taking precedence over the rest. Thereby, the Lega is the party that comes closest to the ideal of populist democracy referred to by Mudde (2007) in the sense that it combines plebiscitary politics, personalization of politics through a strong chief executive who does not depend on Parliament, and strong criticism of the judiciary for contradicting the will of democratically elected institutions. The democratic agenda of Italian populist parties can be explained by some contextual factors, such as a greater tradition of direct democracy, the normalization of populism after years in the institutions, as well as a deep distrust of Italians toward the political class.

By contrast, the democratic programs of populist left and populist right parties in Spain and Portugal differ greatly, as do their views on their countries' authoritarian past and democratic transition. This, together with strong ideological differences in the sociocultural and economic dimensions, makes any possibility of cooperation in the institutions unfeasible. They only agree on the need to enhance the representativeness of the system, improve the independence of the judiciary, and facilitate citizens' access to justice, but they hold very different conceptions of democracy. While Podemos and the BE hold a popular conception of democracy, proposing to strengthen those mechanisms that allow the direct expression of the popular will, Chega defends a more conservative vision of democracy in its representative version, while Vox, subordinates it to national unity. These two parties also display an anti-pluralist conception of democracy when they propose outlawing or withdrawing public support for certain organizations on ideological grounds. The fact that neither Chega nor Vox appeals to popular sovereignty makes us question the role that populism plays in these parties. The results suggest, in line with other research, that populism is used more as a discursive framework at the service of their nationalist agendas and as a strategy to break into politics than as an ideological principle guiding their programs (Fernández-García and Valencia 2022).

To recapitulate, in this chapter, we have shown that populist parties in Southern Europe coincide in their promises to improve the representativeness of the system but differ in their conceptions of democracy. While left-wing parties (including the M5S) defend participatory democracy and promise to reinforce its plebiscitary character (especially M5S and Podemos, but also the Left Bloc), radical right parties in Spain and Portugal maintain a more representative vision of democracy, based on national sovereignty and professing a certain hostility toward pluralism and civil society. The Lega is the political party that comes closest to the ideal of populist democracy, combining plebiscitary politics, personalization of politics, and hostility toward the judiciary.

Bibliography

Albertazzi, D., A. Giovannini, and A. Seddone. 2018. "No Regionalism Please, We Are Leghisti!' The Transformation of the Italian Lega Nord under the Leadership of Matteo Salvini." *Regional & Federal Studies* 28 (5): 645–671. https://doi.org/10.1080/13597566.2018.1512977.

Bonikowski, B., et al. 2019. "Populism and Nationalism in a Comparative Perspective: A Scholarly Exchange." *Nations and Nationalism* 25 (1): 58–81. https://doi.org/10.1111/nana.12480.

Canovan, M. 2002. "Taking Politics to the People: Populism as the Ideology of Democracy." In *Democracies and the Populist Challenge*, edited by Y. Mény and Y. Surel, 25–44. Basingstoke: Palgrave Macmillan.

Huber, R. A., and Schimpf, C. H. 2017. "On the Distinct Effects of Left-Wing and Right-Wing Populism on Democratic Quality." *Politics and Governance* 5 (4): 146–165. https://doi.org/10.17645/pag.v5i4.919.

Hutter, S., H. Kriesi, and G. Vidal. 2018. "Old versus New Politics: The Political spaces in Southern Europe in Times of Crises." *Party Politics* 24 (1): 10–22. https://doi.org/10.1177/1354068817694503.

Carvalho, J. 2022. "Understanding the Emergence of Extreme Right Parties in Portugal in the Late 2010s." *Parliamentary Affairs*, gsac001. https://doi.org/10.1093/pa/gsac001.

Chiaramonte, A. et al. 2018. "Populist Success in a Hung Parliament: The 2018 General Election in Italy." *South European Society and Politics* 23 (4): 479–501. https://doi.org/10.1080/13608746.2018.1506513.

Della Porta, D. et al. 2017. *Movement Parties against Austerity*. Cambridge: Polity Press, 2017.

Fernández-García, B., and O. Luengo. 2019. "Electoral Scenarios of Success for Anti-Establishment Political Parties in Western Europe: A Fuzzy-Set Qualitative Comparative Analysis." *Journal of Contemporary European Studies* 27 (1): 77–95.

Fernández-García, B., and A. Valencia-Sáiz. 2022. "Populismo y nacionalismo en el contexto de las elecciones catalanas de 2021: el populismo al servicio de agendas nacionalistas enfrentadas." *Revista Española de Ciencia Política* 59:13–42. https://doi.org/10.21308/recp.59.01.

Ivaldi, G., M. E. Lanzone, and D. Woods. 2017. "Varieties of Populism across a Left-Right Spectrum: The Case of the Front National, the Northern League, Podemos and Five Star Movement." *Swiss Political Science Review* 23 (4): 354–376 https://doi.org/10.1111/spsr.12278.

Mudde, C. 2007. *Populist Radical Right Parties in Europe*. Cambridge: Cambridge University Press.

Stavrakakis, Y., and G. Katsambekis. 2019. "The Populism/Anti-Populism Frontier and its Mediation in Crisis-Ridden Greece: From Discursive Divide to Emerging Cleavage?." *European Political Science* 18:37–52. https://doi.org/10.1057/s41304-017-0138-3.

Valencia-Sáiz, A. 2021. "Estado y democracia en el siglo XXI: ¿Más Estado frente a las democracias fatigadas y en cuarentena?." In *Tras las huellas de Leviatán*, edited by José M. Canales Aliende, Santiago Delgado Fernández and Adela Romero Tarín, 1–18. Granada: Editorial Comares.

Vallespín, F., and M. Bascuñán. 2018. *Populismos*, Madrid: Alianza Editorial.

CHAPTER 11

Nordic Populism: Conjoining Ethno-Nationalism and Welfare Chauvinism

Eirikur Bergmann

Introduction

Populist parties in the Nordic countries part to a significant degree from most nativist populists in Western Europe by not being clearly positioned on the right-wing of the socioeconomic spectrum. Rather than being established around traditional right-wing neoliberal rhetoric, they rose on a new sociocultural master frame of combining ethno-nationalism and anti-elite populism with welfare chauvinism.

The Nordic populists skillfully played on a nostalgic wish of going back to a simpler and happier time. The Sweden Democrats, for example, reached real tactical breakthrough by shrewdly adopting the traditional social democratic notion of the People's Home (*Folkehemmed*). This was a classical discursive creation of a Golden Age when the close connection between the ethnic people, democracy, and welfare are emphasized in an exclusionary understanding of the nation abandoning their long-asserted promise of the People's Home, the all-embracing welfare society.

In this chapter, I will explore how the Nordic populist parties presented immigration as a threat to the promise of universal welfare for the native population. Rather than primarily referring to the social-economic situation of the ordinary people they, instead, adopted a new populist winning formula of combining socioeconomic left-wing views with hard-core right-wing conservative sociocultural ideas.

Before delving into Nordic nativist populism more closely, it is first necessary to briefly frame how I understand the phenomena here under examination. In previous research, I have detected three distinctive waves of Neo-Nationalism in the postwar era, each rising in the wake of crisis (Bergmann 2020). On the canopy of these waves, nativist populists have since moved from the fringes and to the mainstream. All these waves were ignited by crises. The first wave rose in Western Europe in the wake of the oil crisis in the early 1970s. The second began after the fall of the Berlin Wall, first mainly in opposition to migrants from Eastern Europe from seeking work in the West. The third wave was triggered by the financial crisis of 2008 and heightened by the refugee crisis of 2015 in the wake of the Syrian War. By the time the COVID-19 Crisis hit in 2020, this prolonged neo-nationalist surge had, for example, brought populists to power in all the four largest democracies in the world, namely, the United States, Brazil, India, and Indonesia.

In my previous research, I have also identified a threefold claim that nativist populists put forth in their support of the people: First, they tend to discursively create an external threat to the nation. Second, they accuse the domestic elite of betraying the people, often even of siding with the external aggressors. Third, they position themselves as the true defenders of the "pure people" they vow to protect, against both the elite and these malignant outsiders, that is, against those that they themselves have discursively created. Now I turn to analyzing the evolution of Nordic Populism on these scales.

Varying evolution in time and space

Nationalism in the Nordic region can be viewed as two-dimensional. In addition to separate nationalisms of each of the Nordic five, a pan-Nordic nationalism can also be detected—what has been branded Nordism or Scandinavianism. The political culture of the region is a product of both. The region likes to consider itself as being a wholistic sociocultural and socioeconomic zone, although consisting of separate nation-states. There are times when the two easily coexist, and there are other times when tension between the two rises to the surface.

Prior to the rise of the third wave of nativist populism, these brands of parties had found success only in two out of the five Nordic states. In the wake of World War II, Denmark had started out being open, tolerant, and social liberal. However, since the 1970s, two populist parties were able to turn the small Nordic state to implement perhaps the toughest legislation on immigration in Western Europe. Since the turn of the millennium, migration became the most discussed topic in Denmark, mainly revolving around concerns over Muslims in this predominantly Christian society.

The OPEC Oil Crisis hitting the Western world hard in the early 1970s led to economic hardship, for example to a spike in unemployment. In Finland, an agrarian populist party survived for a while in the wake of World War II. It was however in Denmark and in Norway that the populist right found real foothold in the Nordic region. Protesting against rising tax levels, the Danish and Norwegian Progress Parties promoted anarcho-liberalism and campaigned against increased economic and bureaucratic burden on the ordinary man. They argued against wide-scope social services, immigration, and cozy consensus politics in these corporatist social democratic welfare states.

This was not the regular right-wing neoliberal rhetoric but rather a new populist version in which charismatic leaders positioned themselves alongside the blue-collar public and against the political elite. The Nordic populist parties started out being fiscally libertarian before moving more toward middle ground on economic policy while turning even further hostile against immigration.

Like in France and many other Western European countries, politics in the Nordic countries were indeed shaken by nativist populist actors in the 1970s, when anti-tax parties rushed to the surface in Denmark and in Norway. Both were among those initiating the first wave of populist politics in Europe. However, the fate of nativist populist parties has varied in the region. While populist anti-tax movements rose early in Denmark and in Norway, they turned more firmly against immigration only during the second wave. It was then first in wake of the financial crisis hitting in 2008 that populists found significant success in Finland and in Sweden. In Iceland, only quasi-populist parties have found marginal success.

Although the parties here discussed share many qualities of populist politics, their policies, style, and impact have varied greatly. The Sweden Democrats (Sverigedemokraterna; SD) were rooted in neo-Nazism and remained furthest out on the fringe in national politics. The Norwegian Progress Party (Fremskrittspartiet; FrP) was perhaps the mildest version of populist parties and won almost full acceptance domestically. The True Finns (Perussuomalaiset; PS)—later referred to as only the Finns Party—was primarily Eurosceptic. The Danish People's Party (Dansk Folkeparti; DF) was most influential and managed to pull the domestic discourse on immigration into its own direction. All of these movements, however, offered an alternative voice to the mainstream by tapping into fears of the ordinary public.

Denmark's earthquake elections

In Denmark, the discourse on immigration drastically changed in the 1970s and 1980s, from emphasizing equal treatment and protecting human rights toward requirements of adhering to fundamental values of the Danish society. This change was led by a flamboyant tax lawyer, Mogens Glistrup, who founded the Danish Progress Party prior to the 1973 General Election, winning with such significant support that the elections were being referred to as the earthquake elections. Nationalism was reawakening and soon immigrants and refugees were, through a culturally based neoracist rhetoric, discursively being constructed as a threat to Danish values and national identity. Maneuvrings of this kind developed much later and to a lesser extent in the other Nordics.

Until this watershed change, Denmark had been considered liberal and tolerant toward diversity and alternative lifestyles, for example, regarding sexuality and substance use, to name but two categories. It was also among one of the most open countries of the world when it came to immigration and asylum. Newcomers gained easy access to civil rights and generous welfare benefits. Imposing Danish values or cultural restrictions on immigrants, which later became commonplace, was absent from political discourse of the time and even not considered legitimate.

Tides turning

Though most mainstream parties opposed this chauvinism, the Progress Party was still tolerated by the political establishment. Contrary to what was the case in Sweden, there was no consensus in Denmark with regard to sequestering the populists. Although at the time never considered an ideal partner, the right-of-center government periodically found a need to strike ad hoc deals with them.

The Progress Party was instrumental in the process of externalizing immigrants and in portraying Denmark as being overrun by foreigners. When discussing Muslims in Denmark, Glistrup once, for example, compared them to a "drop of arsenic in a glass of clear water." He referred to them as foreign invaders, aiming to "colonize" Denmark. By adding thick anti-immigrant rhetoric to its anti-tax policy, the party was once again garnering more support. Full acceptance was, nonetheless, still far away.

Internal splits were also tearing the Progress Party apart. The likable Pia Kjærsgaard, who led the more moderate faction, exited the party in the early 1990s to form the Danish People's Party in 1995, which domestically was to become one of the most influential populist right parties in the world.

The Progress Party in Norway grew to simultaneously become perhaps the mildest and most successful populist right political party in Europe. By the late 1980s, the anti-immigrant stance had surpassed that of the anti-tax heritage, tapping into concerns with increased flow of refugees and asylum seekers. Prior to that, Norway was both very homogeneous and held, perhaps, the most liberal immigrant policy in the region.

One example of the hardened anti-immigrant rhetoric came in the 1987 election campaign. Carl I. Hagen quoted a letter he claimed he had received from a Muslim called Mustafa, effectively describing a conspiracy of Muslim immigrants planning to take over Norway. This was quite remarkable as Muslims accounted for only a fraction of the population. Still, he did not hesitate to uphold the Eurabia conspiracy theory (Bergmann 2021). Although the letter proved to be his own fabrication, in fact a full-fledged political forgery, this did not prevent the party from winning over 12% of the vote—mainly on the anti-immigrant platform.

In passing the psychological 10% mark in electoral support, the party in effect graduated into being taken fully seriously in Norwegian politics.

Moving toward the mainstream

In Scandinavia, nativist populism was also being remodeled during the more overall second wave of nativist populism, starting in wake of the end of the Cold War. By carefully crafting their message to become more socially acceptable, the Danish People's Party was fast moving into the mainstream, toning down Glistrup's anti-tax rhetoric, but still maintaining hardcore anti-immigrant policies. The DF campaigned against Denmark becoming multiethnic and what it called foreign infiltration. In economic terms, the party moved much more middle ground, for example, emerging as a staunch defender of the Danish welfare state. Anti-immigration was becoming the core to its politics, with claims that migrants were a threat to the welfare system, which the party vowed to protect.

The FrP's position moved in a Christian conservative direction to protecting Norwegian culture against foreign influences and preventing the welfare system from being exploited by immigrants and asylum seekers. In a classical welfare chauvinistic way, the new mantra was putting "our people first." Another sign of the move away from socioliberalism toward a more authoritative direction was the new emphasis on law and order, for example, in arguing that the system favored criminals over their victims. The immigrant issue was gradually to take up more space in the party's program and discourse until it came to the forefront of its agenda.

Finding legitimacy

The 9/11 attacks in the United States brought new support for the Danish People's Party. Most parties in the mainstream had consistently and firmly opposed the DF's anti-Muslim politics, and the party was harshly criticized for flirting with racism. This was drastically altered after the horrendous event. The DF was gaining legitimacy and was from then on positioned as one of the permanent parties in Danish politics. Since immigration became perhaps the country's most salient political issue, Kjærsgaard was able to present herself and the DF as a credible alternative to the established parties.

For many, the 9/11 terrorist attack served as a validity of the DF's criticism of Islam. Many of the mainstream parties soon started to follow DF's line on immigration and a relatively widespread consensus emerged on a need to stem migration and impose stricter demands on foreigners to integrate and adhere to the Danish way of life. Subsequently, immigration was the most covered political topic in media (Roemer and Van der Straeten 2004; Stainforth 2009).

The anti-immigration rhetoric of the DF revolved around three main themes: first as a threat to Danish culture and ethnic identity; second, as a cause of crime; and third, as a burden on the welfare state. Their argument was placed within an ethno-pluralist narrative, based on the doctrine that even though nations were equal they should be kept separate.

The party was especially successful in linking other political issues to immigration, such as welfare, the state of the economy, and anti-elitism (Anders Jupskås 2015a). Immigration was also directly linked to gender issues, maintaining that Islam was incompatible with the level of women's liberation in Denmark. In this regard, the veiling of Muslim women became a central and symbolic issue.

Securing 12% of the vote in the 2001 election and becoming the third-largest majority in the country marked the long and successful journey of the DF from the cold fringes to the very core of Danish politics. The party's new position of power was cemented when subsequently backing a minority government of the main right-of-center party. Over the coming decade, the DF was able to push through restrictions on immigration, tightening demands for integration, implementing tougher measures on crime through stricter sentences, and increasing public welfare for the elderly. Gradually, the DF rhetoric became the dominant political discourse on migration and Muslims. Arguing that cultural racism had found especially fertile territory in Denmark, Karen Wren (2001) maintains that absence of significant counter-rhetoric has also become institutional and part of the very fabric of Danish society. Even many on the left flank of Danish politics came to accept the anti-immigrant discourse.

Milder Norwegians

Although the populism of the Norwegian Progress Party was always milder than that of its Danish counterpart, the development of the two parties followed a similar trajectory. The FrP moved from problematizing migration merely on economic grounds to also voicing concerns regarding its effect on Norway's culture (Hagelund 2003). The party argued that in order to prevent ethnic conflict in Norway, immigration and asylum sought from outside the Western culture complex had to be stemmed. This was a classic nationalist ethno-pluralist doctrine, emphasizing the importance of keeping nations separate, without openly claiming any sort of superiority.

Carl I. Hagen argued that non-Western immigration would bring a culture of violence and gang mentality. Almost from the outset, the FrP found greater acceptance in society than what similar parties had enjoyed in most other countries. It thus found legitimacy much earlier than many of its counterparts in neighboring countries. In exchange for supporting the right-of-center government, Hagen was, for example, able to secure the influential parliamentary positions.

The anti-immigrant position of the FrP was based on a new master frame according to which immigrants were presented as economic burden and a cultural threat rather than being biologically inferior (Rydgren 2007). Anders Hellstrom (2016) documents how the immigration issue gained salience in the party's repertoire in the 1990s when warning against danger of cultural heterogeneity. He insists that immigration was in that way transformed from an economic to a cultural issue.

The welfare chauvinism of the FrP is, for example, illustrated in the way Anders Jupskås (2015b) identifies its distinctive narratives on immigration. First, that immigrants cost too much. Second, that they exploit "our" welfare. Third, that they are more prone to committing crimes than the native population. Fourth, that they undermine the Norwegian way of life. And lastly, that they challenge Norway's values—mainly liberal values. Thus, when combined, that they threaten Norway's economy, welfare system, security, culture, and liberal values.

Jupskås documents that the first two frames were present from the outset, that the second two narratives emerged in the 1980s, but that the last one, regarding posing a challenge to liberal values, was presented only after 9/11. In any event, the cultural emphasis in the anti-immigrant rhetoric, that is, on rules, norms, and values, rose to prominence in Norway only in the 1990s. Simultaneously, the importance of the economic frames gradually decreased over that same time frame.

Despite their effort in distancing themselves from the Danish People's Party, the anti-immigration rhetoric of the Norwegian FrP gradually grew more distinctively anti-Muslim. Already in 1979, Carl I. Hagen described Islam as a "misanthropic and extremely dangerous religion" (quoted in Jupskås 2013). Since then, their anti-Islam rhetoric just grew firmer. Muslim immigration was linked to terrorism, forced marriage, and crime (Bergmann 2017). They were portrayed as a burden on the welfare system and as a threat to Norwegian culture. Furthermore, the FrP identified a need to fight against Sharia laws filtering through in Norway.

Cultural nationalism

The cultural nationalism in the Danish People's Party's discourse was, for example, found in its emphasis on Christian values and the link between the state and the Evangelic-Lutheran Church. On that ground, the party positioned itself as the protector of Danish culture. In a word, of Danish-ness (*Danskhed*). In doing so, DF representatives often referred to specific Danish values, which primarily consist of Christian values and family values in addition to Danish cultural heritage, all framed within the parameters of the Danish national identity (Gad 2010).

The party clearly defined nationality by ethnicity. Still, although they were highly instrumental in the "othering" process of foreigners, it should, however, be stressed that no evidence of outright racism was found in the party's material. While avoiding being openly racist, the DF was especially skillful in separating immigrants from ethnic Danes, that is, in distinguishing between "others" and "us." Its nationalism, thus, combined both cultural and ethnic elements.

This identity-based rhetoric was also a moralist one. In firmly relying on a moral frame of "us," "others" were negatively represented as culturally inferior (e.g., Boréus 2010). Swedish political scientist Jens Rydgren (2010) defines this as a "neo-racist rhetoric," in which national values were portrayed as being under threat by immigration. Karen Wren (2001) described this depiction in Denmark as a historically rooted set of traditions, which are under threat from globalization, the EU, and from "alien" cultures.

On law and order, the DF started out from quite an authoritarian standpoint. The party emphasized traditional Christian family values. However, when criticizing Islam for intolerance, they would move to place themselves on the side of social liberalism. Islam was, for instance, identified as an enemy of the LGBTQ community, with the party emphasizing that "in recent decades, homosexuals have come under pressure from intolerant Islamic groups" (see Moffitt 2017). The DF vowed to work determinedly against oppression and discrimination against homosexuals. The Danish People's

Party had, in effect, turned around to become the protector of women and gay rights.

True Finns and the crisis

Nativist populism rose in the other Nordic countries only during the Third Wave. Although Finland had surely seen its fair share of wide-ranging nationalist movements, populist right-wing parties like those in neighboring countries rose to prominence only when the True Finns Party surged in wake of the Euro Crisis hitting in 2009. Their charismatic leader, Timo Soini, was quick to position his party against EU bailout for crisis-ridden countries in Southern Europe. Soini saw his party as a forceful channel for the underclass. He called for Greece to be expelled from the Eurozone and said: "We won't allow Finnish cows to be milked by other hands" (quoted in Judis 2018).

In the European Parliament elections of 2009, the True Finns won almost a tenth of the vote. Two years later, they surged in the general elections, landing almost a fifth of the vote. Their success came by hijacking almost the entire political agenda when debating the Euro Crisis.

Prior to finding success, they had widely been dismissed as a joke, a harmless protest movement, and a nuisance on the fringes of Finnish politics (Raunio 2013). Their discourse was deemed to be aggressive and crude, and the media mostly only saw entertainment value in them. After the 2011 election, however, they had surely become a force to be reckoned with. They clashed with the mainstream parties and called for ending of the one-truth cozy consensus politics of the established three parties. Soon, some of mainstream parties began to follow suit and came to adopt much of their anti-EU rhetoric.

In the 2015 election, Timo Soini led his party to government for the first time. Since then, it saw diminished support. Contrary to the Progress Parties of Denmark and Norway, the Finnish populists never flirted with neoliberalism. Rather, they inherited the centrist economic policy of the SMP. Its right-wing populism was thus never socioeconomic, but rather only sociocultural.

Three main themes emerged as the political platform of the Finns Party. First, resurrecting the "forgotten people," the ordinary man, to prominence and speaking in their name against the elite. The phrase "forgotten people" referred to the underprivileged ordinary citizen neglected by the political elite. Second, fighting against immigration and multiculturalism. Third, stemming Europeanization of Finland.

Like both the Danish People's Party and the Progress Party in Norway, the Finns Party was welfare chauvinist. On ethno-nationalist grounds, they emphasized first protecting native Finns but excluding others. On this platform, a more radical and outright xenophobic faction furthermore thrived within the party. Jussi Halla-aho, who became perhaps Finland's most forceful critic of immigration and multiculturalism, led the anti-immigrant faction. After the internal split, which, for example, led to the exit of Timo Soini and many of the more moderate factions of the party, Halla-aho became the party leader in 2017.

Jussi Hallo-aho has frequently been accused of racial hatred (see Dunne 2014). He contributed extensively to the anti-immigration online forum Homma. He wrote that "we will fight until the end for our homeland and one true Finnish nation. The victory will be ours" (quoted in Winneker 2015). The shift in the rhetoric, from placing the EU and its bailout program for crisis-ridden countries in Southern Europe as the main external threat to Muslim migrants replacing Brussels as the arch enemy of the Finnish people, simply follows the progression in time, from the Euro Crisis to the Migration Crisis.

In the 2019 parliamentary elections, the Finns Party became the second largest, following closely on the heels of the Social Democrats. The liberal democratic mainstream in Finland responded by forming a five-party coalition, which mainly served to keep the Finns Party out of government.

The Swedish exception

Nativist populists did not find significant success in Sweden until 2010, when the Sweden Democrats entered Parliament. Until then they had been kept firmly on the fringes of Swedish politics. Sweden had accepted more refugees and asylum seekers per capita than any other country in Europe. The Sweden Democrats forcefully criticized both the open-door policy and what they called a lenient immigration policy of the mainstream parties. They insisted that it had caused segregation, rootlessness, criminality, conflict, and increased tension in society (Hellstrom 2016). They implied that the Social Democrats had effectively turned several city suburbs into foreign-held territories, which were occupied by Muslims who were the country's greatest foreign threat and who had even partially introduced Sharia laws on Swedish soil (Åkesson 2009).

Leader of the Sweden Democrats Jimmie Åkesson noted that Muslim refugees posed the "biggest foreign threat to Sweden since the Second World War" (quoted in Becker 2019). He argued that Sweden should be kept as "an ethnically and culturally homogeneous nation" and warned against emergence of a multicultural society. The party emphasized national separatism based on biological and cultural differences.

Prior to the 2010 electoral breakthrough, the SD had been widely dismissed as an evil outsider. In 1998, their share of the vote was not even 0.5%. In 2006, they gained some attention when almost 3% of the electorate voted for them, though falling short of the 4% Parliament threshold. By 2018, their share of the vote had risen to 17.6%. In the 2022 general elections they snapped a fifth of the vote and entered into coalition negotiation, thus marking their full acceptance into Swedish politics.

Although the SD's move from the radical right fringe of xenophobic and neo-Nazi extremism was initiated earlier, its full transformation was first achieved after young Per Jimmie Åkesson and his clan took over the helm in 2005. They rerouted away from the party's previous neo-Nazi past and instead turned toward the model of Danish People's Party, National Front in France, and the Austrian Freedom Party.

The new leadership set out to systematically abandon extreme and banal views, such as open biological racism (Widfeldt 2015). Furthermore, members expressing extremist views risked expulsion. In November 2011, Jimmie Åkesson announced a policy of zero-tolerance for racism. Several expulsions followed. With the rascals out, the most severe stumbling blocks to electoral success had been removed from their path. Slowly, the party was eventually able to reach the ears of the electorate, and in doing so, even win almost full legitimacy.

Since cleaning up its image, the SD was able to travel far from its neo-Nazi origin, claiming to be an alternative but legitimate voice. They positioned themselves as social conservative protectors of the Swedish national identity and traditional family values as well as advocators of law and order.

Put more simply, they maintained that they were speaking on behalf of the ordinary man who the establishment had left behind. They accused the ruling elite of being preoccupied with interests of the privileged few. Despite this effort, the SD was not fully able to fend of accusations of extremism, such as of its ongoing and not-so-well-hidden xenophobia and of still-visible links to neo-Nazi forces.

In an ethno-pluralist "equal but separate" doctrine, the SD avoided openly describing Swedish culture as superior. Instead, Swedish culture and identity were portrayed as being unique and clearly distinct from others. Each nation was understood here to possess one ethnically determined culture. The Swedish culture thus became a dividing line separating the native population from others in society who were presented as a threat to internal social cohesion. Arguing that each nation embodied a singular culture based on ethnicity, they said it was, thus, the responsibility of the Swedes to protect their own culture and identity from external contamination. On this ground, their 2011 manifesto emphasized turning Sweden back into a culturally homogeneous society, where the interest of the native population always came first.

In maneuvering their way into a position of at least limited legitimacy, the real tactical breakthrough came by shrewdly adopting the social democratic notion of the "People's Home" (*Folkehemmed*). This was also similar to the moves made by both the Danish People's Party and the Norwegian Progress Party. Jimmie Åkesson claimed that the Social Democrats had abandoned their long-asserted promise of the People's Home: the all-embracing welfare society. Instead, he insisted that the SD was now the true representative of the People's Home. The SD skillfully played on the nostalgic wish of going back to a simpler and happier time.

Vitally for achieving this discursive move, they were able to attach their own nationalist agenda of protecting the native population to the unifying metaphor of the People's Home, which in its essence contained the Swedish national identity (Hellstrom 2016). Furthermore, they accused the Social Democrats and other mainstream parties of abandoning the people, and working only on behalf of its own interest or for external forces, aiming for rapid internationalization and for promoting multicultural views.

The SD was firmly socioculturally conservative, but unlike many nativist populist parties in neighboring countries, it was not at all neoliberal. In fact, the SD attacked the Social Democrats for having weakened the welfare state and for having lowered the benefits much to the suffering of native Swedes, who relied on the system. In this regard, they adopted the winning formula of the Danish People's Party. Nordic populists, indeed, generally unite in embracing the newer winning formula of linking people and culture to the nation-state, that is, in protecting the redistributive welfare state for only the ethnic population, and, thus, placing migrants as a threat to it.

The new master frame was in combining ethno-nationalism and anti-elite populism with welfare chauvinism. Jimmie Åkesson maintained that the unique Swedish welfare system could not handle too much immigration. He thus presented welfare and immigration as mutually exclusive and asked the electorate to choose. By discursively stealing back the metaphor of the People's Home, the SD set out to achieve several goals at once. The first was simply to capitalize on the myth of the Swedish heritage. Second was to position themselves as the true representatives of the welfare society—the defining factor of the Swedish national identity. Third, to simultaneously criticize the current leadership of the Social Democrats for having let down the native population for a naive celebration of multiculturalism. A final positive side effect was the portrayal of the contemporary Social Democrats as alienated elitists—out of touch both with its past and present society.

This is the classical three-phase discourse of nativist populist that was framed in the introduction to this chapter: First, Muslim migrants are placed as the threat to the ethnic and cultural nation; second, the Social Democratic leadership is accused of betraying the people; while, lastly, the SD position themselves as their protectors.

In line with its socioconservative stance, the SD was initially skeptical on the issue of gay rights. Over time, however, the party repositioned itself as protectors of homosexuals against a threat to sexual liberalism accompanying mass Muslim migration. In 2010, the party, for example, published a report titled "Time to Speak Out About Rape." The focus was however not on the crime in general, but rather on Muslim immigrants raping native Swedish women, with the report claiming that Sweden was experiencing a rape wave which was a direct consequence of immigration (Moffitt 2017).

The newfound social liberalism was nevertheless always quite selective and seemed, mostly, to be aimed against Muslim socioconservativism.

Icelandic nationalists

Until the 2017 parliamentary elections, when at least two quasi-populist parties passed over the threshold and took up seats in Parliament, such parties had not found significant electoral success in Iceland. I have identified three main reasons halting their rise (Bergmann 2017). First, nationalism was never a discredited ideology in Iceland, like it was in most other Western European countries after World War II. The small island country gained its independence from Denmark in 1944 and its postcolonial national identity was firmly based on nationalistic sentiments (Bergmann 2014a). There was, thus, no need for challenging the political establishment with nationalistic views from the fringe as nationalism had never been marginalized.

Second, nativist populist parties in Europe have found most success when opposing mainly Muslim migrants. Muslims are scarce in Iceland, and there are no areas where the semantics of an Arab culture dominates the scene. And third, populist parties have usually found success when under leadership of charismatic leaders. Until recently, populist radical right parties in Iceland were rather unlucky in this regard.

On the heels of the Financial Crisis that hit Iceland especially hard in 2008, quite a few populist protest movements emerged (Bergmann 2014b). A completely renewed leadership also took over the country's old agrarian party, the Progressive Party (PP), which was rapidly retuned in a more populist direction; geared against foreign creditors, international institutions and eventually partly toward anti-Muslim rhetoric—even in the absence of a significant Muslim population. After a shake-up within the party, the more populist elements left the PP and established a new construct called the "Centre Party."

Another quasi-populist party also found support in the 2017 election. The People's Party was prone to uphold welfare chauvinism. Its leader, Inga Sæland (2016), for example, countered that the cost of asylum seekers could be used to help poor Icelanders instead. She insisted that while lower-income Icelanders suffered hardship, asylum seekers, funded by the state, were living in comfort. Rhetorically, she asked whether that money might instead be better used to help poor Icelanders.

Moving into a Position of Power

The Danish People's Party gradually grew to become the perhaps most influential political party in the country—a position it held for almost two decades. After landing in opposition, the DF went from strength to strength. In the 2014 European Parliament elections, they came out on the very top. In the following year, the DF won a fifth of the vote in the general elections and became the largest party on the right flank in Denmark. Under leadership of Kristian Thulessen Dahl, who had replaced Pia Kjærsgaard at the helm—she became Chair of Parliament—the DF went back to supporting Venstre's right-wing minority government. The DF did not face many obstacles on its road to hardening the already punitive Danish immigration policy even further.

When analyzing the success of the Danish People's Party, a specific winning formula can be detected. Rather than adhering to the well-known populist formula of combining an anti-immigrant stance with neoliberal economic policies, the DF instead combined social welfare policy and nationalist-chauvinist ideas. Here, the party did strike a chord with the less-educated voters who in the past had voted for the Social Democrats.

The DF successfully transformed from being a fringe party with marginal impact to become one of the most influential parties in Danish politics. Interestingly, the party achieved this by changing the political discourse in Denmark on immigration and Islam rather than by altering much of its own message. Their once condemned policies not only became fully normalized but also much more widely supported in society. Generally, the debate had shifted from ways of accommodating migrants, as it had centered on in the 1960s, to measures of expelling them from the country.

Frustrated by the shifting allegiance to the Danish People's Party, the Social Democrats—the once hegemonic power in Danish politics—started to move in the direction of the DF. With Mette Fredriksen assuming stewardship in 2015, the Social Democrats took several steps to further abandon their former socioliberal stance against the DF's callous immigration policy. Instead, they made it their own, for instance, by proposing a cap on non-Western immigrants and shipping asylum seekers to reception centers in North Africa. In the so-called Paradigm Shift legislation of 2019, the Social

Democrats even came to support the right-wing government's increased restrictions on immigrants. The band of measures, for example, included a burqa ban, and it increased the automatic repatriation of refugees out of Denmark—by then, however, Denmark was all but closed to refugees.

By the 2019 general elections, the DF had fallen victim to its own success and saw its support go down by more than half. The downfall was mainly caused by other parties closing in on their space, largely by copying DF's policies. First, the right-of-center Venstre had regained some of its lost support by adopting the strict anti-immigrant stance of the DF, followed by the Social Democrats who, leading up to the 2019 elections, vigorously targeted the more authoritarian working-class voters.

Simultaneously, the DF also felt squeezed from the other side, from the even further and more extreme right. In addition to others stealing their anti-immigration policies, two new parties, positioned further out on the fringe, ran with far more extremist views than had been heard before in Danish politics—including a call for expelling all Muslims out of the country.

The two new parties, New Right and Hard Line, emerged from the outliers to challenge the DF. New Right was much more firmly nativist, anti-EU, and economic right-wing than the DF, while the Hard Line was outright racist. In other words, the DF was outflanked.

After becoming an establishment party in a position of power themselves, the DF was no longer seen as a challenger. Instead, it had become the new mainstream and was now contested from the outer periphery. The difference was, though, that after they had, over decades, gradually been able to turn the discourse on immigration to become much tougher than before, the new challenger parties had to go much further in their defiance than their predecessors ever did.

Although the style of the new parties and their position in Danish politics was perhaps comparable to the Progress Party and the Danish People's Party when they had emerged onto the scene in Danish politics in their own time, the stance of the new parties was much tougher. As a result, the anti-immigrant field had become much more fragmented in Danish politics. However, only the milder of the two, namely the New Right, won seats in Parliament, while the Hard Line fell just short of the threshold.

What stands out from the 2019 election is that even though the DF massively lost support, their politics was still the greater winner. In fact, political positions that previously had been kept out on the fringe were now the new normal. After the election, Mette Fredriksen went on to lead a Social Democratic minority government, which continued to uphold much of the immigration policy pushed through by the Danish People's Party.

Sneak Islamization

Further north, immigration had also evolved to become the most discussed issue by the Progress Party of Norway, mentioned twice more often in the 2009 election campaign than health care, the next most frequent topic of party members. Party leader, Siv Jensen, who had succeeded Carl I. Hagen in 2006 warned against what she referred to as "sneak Islamisation" (quoted in Jupskås 2015b). The notion alludes to a hidden process already being in place, which eventually would alter Norway and turn it away from its liberal Christian roots toward becoming a Muslim-based society. In flirting with the Great Replacement conspiracy theory, Siv Jensen maintained that demands of the Muslim community such as on halal meat being served in schools, the right to wear hijab, and of public celebration of Muslim holidays were all examples of such sneak Islamization.

Despite the tough anti-Islam rhetoric, the FrP succeeded in portraying itself as a much milder nativist populist party than those on the continent. They refused being compared to other parties such as the Danish People's Party or the French National Front (now National Rally). Siv Jensen was also successful in broadening the FrP's political platform, which eventually brought it closer to the mainstream. Their success in this regard is evident, for example, in the fact that they never faced similar boycotting attempts and isolation by the political establishment that several other populist parties suffered from.

In the 2009 general elections, the FrP won almost a quarter of the vote, by then the best result of any populist party in the region and among the very best Europe-wide. Despite this strive of distancing itself from extremist parties elsewhere, the FrP always had a clear populist verve. They firmly positioned themselves as defenders of the ordinary people. Similar to the Danish People's Party, they successfully tapped into the voter base of the Labor Party and repositioned themselves as Norway's worker's party. Their voter base was also like populist parties elsewhere, mainly the undereducated working-class or unemployed of the youngest and oldest voter groups. Surveys showed that the most important issue for their supporters was indeed immigration, law and order, care for the elderly, and reduced taxes (Jupskås et al. 2016). Similar to the influence of Danish People's Party in Denmark, it has also been documented how both the Labor Party and the Conservative Party of Norway gradually came to adopt much of the FrP's rhetoric on immigration (Simonnes 2011).

Although the FrP was of a relatively milder kind within the realm of nativist populism, Norway has still seen its fair share or violent radical right extremism. The most horrible and traumatic incident was the terrorist attack of Anders Behring Breivik on July 22, 2011, killing 77 people in a bomb blast in the administration quarter in Oslo, and in a gun massacre at the Labor Party Youth movement camp in Utøya, 38 kilometers west of Oslo.

Breivik previously belonged to the FrP but had not found success in meeting his ambition. The attack caused the Progress Party grave difficulty and threatened its hard-earned legitimacy. The party leadership campaigned vigorously to disown him and instantly toned down its anti-Muslim rhetoric. Still, the FrP faced a severe backlash in the 2011 local elections.

However, the setback proved to be only temporary. Two years later they had won back much of lost support and landed in government as a junior partner in a minority coalition with the Conservative Party.

The Breivik attack reviled a hidden subculture in Norway, simmering under the surface on the internet, which involved a network of racist and Islamophobic groups operating around the country. Their overall narrative was of unraveling a socioliberal cabal conspiring with Islamic forces of turning the continent into Eurabia. Numerous other radical right movements have existed in Norway. Norwegian racism usually does not accept being racist at all. Public versions had indeed surely and squarely moved away from being biology based toward much rather being cultural. However, such examples still did exist (see Booth 2014).

As discussed, although the initial response to Breivik's attack were severe and almost universal, it did not lead to the demise of nativist populist tactics.

Nordic after COVID-19

It was interesting how the COVID-19 pandemic served to reaffirm the old dividing lines between the Nordic countries. The region saw vastly contradicting response to the crisis. Denmark was one of the first in the world to impose draconian lockdown measures, suspending some traditional human rights, such as even closing borders to its Nordic neighbors. Sweden, however, became the posterchild of light touch restrictions, limiting their actions to almost only issuing general guidelines to the public and urging for caution.

In Denmark, authorities were fast in linking the crisis with others. The prime minister of the mainstream Social Democratic Party said that it was unacceptable how many people who were "not of a Western decent," as she phrased it, were roaming around the streets while infected.

Identifying the winning formula of Nordic nationalist populism: Welfare chauvinism

As noted earlier, the Nordic neo-nationalists distinguish themselves from many of their counterparts on the European continent by emphasizing on the protection of their countries' vast welfare systems for the domestic population. Across the region, Muslim migrants were portrayed as burden on the welfare system; this is what is called welfare chauvinism. The Nordic populists skillfully played on a nostalgic wish of reverting to a simpler and happier time.

As has been established in this chapter, nativist populist parties in the Nordic countries differ to a significant degree from most populists in Western Europe by not being clearly positioned on the right-wing of the socioeconomic spectrum. Instead of basing their discourse on traditional right-wing neoliberal rhetoric, they rose on a novel sociocultural master frame of conjoining ethno-nationalism and anti-elite populism with welfare chauvinism. In other words, rather than primarily referring to the social-economic situation of the ordinary people, they, instead, adopted a new populist winning formula: that is, combining socioeconomic left-wing views with hard-core right-wing conservative sociocultural ideas.

Bibliography

Åkesson, J. 2009. "Muslimerna är vårt största utländska hot." Aftonbladet, October 19. http://www.aftonbladet.se/debatt/debattamnen/politik/article12049791.ab.

Becker, J. 2019. "The Global Machine Behind the Rise of Far-Right Nationalism." *New York Times*, August 10. https://www.nytimes.com/2019/08/10/world/europe/sweden-immigration-nationalism.html.

Bergmann, E. 2014a. "Iceland: A Postimperial Sovereignty Project." *Cooperation and Conflict* 49 (1).

Bergmann, E. 2014b. *Iceland and the International Financial Crisis: Boom, Bust and Recovery.* New York: Palgrave Macmillan.

Bergmann, E. 2017. *Nordic Nationalism and Right-Wing Populist Politics: Imperial Relationships and National Sentiments.* New York: Palgrave Macmillan.

Bergmann, E. 2020. *Neo-Nationalism: The Rise of Nativist Populism.* New York: Springer Nature.

Bergmann, E. 2021. "The Eurabia Conspiracy Theory." In *Europe: Continent of Conspiracies: Conspiracy Theories in and about Europe*, edited by A. Önnerfors and A. Krouwel, 36–53. London: Routledge.

Booth, M. 2014. *The Almost Nearly Perfect People: The Truth about the Nordic Miracle.* London: Jonathan Cape.

Boréus, K. 2010. "Including or Excluding Immigrants? The Impact of Right-Wing Populism in Denmark and Sweden." In *Diversity, Inclusion and Citizenship in Scandinavia*, edited by B. Bengtsson, P. Strömblad, and A.-H. Bay, 127–158. Newcastle upon Tyne: Cambridge Scholars Publishing.

Dunne, D. 2014. "Finns Party MP Remains Defiant After Race Hate Conviction." *Helsinki Times*, August 7.

Gad, U. P. 2010. "(How) Can They Become like Us? Danish Identity Politics and the Conflicts of 'Muslim Relations.'" *Museum Tusculanum*, 3.

Hagelund, A. 2003. "A Matter of Decency? The Progress Party in Norwegian Immigration Politics." *Journal of Ethnic and Migration Studies* 29 (1): 47–65.

Hellstrom, A. 2016. *Trust Us: Reproducing the Nation and the Scandinavian Nationalist Populist Parties.* Oxford: Berghahn Books.

Judis, J. B. 2018. *The Nationalist Revival: Trade, Immigration, and the Revolt Against Globalization.* Colombia: Columbia Global Reports.

Jupskås, A. R. 2013. "The Progress Party: A Fairly Integrated Part of the Norwegian Party System." In *Exposing the Demagogues: Right-wing and National Populist Parties in Europe*, edited by K. Grabow and F. Hartleb, 205–236. Maastricht: Centre for European Studies.

Jupskås, A. R. 2015a. "Institutionalized Right-Wing Populism in Times of Economic Crisis: A Comparative Study of the Norwegian Progress Party and the Danish People's Party." In *European Populism in the Shadow of the Great Recession*, edited by T. Pappas and H. Kriesi, 23–40. Colchester: ECPR Press.

Jupskås, A. R. 2015b. *The Persistence of Populism. The Norwegian Progress Party 1973–2009.* Oslo: University of Oslo.

Jupskås, A. R., E. Ivarsflaten, B. Karlsnes, and T. Aalberg. 2016. "Norway: Populism from Anti-Tax Movement to Government Party." Unpublished Working Paper.

Moffitt, B. 2017. "Liberal Illiberalism? The Reshaping of the Contemporary Populist Radical Right in Northern Europe." *Politics and Governance* 5 (4): 112–122. https://doi.org/10.17645/pag.v5i4.996.

Raunio, T. 2013. "The Finns: Filling a Gap in the Party System." In *Exposing the Demagogues: Right-wing and National Populist Parties in Europe*, edited by K. Grabow and F. Hartleb. Maastricht: Centre for European Studies, 133–160. Konrad Adenauer Stiftung. PP 133-160

Roemer, J. E., and K. Van der Straeten. 2004. "The Political Economy of Xenophobia and Distribution: The Case of Denmark." Working Paper 2004–2003, Laboratoire d'Econométrie de l'Ecole Polytechnique.

Rydgren, J. 2007. "The Sociology of the Radical Right." *Annual Review of Sociology*, 33:241–262.

Rydgren, J. 2010. "Radical Right-Wing Populism in Denmark and Sweden: Explaining Party System Change and Stability." *SAIS Review of International Affairs* 30 (1): 57–71.

Sæland, I. 2016. Facebook post, February.

Simonnes, K. 2011. "I stjalne klær? En analyse av endringer i Høyres, Arbeiderpartiets og Fremskrittspartiets innvandrings-og integreringspolitikk fra 1985 til 2009." University of Oslo. https://www.duo.uio.no/handle/10852/13210.

Stainforth, T. 2009. "The Danish Paradox: Intolerance in the Land of Perpetual Compromise." *Review of European and Russian Affairs* 5 (1).

Widfeldt, A. 2015. *Extreme Right Parties in Scandinavia*. New York: Routledge.

Winneker, C. 2015. "Finnish Politician Declares War on 'Multiculturalism.'" *Politico*, July 27. http://www.politico.eu/article/finland-immonen-stubb-immigration-multiculturalism/.

Wren, K. 2001. "Cultural Racism: Something Rotten in the State of Denmark?." *Social & Cultural Geography* 2 (2): 141–162.

Conclusion: What Lies Ahead

Carlos García-Rivero

Populism is now part of our ordinary political vocabulary and populist parties are now part of our political environment, and, bearing in mind the results presented in this volume, populist parties will be part of our political scenario and for long. At the time of writing, populist parties have already managed to consolidate their political presence in the Nordic countries, Southern Europe, as well as Western and Eastern Europe. Led by historical grievances, perceived corruption, and economic crisis, their antiestablishment and anti-oligarchy discourse has penetrated into society appealing ordinary citizens from left to right.

The basic conclusions reached in this volume are as follows

- In 2010, a wave of populist parties began to access institutions all over a Europe severely affected by the 2008–2012 economic crisis.[1]
- There are two common factors that propel populism support: political polarization and authoritarian values. On the one hand, polarization enhances the political participation of more authoritarian citizens, but on the other, it deactivates more moderate sectors of the electorate, leaving the political scenario at the mercy of populist supporters. As long as polarization remains, democrats will deactivate their participation and autocrats will increase their activism, gaining a larger share of the political terrain. Furthermore, authoritarian values are spreading throughout society, and this is a major factor behind the satisfaction with a deteriorating democracy, especially in Eastern Europe

---

1   Nordic populism is a case apart, as it is mainly based on what Bergmann termed *welfare chauvinism*, which basically consists in emphasizing protection of their countries' vast welfare systems for the domestic population, and it has been growing steadily for decades in all Nordic countries.

- There is a clear East-West divide, with Eastern European democracies deteriorating at a faster pace,[2] and this is exacerbated by the fact that citizens, as stated above, seem to be satisfied with this process.
- Southern, Western, and Nordic Europe are also following the path of Eastern Europe, albeit at a different pace.
- There is a high level of congruence among populist party voters at different levels of electoral calls and among populist party voters and representatives, enhancing these parties' capacity to maintain their electoral share election after election. The evolution of vote share since 2010 in European elections evidences this.

Regarding polarization, Figure C.1 presents data on political polarization in Europe by regions and in the whole of the European Union. As noted in Chapter 3, there is an evident wave of populism in Europe. This will certainly have an illiberal impact on democracies, and although there are many factors behind this, a major one is polarization. Enrique Clari and Carlos García-Rivero pointed out that polarization makes moderate democrats decrease their political participation whereas it boosts authoritarian citizens' engagement in politics.

Evidently, since 2010, political polarization has increased dramatically all over Europe, but more pronouncedly in Eastern Europe. Interestingly, in Chapter 3, Clari-Galán noted that the wave of populism started in 2010, and it is also since 2010 that polarization has risen exponentially.

Eastern Europe evidences a higher level of polarization, and this tallies with results presented in Chapter 3, when saying that "in ex-communist countries, the increasing correlation between populism and anti-pluralism goes further back in time and has remained stable but very high since 2007." The question that arises is why in Eastern Europe populism, anti-liberalism and anti-pluralist ideas have taken root so firmly. Possibly, Eastern Europe is differentiated by its own history. Former communist countries' different transitions—configuration of nation-states, transition to market economy and capitalism, and, finally, transition to democracy—were more or less finalized in the decade after 1990, whereas in Western Europe the same process took four centuries.

---

2 In fact, Eastern Europe, together with Central Asia, is the area worst affected by autocratization worldwide (Varieties of Democracy Institute 2021)

In Eastern Europe, changes began with Poland started with the founding of Solidarity, an independent trade union, and the entire region followed, led by international institutions such as IMF and the EU. Transitions to democracy ran parallel to the transition to market economy and capitalism, with citizens often misunderstanding the aim and meaning of both democracy and capitalism (Haynes 1996; Hofferbert and Klingemann 1999; Ghodsee and Orenstein 2021). As a result, economic progress is often linked to support for democracy: if the economy flourishes, democracy as a regime thrives. Finally, decades of a totalitarian past also left a legacy in the political culture, and political rights and liberties may not be so closely rooted in the idea of democracy as in the West (Tismaneanu 2007; Jones 2019).

As pointed out by José Rama and Andrés Santana in Chapter 9, satisfaction with democracy affects the vote for populist parties, not only but especially in Eastern Europe. In this region, satisfaction with democracy "increases rather than curtails [populist] electoral prospects." As in Eastern Europe, satisfaction with democracy runs divergent to level of democracy (Chapter 1); it follows that the lower the quality of democracy, the higher the satisfaction and, hence, the higher the prospects for the electoral success of populist parties in Eastern Europe. Further still, with a high level of party voter-representative political congruence enhancing the voter-party link.

Therefore, it is *logical* that populist parties in office in Eastern Europe such as Fidesz in Hungary or Prawo i Sprawiedliwość in Poland aim to dismantle democratic liberties and rights, as the lower the quality of democracy, the higher the satisfaction (Chapter 1) and, hence, the higher their expectations of electoral success (Chapter 9). Latest elections in Hungary evidence this: the ruling party, highly criticized by the European Union for its anti-liberalism policies, has increased its electoral share from 47.89% in 2018 to 52.52% in 2022.

The only legal resource at hand for the European Union to promote and safeguard EU values and to stop populist parties from dismantling liberal democracy once in office is to activate Article 7 of Treaty of the European Union. However, as Clara Portela and Ruth Ferrero Turrión pointed out in Chapter 8, once a populist party comes to power in one of the member states, the EU is ultimately unwilling to do anything about it. While suitable instruments to address democratic backsliding among EU members are in place, inhibitions about their activation are such that, instead of deploying

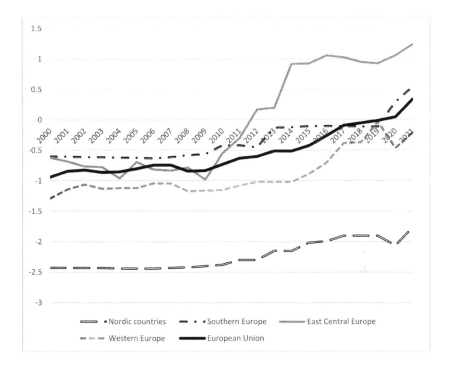

Figure C.1 Political polarization in Europe

Source: Varieties of Democracy Institute (2021).

them, the institutions continue to devise new procedures to act as antechambers to a sanctions mechanism that exists only on paper.

Overall, we are witnessing a vicious circle that feeds back on itself. A populist party in office dismantles democracy, satisfaction with democracy increases, at the same time increasing the populist party in office's electoral expectations, especially in Eastern Europe, and all this with the EU's Article 7 inactivated.

Largely, the future of democracy in Europe is at stake, with populist parties having room to maneuver. Authoritarian values are spreading throughout society, and this justifies a rising satisfaction with democratic deterioration. Political polarization fuels this process and, to make matters worse, it is on the rise. Interestingly, although populism has established itself more firmly in Eastern Europe, the rest of Europe is not immunized. In fact,

Southern, Nordic, and Western Europe are following suit as the recent electoral results in Sweden or Italy show.

Tellingly, we may be witnessing the emergence of a new political cleavage based on the conception of democracy itself: liberal democracy versus populist democracy. If citizens realize the real impact and consequences of the latter, they may return to more moderate positions on the left or right; otherwise, democracy in Europe as we used to know it will become an endangered species.

Bibliography

Ghodsee, K., and M. Orenstein. 2021. *Taking Stock of Shock: Social Consequences of the 1989*. Oxford: Oxford University Press.

Haynes, M. 1996. "Eastern European Transition: Some Practical and Theoretical Problems." *Economic and Political Weekly* 31 (8): 467–471.

Hofferbert, R. I., and H. Klingemann. 1999. "Remembering the Bad Old Days: Human Rights, Economic Conditions, and Democratic Performance in Transitional Regimes." *European Journal of Political Research* 36:155–174. https://doi.org/10.1111/1475-6765.00466.

Junes, T. 2019. "Illiberalism in Eastern Europe Is a Legacy of 1989." *Open Democracy*. https://www.opendemocracy.net/en/can-europe-make-it/illiberalism-eastern-europe-legacy-1989/.

Tismaneanu, V. 2007. "Is East-Central Europe Backsliding? Leninist Legacies, Pluralist Dilemmas." *Journal of Democracy* 18 (4): 34–39.

Varieties of Democracy Institute. 2021. *Autocratization Turns Viral—Democracy Report 2021*. Gothenburg: V-Dem Institute.

About the Contributors

Javier Antón-Merino is adjunct professor at the University of Burgos, Spain. He studied political science at Universidad Complutense de Madrid and holds a PhD in law, government, and public policy from Universidad Autónoma de Madrid. His areas of interest include federalism, nationalism, and populism.

Eirikur Bergmann is professor of politics at Bifröst University in Iceland. Author of nine academic books and numerous journal articles, he writes mainly on nationalism, populism, conspiracy theories, European integration, and participatory democracy. Bergmann has also authored three novels published in Icelandic. His latest book titled *Neo-Nationalism: Rise of Nativist Populism* was published in 2020.

Hans-Georg Betz is professor of politics at the University of Zürich, Switzerland, and a leading expert on populism and the radical right in affluent liberal democracies. He has written several seminal books and articles on radical right-wing populism, nativism (both past and contemporary), and Islamophobia. Betz currently serves as an adjunct professor at the Institute of Political Science at the University of Zürich, where he teaches advanced courses on populism and globalization. Before coming to Switzerland, he taught at York University in Toronto, the Paul H. Nitze School of Advanced International Studies in Washington, DC, and the Loyola University Rome Center in Italy. He was also a joint visiting chair at Columbia University/New York University in New York City. His main publications include *Radical Right-Wing Populism in Western Europe* (1994), *La droite populiste* *en Europe Extrême ou démocrate?* (2004), as well as a number of articles in leading political science journals, such as *Comparative Politics, Comparative Political Studies, The Review of Politics,* and *Socio-Economic Review*. He has also contributed several chapters to edited volumes on the subject, most recently to *The Oxford Handbook of the Radical Right* (2018) and *Political Populism: A Handbook* (2017).

Enrique Clari is a PhD candidate at Valencia University, Spain. He holds an MA from the London School of Economics and Politics, United Kingdom. His research focuses on democratization, autocratization, and value change in contemporary Europe.

Belén Fernández-García is a postdoctoral researcher at the University of Málaga. She was a visiting scholar at the Amsterdam Institute for Social Science Research, the Netherlands, and the Institute for German and International Political Party Law and Research, Düsseldorf, Germany. She was also a postdoctoral researcher at the Institute of Social Sciences, University of Lisbon, Portugal. Fernández-García has received her PhD in political science from the University of Granada, Spain, and her principal research interests lie in the area of populism, the radical right, political parties, and political communication. Her most recent publications include *En los márgenes de la democracia liberal: Populismo, nacionalismo y radicalismo ideológico en Europa* (with Ángel Valencia-Sáiz, 2022); "Demonization of Political Discourses? How Mainstream Parties Talk about the Radical Populist Right" (with Jakob Schwörer) in *West European Studies* (2021); and "Religion on the Rise Again? A Longitudinal Analysis of Religious Dimensions in Election Manifestos of Western European Parties" (with Jakob Schwörer) in *Party Politics* (2021).

Ruth Ferrero-Turrión is associate professor of political science at Universidad Complutense de Madrid (UCM) and associate researcher at Complutense Institute of International Studies (ICEI-UCM). She has received the Research Award in European Studies from the European and Ibero-American Foundation of Yuste in 2019. She is holds a PhD in political science and international relations, an MPhil in Eastern European studies from Universidad Nacional de Educación a Distancia (UNED), a degree in political science and sociology from the Complutense and Newcastle upon Tyne universities, a postgraduate degree in political science and constitutional law from the Center for Political and Constitutional Studies, as well as a Diploma in Specialization in European Union granted by the Diplomatic School. She has held academic positions at Carlos III University, Comillas Pontifical University, the International University of Andalusia, and the UNED. She has also been a research fellow at Columbia University (NYC), at the London School of Economics (LSE), Babes-Bolyai University (Romania), the Hungarian Institute of International Relations, the Open Society Foundation of Sofia, non-Visegrad fellow at the Institute of International Relations in Prague, and visiting fellow at Leipzig University. Likewise, she has been visiting professor at the universities of Coimbra, Bochum, Florence, and Warsaw.

Carlos García-Rivero is associate professor of political science at Valencia University, Spain, and a research associate at the Centre for International and Comparative Politics, Stellenbosch University, South Africa. He was also a lecturer at Burgos University, Spain, and Saint Louis University (Madrid Campus). His research has focused on political culture, democratization, and electoral behavior at both elite and mass levels, mainly in sub-Saharan Africa and in Islamic parties and democracy in North Africa and the Middle East. His research has been published in journals such *as Party Politics* and *Government and Opposition*. In 2009, together with Hennie Kotzè, he received the "best article prize" from the Spanish Association of Political Science for their article "Opposition Politics and Party Support: An Elite-Mass Analysis" (2008). In 2021, he was awarded, together with Enrique Clari, the "best paper presentation prize" at the national online congress of the Spanish Association of Political Science. He also served as a political analyst at the Ministry of Defense in Spain on International Humanitarian Crisis Management and has acted as an electoral observer for the Organization for Security and Co-Operation in Europe.

Hennie Kotzè was chair of the Department of Political Science at the University of Stellenbosch from 1986 to 2002, where he taught research methodology, public policy-making, and political behavior. He was also the dean of the Faculty of Arts and Social Sciences at the University of

Stellenbosch for ten years and is presently a research fellow in the Centre of International and Comparative Politics at the same university. He also held lectureships at the University of South Africa (UNISA) and Johannesburg University. Kotzè is currently engaged in research on the process of democratic consolidation in South Africa and value change at both the elite and mass levels in Africa. He has authored and/or coauthored four books, edited six volumes, and written over 80 academic articles on comparative politics.

Marta Méndez-Juez is senior lecturer in political science at the University of Burgos, Spain. She is the author of several publications on topics such as transparency, reuse of public data, modernization, reform, quality of public services, evaluation of public policies and programs, as well as citizen participation. She was a postdoctoral researcher at the University Institute of Democracy, Peace and Security at the National Autonomous University of Honduras. She has completed a stint in the Ex-Post Unit of Public Policy Evaluation of the Directorate General of Parliamentary Research Services at the European Parliament in Brussels.

Sergio Pérez-Castaños is associate professor of political science at the University of Burgos, Spain. He is a part of several research projects, both at national and international levels, on issues such as political congruence, populist discourse, federalism, and political communication among others, which are his main research areas. He has led the Spanish national section of the European Election Monitoring Centre and is a member of the Spanish Political Science Association Board. He has delivered lectures and workshops to students in universities at Coimbra (Portugal), Macerata (Italy), and Naples (Italy).

Clara Portela is a full-time faculty member in political science at the University of Valencia, Spain, having previously served in a similar role at Singapore Management University, Singapore, and as a research fellow at the Institute for Security Studies of the European Union in Paris. Her research focuses on arms control, multilateral sanctions, and EU foreign policy. She holds a PhD from the European University Institute in Florence and an MA from the Free University of Berlin. She is the recipient of the THESEUS Award for Promising Research on European Integration. Portela has been a visiting professor at the OSCE Academy in Bishkek, the College of Europe, and the University of Innsbruck.

José Rama is lecturer at the Universidad Autónoma de Madrid. He was also a lecturer of comparative politics at Universidad Carlos III, Madrid, and of quantitative methods at King's College London. He has published in *Journal of Democracy, Party Politics, European Political Science Review, Political Studies Review*, and *Government and Opposition*, among others. His recent coauthored book titled *VOX: The Rise of the Spanish Populist Radical Right* was published in 2021.

Ángel Rivero is associate professor in the Department of Politics and International Relations at the Universidad Autónoma de Madrid, where he teaches political theory. He holds a PhD in philosophy from the UAM and a BSc (Hons.) in social sciences with politics and sociology from the Open University (United Kingdom). He was a Fulbright Visiting Scholar at the Graduate Faculty of Political and Social Science, New School for Social Research, New York, and was the head of the Department of Politics and International Relations at UAM (2000–2003).

Andrés Santana is associate professor at the Universidad Autónoma de Madrid. His work has been published in *Journal of Elections, Public Opinion and Parties*; *Social Politics*; *Politics & Gender*; *East European Politics*; *Problems of Post-Communism*; and *European Sociological Review*, among others. He is the author of ten books and several book chapters.

Ángel Valencia-Sáiz is professor of political science and administration at the University of Málaga, Spain. His broad field of research is political theory, and his work focuses specifically on green political theory, the comparative analysis of environmental movements and parties, and the study of environmental policies, in addition to the crisis of democracy; he has been a part of several national research groups working on these issues. He has published numerous articles on these topics in leading national and international journals as well as chapters in edited collections. He is the author of *Citizenship, Environment, Economy* (with Andrew Dobson, 2005); *La Izquierda Verde* (2006); *Ciudadanía y Conciencia Medioambiental en España* (with Manuel

Arias Maldonado and Rafael Vázquez García, 2010); *Política y Medio Ambiente* (2014); *Democracia verde* (with Rafael Enrique Aguilera Portales, 2016); and coeditor of *En los márgenes de la democracia liberal: Populismo, nacionalismo y radicalismo ideológico en Europa* (with Belén Fernández-García, 2022). From 2010 to 2013, he was a senior researcher in the area of political science at the Andalusian Studies Centre (Spain). He was a visiting scholar at the Keele University (United Kingdom), Universitá Degli Studi Di Bari (Italy), and the Universidad Autónoma de Nuevo León (México). He was also a member of the Board of Directors of the Spanish Association of Political Science and a columnist for several newspapers such as *La Opinión de Málaga*, *Sur*, and *El País*.

Index

A
accession criteria 176
Alternative für Deutschland (AfD) 2, 69, 76, 90–92, 121, 154, 184, 198, 200, 207, 209
anger 79, 80, 82, 84, 88–90, 92, 128
antiestablishment 217, 231, 235, 262
anti-pluralism 7, 24, 51, 52, 56, 57, 59–61, 68, 106, 231, 263
anti-pluralist 3, 4, 7, 23, 24, 27, 31, 52, 55, 56, 59–61, 68, 106, 108, 237, 263
article 7 TEU 9, 172–176
austerity 4, 128, 216, 217
authoritarian values 7, 16, 21, 27, 29, 30, 104, 105, 114, 262, 265
authoritarianism 18, 19, 24, 27, 29–31, 37, 44, 48, 49, 68, 100, 102, 104, 105, 108, 110–116, 118, 120, 127, 179, 185, 221

B
Breivik attack 258

C
chauvinism 10, 63, 240, 243, 247, 253, 254, 259, 262
Christian Social Union 82, 154
citizen 4, 91, 137, 156, 158, 159, 219, 225, 229, 232, 233, 250, 270
compliance dilemma 178, 185
Conservative Party of Norway 258
Copenhagen criteria 174, 176
corrupt elite 6, 41
critical citizens 22, 27, 102, 103, 115
cross-sectional 8, 16, 99, 100, 114, 118, 134

D
Danish People's Party 2, 198, 243–245, 247, 250–253, 255–258
Danish-ness 248
Dansk Folkeparti 243
Danskhed 248
demagogue/demagoguery 37
democratic backsliding 7, 15, 44, 51, 54, 60, 99, 100, 118, 174, 175, 185, 264
democratization 40, 48, 232, 236, 268, 269
Denmark 2, 3, 76, 110, 197, 198, 242–246, 248, 249, 254–256, 258, 259
Dansk Folkeparti (DF) 69, 121, 198, 243, 245, 246, 248, 255, 256
dictatorship 45, 67, 232
Die Linke 154
diffuse support 17, 23, 27, 100, 103, 113

E
economic crisis 4, 9, 10, 49, 131, 133, 147, 153–159, 164, 166, 216, 217, 219, 262,
electoral authoritarianism 179
elite 6, 8, 9, 41, 46, 67, 77, 79, 92, 100, 131, 132, 149–152, 154, 156–162, 220, 240–242, 250, 252, 253, 259, 269, 270
ethno-nationalism 10, 83, 240, 253, 259
EU 4, 9, 15, 56, 158, 159, 163, 167, 172–178, 180–184, 186, 187, 196, 197, 224, 248–250, 256, 264, 270
European democracy 1, 51
European Parliament 1, 129, 173, 178, 180, 181, 196, 198, 249, 255, 270
European Union 4, 80, 132, 135, 152, 153, 156, 157, 167, 173, 196, 233, 263, 264, 269, 270

Index

F
fake democracy 39
Fidesz 2, 6, 66, 69, 89, 121, 174, 176, 179, 180, 183, 184, 185, 198, 200, 205, 207, 209–211, 264
financial crisis 26, 76, 92, 111, 154, 241, 242, 254
Finland 2, 3, 193, 197, 198, 242, 249, 250
Folkehemmed 240, 252
Folkpartiet liberalerna 154
FPÖ 6, 69, 121, 143, 196, 198, 200, 207, 209
France 2, 3, 44, 45, 75, 76, 79, 92, 121, 128, 193, 197, 198, 207, 242, 251
Fratelli d'Italia 75, 198
Free Voters 154
Fremskrittspartiet (FrP, Norwegian Progress Party) 121, 242, 246–248, 257, 258
funding conditionality 186

G
Germany 2, 3, 8, 9, 27, 83, 84, 90–92, 111, 132, 146, 147, 150, 153, 154, 160–162, 164, 166, 197, 198, 207, 268
Glistrup, Mogens 243
Greece 2–4, 6, 10, 27, 40, 216–218, 220, 223, 249

H
Hard Line 256
hegemony 38, 39, 85
humiliation 89, 91
Hungary 2, 3, 6, 18, 19, 27, 51, 89, 92, 99, 111, 128, 173, 174, 176–185, 193, 197, 198, 207, 211, 264

I
Iceland 111, 242, 254, 267
ideological congruence 8, 9, 146–155, 164, 165
ideology 36–38, 41–43, 48, 49, 53, 63, 67, 68, 76, 126, 132, 135, 139, 140, 148, 181, 193, 195, 200, 203, 220–222, 254
illiberal 3, 4, 7, 8, 22, 23, 25–27, 29, 53, 54, 59, 68, 99, 100, 102, 117, 180, 194, 211, 263

IMF 216, 264
immigrants 24, 152, 153, 166, 243–245, 247, 248, 253, 255, 256
internal sanctions 9, 172, 173, 176, 186
Italy 1–4, 6, 10, 27, 75, 84, 150, 197, 198, 207, 216–218, 223, 225, 266, 267, 270, 272

K
Kjærsgaard, Pia 244, 255
Kristdemokraterna 154

L
leader 22, 37, 38, 43, 45, 47, 48, 100, 157, 164, 220, 249–251, 254, 257
left-right self-placement 108, 148, 149, 152, 154, 156, 157, 159
left-wing 10, 54–56, 62, 63, 65, 66, 88, 129, 216, 220, 223, 234, 236, 237, 240, 259
Lega Nord 77, 84, 121
LGBTQ 248
liberal democracy 4, 6, 7, 9, 18, 19, 22–24, 27, 31, 36, 39, 43, 44, 46–49, 51–54, 68, 78, 100, 106, 108, 195, 221, 264, 266
Liga Polskish Rodzin 154

M
M5S 6, 63, 65, 69, 217, 218, 221–227, 235–237
mass 21, 27, 45, 88, 150, 154, 253, 269, 270

N
nativism 10, 24, 30, 127, 132, 267
nativist populism 241, 244, 249, 258, 267
neo-Nazi 251, 252
neoliberalism 249
neoracist 243
New Right 256
Nordic Europe 263
Nordic Populism 10, 240, 241, 262
Nordism 241
Norway 2, 111, 242, 244, 246–250, 257, 258
Norwegian Labor Party 257, 258
Norwegian Progress Party 242, 246, 252
nostalgia 80, 81, 88, 89, 92

Index

O
oligarchy 7, 38–42, 45, 46, 48, 49, 126, 262
Orbán, Viktor, 89, 181

P
parliamentarians 8, 9, 147, 151, 154, 156, 163, 165, 223
party representatives 8, 9, 147–149, 151, 157, 158, 164–166
party systems 59, 147
Perussuomalaiset (PS, True Finns) 121, 198, 243, 249
plebiscitary democracy 39, 234
Podemos 59, 63, 69, 79, 128, 130, 217, 219, 221, 222, 228–230, 232, 235–237
Poland 1–3, 6, 8, 9, 18, 19, 27, 51, 83, 99, 111, 128, 146, 147, 150, 153, 160–162, 164, 166, 173, 174, 176–185, 193, 197, 198, 207, 211, 264
polarization 8, 20, 23, 24, 26, 27, 31, 47, 99–104, 106, 108–119, 220, 262, 263, 265
Polish Peasants Party 154
Polish Solidarity 154, 232, 264
political conditionality 174
political congruence 8, 146, 147, 264, 270
populism 1, 4, 6, 7, 9, 10, 36–49, 51–61, 68, 75–78, 81, 83, 87, 89–92, 97, 118, 126, 127, 155, 156, 186, 193–195, 200, 215–218, 220–223, 228, 232, 233, 237, 240, 241, 244, 246, 249, 253, 258, 259, 262, 263, 265, 267, 268
populist democracy 7, 36, 37, 46–48, 221, 237, 238, 266
populist parties 1, 4, 6, 7, 9, 10, 19, 51–54, 56–60, 63, 68, 70, 150, 152, 155, 163–165, 186, 191, 194, 202, 215, 218, 220, 221, 235–237, 240, 242, 243, 252, 254, 257, 259, 262, 264, 265
populist radical right parties 4, 8, 15, 53, 55, 81, 82, 100, 121, 125, 132, 147, 193, 198, 203, 220, 254
Portugal 1–3, 10, 58, 76, 127, 150, 216, 217, 219, 223, 232, 237, 238, 268, 270
Prawo i Sprawiedliwość (PiS, Law and Justice) 2, 6, 66, 69, 121, 154, 174, 176, 179–81, 183, 184, 198, 200, 205, 207, 209–11, 264
Progress Party 2, 242–244, 246, 250, 252, 256–258
PRRP 26, 103–105, 107, 109, 112, 113, 117, 125, 127, 130, 131, 137, 151, 194, 195, 197, 199–202, 205, 207, 208

Q
quality of democracy 6, 10, 15, 16, 22, 28, 29, 211, 264

R
radical right populism 7, 75, 76, 81, 83, 89, 91, 92, 126
Rassemblement national 2, 75, 76
real democracy 39, 42, 43, 45, 46
recognition 7, 77, 79, 91, 92, 182
refugees 88, 182, 243, 244, 250, 251, 256
resentment 79, 80, 82, 84, 89, 90
right-wing 11, 19, 31, 56, 57, 62, 63, 65, 66, 68, 130, 132, 138, 139, 142, 165, 202, 218, 219, 221, 223, 235, 240, 242, 249, 255, 256, 259, 267
rule of law framework 175, 178, 179, 182, 186
rule of law mechanism 175, 182

S
Samoobrona Rzeczpospolitej (SRP) 69, 154
sanctions 7, 9, 172–178, 183, 185–187, 265, 270
satisfaction with democracy 6, 9, 10, 16–19, 21, 29, 105, 107, 113, 194, 200, 203, 205, 206, 264, 265
Scandinavianism 241
Southern Europe 10, 26, 27, 61, 215, 217, 221, 235, 237, 249, 250, 262
sovereignty 10, 40, 44–48, 52, 88, 89, 132, 216, 220, 224, 226, 227, 230, 231, 233, 234, 237, 238

Spain 2–4, 8–10, 27, 67, 76, 79, 111, 127–133, 139, 140, 142, 150, 193, 197, 198, 207, 216, 217, 219, 228, 230–232, 237, 238, 267–272
state capture 180
Sverigedemokraterna (SD, Sweden Democrats) 2, 75, 121, 154, 196, 200, 207, 209, 240, 242, 250, 251–53
Sweden 1–3, 6, 8, 9, 75, 110, 146, 147, 150, 153, 164, 166, 193, 196–198, 207, 240, 242, 243, 250–253, 259, 266
Swedish Centerpartiet 154
Swedish Moderaterna 154
Swiss People's Party (SVP) 58, 69, 86–89, 121
SYRIZA 6, 69, 216

T
terrorist attack 245, 258
time-series 8, 99

U
Unidas Podemos 59

V
victimization 89
voter 4, 8, 9, 82, 125, 126, 129–133, 136, 138–143, 147, 149–152, 156, 160–162, 164, 194, 257, 258, 264
Vox 2, 8, 59, 65, 67, 69, 121, 125–134, 136–143, 198, 200, 207–209, 219, 230–232, 236, 237, 271

W
welfare 4, 10, 57, 61–63, 65, 88, 240, 242, 243, 245–247, 250, 252–255, 259, 262
welfare chauvinism 10, 63, 240, 247, 253, 254, 259, 262